CHEMICAL AND BIOLOGICAL WARFARE

A Reference Handbook

Other Titles in ABC-CLIO's
CONTEMPORARY
WORLD ISSUES
Series

Books in the Contemporary World Issues series address vital issues in today's society such as genetic engineering, pollution, and biodiversity. Written by professional writers, scholars, and nonacademic experts, these books are authoritative, clearly written, up-to-date, and objective. They provide a good starting point for research by high school and college students, scholars, and general readers as well as by legislators, businesspeople, activists, and others.

Each book, carefully organized and easy to use, contains an overview of the subject, a detailed chronology, biographical sketches, facts and data and/or documents and other primary-source material, a directory of organizations and agencies, annotated lists of print and nonprint resources, and an index.

Readers of books in the Contemporary World Issues series will find the information they need in order to have a better understanding of the social, political, environmental, and economic issues facing the world today.

CHEMICAL AND BIOLOGICAL WARFARE

A Reference Handbook

Al Mauroni

CONTEMPORARY WORLD ISSUES

A B C CLIO

Santa Barbara, California
Denver, Colorado
Oxford, England

Library of Congress Cataloging-in-Publication Data

Mauroni, Albert J., 1962–
   Chemical and biological warfare : a reference handbook /
Al Mauroni. — 1st ed.
     p. cm. — (Contemporary world issues)
   Includes bibliographical references and index.
    ISBN 1-85109-482-2 (hardcover : alk. paper) —
    ISBN 1-85109-487-3 (e-book)
   1. Biological warfare. 2. Chemical warfare. I. Title. II. Series.
UG447.8.M33 2003
358'.34—dc21

                              2003008653

08 07 06 05 04   10 9 8 7 6 5 4 3 2

This book is also available on the World Wide Web as an e-book. Visit abc-clio.com for details.

ABC-CLIO, Inc.
130 Cremona Drive, P.O. Box 1911
Santa Barbara, California 93116–1911

This book is printed on acid-free paper ∞.
Manufactured in the United States of America

To my parents,
Al and Jan

Contents

Preface

Truly understanding chemical and biological warfare requires deciphering this complex, technically challenging, emotional, and politically sensitive topic. There are many aspects of chemical and biological warfare: There is the purely scientific arena, where researchers seek to identify and manufacture liquids and vapors so toxic that drops can kill an adult in minutes, or to culture deadly microorganisms that can lay waste to a city's populace or a country's crops. There is the military aspect, where countries seeking an advantage over their adversaries employ weapons that can at best disable thousands and can at the least demoralize enemy forces and turn the tide of battle. There is the moral side, where critics see these weapons as uncontrollable and too liable to kill noncombatants as well as soldiers, and where some describe these weapons as tools for cowards. There is the political aspect, as governments try to stem the proliferation of material and technology to other adversarial nations or terrorist groups.

The common view of chemical and biological weapons is that they are a "poor man's atomic bomb,"[1] that they are vile instruments of terror that civilized nations just do not use. This naive and narrow viewpoint ignores the fact that nations owning nuclear weapons have also developed chemical and biological weapons, not content with the nuclear weapons' more destructive capability. This view disregards the fact that more countries are investing in chemical and biological weapons programs than in the past, despite the alleged perception that the world finds these weapons "immoral." Countries invest in chemical and biological warfare for very rational reasons: These weapons can be delivered effectively, they can be used to combat insufficiently trained or equipped modern forces or insurgents, and they shorten conflicts that might otherwise be very long and expensive. One country that once felt that these weapons were a rational investment was the United States.

Between 1918 and 1990, the United States made significant investments in maintaining an effective chemical weapons capability. This was primarily because the U.S. government wanted to be able to warn its enemies that they would be attacked with chemical weapons if they employed such means against U.S. forces. The U.S. military did not want to be strictly on the defensive, allowing an adversary to choose the time and place of chemical weapons attacks. Between 1942 and 1969, the U.S. government similarly invested in a biological weapons capability, primarily as a retaliatory threat, again to counter threats from adversaries that were thought to have an offensive biological warfare capability.

Although the United States has abandoned the strategy of employing these weapons, they are still a modern-day threat. President George W. Bush clearly stated this view, noting that "the United States of America will not permit the world's most dangerous regimes to threaten us with the world's most destructive weapons."[2] Deputy Secretary of Defense Paul Wolfowitz echoed this sentiment: "[Asymmetric threats] include forms of warfare that most civilized nations long ago renounced: chemical and biological weapons and the intentional killing of civilians through terrorism."[3] In a 2002 *Meet the Press* discussion, National Security Advisor Condoleezza Rice noted that the Bush administration wanted to "send a very strong signal to anyone who might try to use weapons of mass destruction against the United States. . . . The only way to deter such a use is to be clear it would be met with a devastating response."[4]

The question is, are chemical and biological weapons really that dangerous? Many people unintentionally (or perhaps intentionally) put them on a par with nuclear weapons in their discussions of "weapons of mass destruction" (WMDs), also known as nuclear, biological, and chemical (NBC) weapons or chemical, biological, and radiological (CBR) weapons. Hollywood producers have not helped allay this image, offering such fictional portrayals as *The Rock*, in which nerve agent–filled guided rockets threatened thousands in San Francisco; nor have famous authors such as Stephen King, whose book *The Stand* shows a military-bred biological organism wiping out most of humanity. Although chemical and biological agents have the potential for large-scale attacks producing massive casualties, this outcome is often only possible if massive amounts—tons of chemicals or hundreds of pounds of biologicals per kilometer—are laid down over an exposed populace, if no protective measures are taken, and if no medical treatment occurs.

The images of huge, rolling clouds of chemical vapors devastating cities of noncombatants along with military forces were derived from World War I stories and from strategic bombing scares from World War II. They have little relevance in today's conflicts. Chemical weapons, developed and tested at government proving grounds, have precise effects, which can be calculated very accurately, on specific areas. This is particularly true for the weapons in the arsenals of smaller countries, few of which have the capability to manufacture, store, and employ thousands of tons of chemical agents in a military operation for a sustained period of time. For instance, if Iraq had fired a chemical-filled ballistic rocket at U.S. forces in 1991 and it had actually worked, the effect would still have been limited to causing casualties in an area of less than five square kilometers. If that area is a city, the weapon will cause hundreds of deaths. But if the area is a patch of desert where Iraq thought there were military forces, the number of deaths might be in the single digits. It is impossible to compare that effect to the effect of a tactical nuclear weapon aimed at the same target.

This blind fear of disastrous effects extends to biological agents as well. Not all biological agents are deadly. Outside of plague, smallpox, and Marburg virus (a relative of Ebola virus), most weaponized biological agents are not lethal at all, merely incapacitating. Brucellosis, Q fever, and cholera will make many people sick for days or (if untreated) weeks, but the actual death rate is relatively low. Some strains of tularemia, if left untreated, can kill up to 30 percent of those infected. Even the recent anthrax mail scare demonstrated this: Of the twenty-two people infected, only five people died. But the concern that there might be additional biological attacks has unleashed literally billions of government dollars in response activities. Much of this response was generated by fear of worst-case scenarios rather than by rational decisions based on more probable outcomes.

The U.S. military has been attacked only once with chemical weapons, and that was more than eighty years ago. Through diplomacy, threats of retaliation, and defensive measures, the United States has avoided suffering massive casualties as a result of chemical or biological warfare, either on the battlefield or in its cities. Yet the Department of Defense's 1997 Quadrennial Defense Review concluded that the threat or use of chemical or biological weapons is a "likely condition of future warfare." For that reason alone, it is worthwhile to try to understand more about this threat. This book will provide some of the tools for students to research the area of chemical and biological warfare and, given that opportunity, to make their own judgments of the facts and opinions of many different agencies.

There is a historical basis for the formation of the current perception of chemical and biological warfare. Understanding that history can deconstruct this warfare's doomsday mystique. This book is not intended to teach readers about the physical properties of chemical and biological agents, nor will it lecture readers on the morality of this form of warfare. It is intended to educate readers on the reasons nations seek this military capability. The fact that nations continue to seek chemical and biological weapons is also evidence that they consider these weapons to be capable, manageable, and necessary instruments of war.

I present the discussion of history with the hope that the reader will take the opportunity to reexamine historical events in the U.S. government's involvement in chemical and biological warfare. There have been many misquoted and inaccurate views of what the U.S. government has done, views that have created inaccuracies that live on in the public consciousness for decades without a basis in the facts. This book is not an attempt to revise history but, rather, to allow those interested to reexamine the past for indications on how to address future threats. Here are the issues on both sides; here are the sources. Let the reader judge.

I would like to thank Mim Vasan and Alicia Merritt of ABC-CLIO for the opportunity to write this book. Many thanks to Eric Croddy and Howard Beardsley for their reviews of the manuscript and, more importantly, for their continued friendship. Kathy Delfosse greatly improved this book with her thorough copy editing. Special thanks to my wife, Roseann, for her unwavering support through this process.

Al Mauroni

Notes

1. First attributed to the speaker of the Iranian parliament Hashemi Rafsanjani in 1988. Quoted in "Chemical and Biological Weapons: The Poor Man's Bomb," draft general report of the Committees of the North Atlantic Assembly (on-line; available: http://www.fas.org/irp/threat/an253stc.htm; accessed March 31, 2003).

2. White House transcript, "President Calls for $48 Billion Increase in Defense Spending," Fort Walton-Beach, Florida, February 4, 2002 (on-

line; available: http://www.whitehouse.gov/news/releases/2002/02/20020204-1.html; accessed November 2, 2003).

3. Remarks by Deputy Secretary of Defense Paul Wolfowitz, Ronald Reagan Building and International Trade Center, November 14, 2001 (online; available: http://www.defenselink.mil/speeches/2001/s20011114-depsecdef.html; accessed November 2, 2003).

4. Quoted in David G. Savage, "Nuclear Plan Meant to Deter," *Los Angeles Times*, March 11, 2002, A-1.

1

Addressing Chemical and Biological Warfare

Many authors, in their reviews of the history of chemical and biological (CB) warfare, start in ancient times with the use of diseased animals to spread infection in besieged castles or to spoil wells in the face of advancing hostile troops. These attempts to use CB warfare agents prior to World War I were clumsy and singular events that really do not represent serious military capabilities. This book will limit its historical review, starting with the true birth of chemical warfare, with its wide-scale use on the battlefields of Europe in 1915, and progressing to the present date. This era—from 1915 to the present—is when all the relevant discussions and controversies have taken place.

As alluded to in the preface, there are many different approaches to studying CB warfare. There is the strict military measure of how effective these special weapons and the defensive tactics required to circumvent them are on the battlefield. In fact, more conflicts have had the threat of CB warfare but no actual use than have actually seen the use of CB warfare. The threat of possible employment of CB weapons by terrorists has recently enjoyed more attention, but such use can be tracked back to terrorist interest during the 1970s and 1980s. There is the political arena of arms control and disarmament, which focuses on convincing nations to eliminate the development and use of such unconventional weapons as CB weapons, nuclear arms, land mines, and so on. There is the scientific review of CB warfare agents, which examines what their physical properties are; how they work against people, animals, and plants; and how future CB warfare threats might be designed. Given advanced laboratory equipment and the ease of obtaining an advanced education, nearly any nation (or affluent terrorist group) that puts its scientific minds to the task could produce these weapons. Of course, successfully employing CB weapons is another matter altogether.

CB warfare is a broad field, and this book will attempt to touch on all aspects of it. A great deal of additional research can be performed to better understand CB warfare; it is merely a matter of deciding what avenue to pursue and what references to use. In approaching this topic, I would make one suggestion: Avoid discussions of the morality of CB warfare and of the possibility of government conspiracies. Discussions that try to evaluate the particular morality of one method of killing people versus another are hard to articulate in other than emotional terms. Usually one sees the morality of war as a function of trying to protect noncombatants, such as civilians, medical professionals, and prisoners of war, from unnecessary suffering. It is not clear (to me, at least) that using a chemical or biological weapon against a military force is somehow worse than ordering an artillery barrage on the same unit. Similarly, the idea that some nebulous government agency is secretly ordering tests of CB weapons on U.S. military or civilian personnel or has covered up adversarial use of CB weapons against U.S. military forces in the past is fraught with advocacy science, unsupported hypotheses, and often out-and-out, transparent exaggeration. Yet many like to think the worst of the government rather than examining the more credible possibilities, and fear of potential mass casualties added to a perception of government conspiracies and bureaucratic ineptness always seems to sell books and movie tickets.

Defining CB Warfare

The Chemical Weapons Convention (CWC) defines a chemical warfare agent as "any chemical which through its chemical action on life processes can cause death, temporary incapacitation or permanent harm to humans or animals. This includes all such chemicals, regardless of their origin or of their method of production, and regardless of whether they are produced in facilities, in munitions or elsewhere." This very broad definition includes the offensive use of riot-control agents (commonly called tear gases) and herbicides, for they have the potential for injuring personnel through their chemical actions. The U.S. military defines chemical warfare agents as "chemical substances that are intended for use during military operations to kill, seriously injure, or incapacitate a person through its physiological effects." This definition deliberately excludes incendiary munitions, riot-control agents, and herbicides, which may be considered chemical munitions but are not considered to be toxic chemical warfare munitions. The U.S. Senate, as part of its advice and consent to the ratification of the CWC treaty, directed that the United States would not be restricted as to the potential military use of riot-control agents. The ideal chemical warfare (CW) agent is highly toxic in small doses; can be manufactured on a large scale with inexpensive, domestically obtainable raw materials; can be weaponized (that is, to be delivered via an artillery projectile, an aerial bomb, a rocket, or a mine) and disseminated without much loss of payload; can be safely handled and transported; and is stable for storage. Chemical warfare is defined as "all aspects of military operations involving the employment of lethal and incapacitating munitions/agents and the warning and protective measures associated with such offensive operations."[1]

In World War I, the major European powers used industrial chemicals as the first CW agents. Although there were thousands of toxic industrial chemicals in use by commercial industries around the world at that time, a very short list soon emerged as the most effective and lethal agents that could be employed on the battlefield. Between the world wars, Germany developed the first nerve agents, which, since World War II, have become the standard for most nations with an offensive CW program today. Some nations continue research to create more-toxic and more-persistent CW agents. Terrorists today could use the same toxic industrial chemicals used in World War I as improvised weapons, using chemicals such as chlorine, chloropicrin, hydrogen cyanide, and phosgene instead of manufacturing military-grade CW agents.

The Biological and Toxins Weapons Convention (BWC) defines biological weapons as "microbial or other biological agents, or toxins whatever their origin or method of production, of types and in quantities that have no justification for prophylactic, protective or other peaceful purposes." The U.S. military defines biological warfare (BW) agents as "those biological pathogens and toxins that are intended for use during military operations to cause death and disease among personnel, animals, or plants, or to deteriorate material." BW agents include bacteria, viruses, rickettsia, and fungi as pathogens, and poisonous toxins derived from biological organisms (such as snake venom, ricin from castor beans, toxins from moldy bread, and the like). Just as with CW agents, the list of BW agents could be very long—there are thousands, if not tens of thousands, of microbial organisms in the natural environment, of which hundreds have the potential for causing some amount of harm to people, livestock, or crops. Some are infectious; many others are not. BW agents that are ideal for military operations are easily disseminated in aerosol form in small amounts over large areas to expose large numbers of people, animals, or crops; have high potency, causing casualties in short order; store well for long periods; and have medical countermeasures that a nation can give to its own troops and civilians.

Most BW agents are grown in laboratories using initial stocks drawn from natural sources and designed for use against specific targets (humans, specific breeds of animals, or specific crops). There are very few BW agents that are lethal to both humans and animals or to both animals and crops. Russia does not agree to including toxins among biological warfare agents, largely because toxins are chemical in nature and can be synthesized in a laboratory. Toxins cannot reproduce and cannot "infect" people who have not ingested the toxin. With a few exceptions, most toxins are relegated to use in assassinations rather than in attacks covering large areas. By weight, toxins are much more lethal than CW agents, but toxins cannot penetrate skin as some CW agents can and they do not act as quickly as CW agents do.

These definitions, developed by arms control negotiators for politicians attempting to draw up internationally accepted rules for warfare, allow for a common understanding of what constitutes CB weapons, but they do not really give one a good understanding of why these weapons were created or of how successful (or unsuccessful) they have been. A review of the history of CB warfare is the best forum for discussing what kinds of CB warfare agents exist, for identifying what defenses can be developed to protect against these agents, and for understanding why nations develop offensive and defensive CB warfare programs.

In the Beginning: World War I

Prior to the outbreak of World War I, attempts were made to at least limit the unchecked destructiveness of war, primarily through international arms control conventions. One early convention was the Hague Declaration Concerning Asphyxiating Gases, signed on July 29, 1899.[2] This short declaration noted that "[t]he Contracting Powers agree to abstain from the use of projectiles the object of which is the diffusion of asphyxiating or deleterious gases." On October 18, 1907, the European nations signed the Hague Convention Respecting the Laws and Customs of War on Land, noting that it was especially forbidden "to employ poison or poisoned weapons."[3] Other clauses in the convention addressed the definition of belligerents, the use of naval contact mines, the use of expanding bullets, and the treatment of prisoners. The common theme was one of protecting both combatants and noncombatants from unnecessary suffering and devastation during times of armed conflict.

The Great War erupted, and soon nations saw massive waves of their men and equipment thrown against each other on the European continent. Far different from earlier conflicts, this war quickly evolved into a deadlock in the trenches, with troops gaining a few miles on one day only to see their gains reversed in the next month. With forces evenly matched, both sides were seeking an advantage to move the conflict forward.

German scientists proposed using toxic chemicals to break the deadlock. They felt that although this approach technically violated the Hague Conventions, it was justified by French use of riot-control agents (ethyl bromoacetate) against German forces in August 1914 (although the effects were practically unnoticeable). The German military leadership was skeptical, but it was willing to try a new approach. The first large-scale gas attack was launched against the British forces on October 27, 1914, using 105 mm artillery shells filled with dianisidine chlorosulfate, a lung irritant. The British did not notice any effects because as the shells exploded, the chemical component was destroyed. Early experiments on the Russian front in January 1915 and against the British in March 1915 using chemical-filled artillery shells (filled with xylyl bromide) did not demonstrate any success. This could have been due to the cold weather and the low volume of chemical agent released by the (relatively) small artillery shells.[4] These observations required a change of operations.

Dr. Fritz Haber, a German scientist and consultant to the German War Office, thought that chlorine gas would be more effective in driving soldiers from their trenches, primarily because it was volatile enough to be driven by the wind and yet would not leave any prolonged aftereffects that might deter attacking forces. Chlorine was available to Germany in large quantities from its commercial dye industry, and using cylinders to disburse the gas would ensure that the new form of warfare would not compete with the demands for high-explosive artillery shells. In January 1915, the German high command approved the concept and decided to implement it at Ypres.[5]

German engineer troops brought thousands of gas cylinders filled with chlorine to the Ypres battlefield, and by March 10 they had positioned the cylinders in their trenches. Because the wind direction was predominantly west to east, they had to wait for optimal wind conditions before releasing the chlorine gas. On April 22, 1915, at five o'clock in the morning, they released 168 tons of chlorine, creating a yellow fog more than five miles wide. Although the attack successfully drove the French and British from the trenches, the German advance was soon stopped by Canadian reinforcements.[6] Because this attack had been viewed as an experiment, the German military command had not planned to reinforce it, and they lost the tactical initiative. The Germans used chlorine again at Ypres on April 24 and four more times in May, gaining ground against the unprepared Allied forces.

Although the Allies initially railed against the use of chemicals, they decided that not having their own gas warfare capability would be far worse than using them, both from a morale perspective and from a tactical perspective. The British released their first chlorine cloud in September 1915, on the Loos battlefield, using thousands of cylinders and releasing more than 150 tons of chlorine.[7] Both sides invested in the development of new gases and new delivery systems to harass and demoralize their opponents. These gases fell into two major classes: nonpersistent gases, and vesicants, or blister agents. The former can be subdivided, according to their effects on personnel, into asphyxiators, or choking gases (affecting the lungs); toxic blood agents (inhibiting the body's ability to transport oxygen through the blood system); sternutators, or sneeze gases (causing vomiting that would force a person to take off his or her gas mask); and lacrimators, or tear gases (irritants).

The choking agents included chlorine, phosgene, diphosgene, and chloropicrin. More than 80 percent of gas fatalities were caused by phosgene, which is more than ten times as toxic as chlorine. The blood agents included hydrogen cyanide, cyanogen chloride, and cyanogen bromide. The sneeze gases were generally arsenic-laced chemicals; not very deadly at first, they had a delayed toxic effect. Tear gases included ethyl bromoacetate, bromoacetone, and bromobenzyl cyanide. Early gas masks protected only the respiratory system, which forced a redesign to protect the eyes from these tear gases. Because these chemicals are lighter than air and disperse quickly, they had to be delivered in massive amounts (through mass artillery barrages, cylinders, or projectors) if they were to have much effect on unprepared troops.

Since these chemicals had odors, and in many cases, colors, troops could often don gas masks before being incapacitated by their effects. Once it was seen that the use of these chemicals would not carry the battles by themselves, both sides used them to harass the enemy. In an effort to improve these weapons, both the Germans and the English investigated vesicants such as mustard agent (often incorrectly referred to as "mustard gas," but actually a liquid) and lewisite, which was developed very late in the war. These liquids inflamed and damaged body tissues, causing temporary blindness, raising huge blisters on unprotected skin, and damaging the respiratory tract if inhaled. Mustard agent is not lethal, and the British initially deliberately ignored it because of this trait, not recognizing its very effective incapacitating capability. Mustard agent was first used by the Germans against the British at Ypres on July 12, 1917, killing eighty-seven and incapacitating 2,000 after a barrage of 50,000 shells. Although phosgene caused the most deaths, mustard agent caused the most injuries of all the war gases. More than eleven months later, British and French forces were using their own mustard projectiles against the Germans. Up to 50 percent of artillery projectiles were chemical-filled by the end of the war.

Both sides developed defensive equipment in response to the gases, including protective masks for humans, dogs, and horses; impregnated clothing for protection against the vesicants; warning horns and gongs; and improvised collective protection shelters in the trenches. When the United States sent the American

Expeditionary Force to France in 1917, the British and French military had to provide U.S. soldiers with protective gear and chemical munitions. The U.S. military had not prepared for gas warfare, despite knowledge of the threat for years. In September 1917, the U.S. Army formed the Gas Service, which had the responsibility to train and equip its forces and to develop an offensive capability designed on the British mortars and French 75 mm artillery. After initial heavy losses due to poor gas discipline, the Americans learned to protect themselves. They recognized the need to develop an inherent military agency to specialize in this area.

The War Department created the Chemical Warfare Service in June 1918 to organize an effort that was being executed by the Bureau of Mines (research and development), the Ordnance Department (production of agents and the filling of chemical shells), the Medical Department (procurement and supply of gas masks), the Signal Corps (procuring gas alarms), and the Corps of Engineers (offensive training and actual employment of gas). On July 1, 1918, Major General William Sibert, the architect of the Panama Canal and former First Infantry Division commander, became the first director of the Army's Chemical Warfare Service. The Army built four CW agent production plants on Edgewood Arsenal in Maryland in 1917–1918 to produce chlorine, chloropicrin, phosgene, and mustard agent. The arsenal produced more than 930 tons of phosgene and 710 tons of mustard agent by the end of the war; although the CW agents were shipped to France, no shells were manufactured in time to support U.S. forces. The American Expeditionary Force's Second Chemical Battalion would use British Stokes mortars and Livens projectors and French artillery batteries during their operations in Europe.

Many U.S. commanders were reluctant to employ a weapon with which they had no experience. Some thought their use of gas weapons would cause the Germans to retaliate with gas against them, and so abstained. When the Germans attacked the American forces with gas regardless, the Americans began to use gas in support of their attacks. General John J. Pershing, commanding general of the U.S. forces, referred specifically to aircraft, tanks, and poison gas as the three weapons making major impacts during the Great War. In a statement still quoted today, he declared, "Whether or not gas will be employed in future wars is a matter of conjecture, but the effect is so deadly to the unprepared that we can never afford to neglect the question."[8]

At the end of the war, nearly one third of all U.S. soldiers evacuated to military hospitals had been a casualty of gas warfare, about 70,000 in all. Of these casualties, slightly more than 1,200 died, or about one in every sixty gas cases. By comparison, artillery in general had caused nearly 75,000 U.S. casualties, of which about one in ten died in the wards. Gas was not a major battlefield killer, but it had a significant emotional impact on how the military and public perceived the conflict.

Congress authorized the permanent formation of the Chemical Warfare Service in 1920, with the rationale that this form of warfare would continue to be a threat. In the bill authorizing the service, Congress stated that the duties of the Chemical Warfare Service

> comprise[d] the investigation, development, manufacture or procurement and supply of all smoke and incendiary materials, all toxic gases, and all gas defense appliances; the research, design, and experimentation connected with chemical warfare and its material; and chemical projectile filling plants and proving grounds; the supervision and training of the Army in chemical warfare, both offensive and defensive, including the necessary schools of instruction; and the organization, equipment, training, and operation of special gas troops.

Because of the visibility of surviving veterans' wounds, gas warfare became a rallying point for postwar arms control efforts. Following the war, a number of treaties addressed chemical and biological warfare. The most important one was the Geneva Protocol of 1925, which called for nations to abstain from the use of chemical or biological weapons in future conflicts. Many nations interpreted this protocol to mean any and all gases, including riot-control agents. Nearly all interpreted it as authorizing a nation to use chemical or biological agents in response to a belligerent's first use of such weapons in a conflict. As such, the protocol did not ban the development and storage of these weapons, merely its first use. At the time, the Senate did not ratify the treaty, stating that it was not realistic to expect a nation to limit itself in its potential defenses against adversaries armed with chemical weapons. This was not an endorsement of gas warfare; rather, the Senate was acknowledging that despite the existence of treaties, gas would be used in future conflicts and the U.S. military had to be prepared.

The Threat Increases: World War II

Prior to the outbreak of war in Europe, there had been indications that the coming conflict would include the use of chemical weapons. An Italian general, Giulio Douhet, came forth with a popular theory on future military operations. He saw the development of bombers and chemical warfare coming together to create a new threat against military forces and the civilian populace. He went so far as to suggest that nations should reduce their procurement of ground and sea forces to focus on air power, for once an opponent's air bases were destroyed, the cities would be next. Gas bombs would demoralize the populace until they forced their government to surrender.[9]

In 1935, Italian forces in Ethiopia successfully employed aerial-delivered mustard bombs and spray tanks against tribesmen in the mountains to quickly conclude the conflict in months, instead of the several years that had been projected. Italy justified this use by stating that Ethiopians had tortured or killed their prisoners and wounded soldiers and that the Geneva Protocol included an exception that allowed gas warfare as a reprisal against illegal acts of war. Japan had experimented with chemical and biological warfare in their invasion of China, using mustard-filled shells and tear gas grenades mixed with smoke screens against Chinese forces and targeting several large cities with biological agents delivered from the air. Although the BW attacks were not militarily significant, they increased the panic and the number of war casualties in China, resulting in a formal protest by the Chinese government to the League of Nations in 1937. The response from the League of Nations against Italy and Japan was relatively mild and only served to increase concerns that future wars would feature the use of poison weapons.

France and England had developed their own chemical warfare stocks, but Germany was forbidden by the Versailles Treaty from developing chemical weapons in their country. Observing the letter of the treaty but not the intent, German scientists traveled to the Soviet Union in the 1920s to cooperatively develop chemical capabilities (both industrial and military). The discovery of nerve agents was an accident, for the Germans were actually developing an indigenous insecticide production capability that was not dependent on oil imports. Once the war started, the Germans did build a limited chemical weapons stockpile, but they assumed that the Allies had already discovered nerve agents; after all, the Allies had not been restricted in their technical research as the Germans had been.[10]

The U.S. government entered World War II with very few chemical weapons in its inventory and with practically no ability to deliver chemical weapons on the battlefield. The U.S. military leadership was very nervous about fighting a two-front war against countries that already had demonstrated a chemical warfare capability. Japan had not ratified the Geneva Protocol, and Germany's ally Italy had already demonstrated its CW ability in Ethiopia. President Franklin D. Roosevelt ordered the development of a retaliatory capability, which resulted in a very large investment in building chemical ammunition plants, testing grounds, and defensive equipment such as chemical agent detectors, protective masks and suits, and decontaminants. This included the formation of Pine Bluff Arsenal, Rocky Mountain Arsenal, Dugway Proving Ground, Camp Sibert, Plum Island, and Camp Beale, among other installations. The United States soon developed huge stocks of mustard agent, lewisite, phosgene, cyanogen chloride, and hydrogen cyanide. The U.S. military built up overseas stockpiles of CW agents, producing more than 146,000 tons by the end of 1945, so they could retaliate quickly if they came under attack by German or Japanese CW munitions. The military had also developed new weapon systems to deliver the agents, including a new 4.2 inch chemical mortar, aerial bombs, and spray generators.

The United States initiated its biological warfare program in 1942, in close cooperation with the Canadian and British governments. During the 1930s, there had been a great deal of research on the practical employment of BW agents in Europe, but not in the United States. Camp Detrick, in western Maryland, sprang into existence in April 1943. It included a number of laboratories and a pilot plant that manufactured weapons-grade botulinum toxin and anthrax spores. Although a larger plant was constructed in Terre Haute, Indiana, and tested with biological simulants—chemicals that have some of the features of a chemical or biological warfare agent that are used by evaluators to assess the agent's effectiveness without actually using toxic substances—it was not ready prior to the invasion of Europe and never manufactured any anthrax.[11]

Americans storming the beaches in Africa, Italy, and Europe all had gas masks, impregnated suits, and information cards detailing the signs and symptoms of gas poisoning. Decontamination troops landed right behind the infantry in the major invasions, ready to clean the beaches in case they had been hit by CW agents. More than 400 chemical battalions and companies, numbering more than 60,000 military personnel at the peak of enlistment, were supporting combat forces with specialized chemical offensive and defensive expertise.[12] Although, for whatever reasons, no nation was willing to use CB weapons, no one was willing to neglect the requirement to defend against their potential use.

Despite the presence of chemical weapon stockpiles in Europe and in Asia, there was no use of chemical weapons by any major power. There has been much speculation as to why nations did not seek to use these weapons to gain a military advantage over their adversaries. All the ground forces had significant defensive capabilities, and all the major powers had the industrial capability to produce CW agents in large enough quantities to allow their armed forces to launch and sustain decisive offensive operations. There was considerable discussion over the use of gas warfare for military operations, including Prime Minister Winston Churchill's calling for plans to defeat a German invasion of the United Kingdom by using mustard agents against the invaders. Although some debated the morality of using these particular weapons, many others had little trouble discussing the use of CB weapons as a method to stop large-scale invasions of their country or to reduce the massive casualties suffered in the Pacific theater, or as retaliatory threats to counter enemy use of the same. The United States, having signed but not ratified the Geneva Protocol, could have unilaterally employed gas against the Axis within the letter (but not the spirit) of international law. In the end, attacking forces relied on the speed and shock of conventional warfare, where the use of gas could have slowed down operations in favor of the defender.

Major General Alden Waitt, the chief chemical officer in 1945 and the assistant chief chemical officer during World War II, appropriately noted that earlier lack of use of toxic gases did not justify the conclusion that they would not be used in the future. The Germans had produced more than a quarter of a million tons of toxic gas, including thousands of tons of tabun nerve agent. Their failure to use this gas was largely attributed to the fear of retaliation. The United States should not, Waitt felt, assume that other nations would refrain from using gas where it could serve their purposes.[13] Congress agreed, and on August 2, 1946, it codified the Army's Chemical Warfare Service as the Chemical Corps (an act that President Roosevelt, an ardent opponent of chemical warfare, had refused to approve).

The Cold War Starts

Following World War II, the United States and the Soviet Union both discovered the German nerve agent production facilities, and both began intense research and development efforts to better understand these new weapons. These nerve agents included tabun, sarin, and soman and are often referred to as the "second generation" of chemical weapons (the first generation being the industrial chemicals and mustard agent employed in World War I). These agents were much more lethal than their predecessors, but it took several years of research to understand their effects and limitations as weapons and how to best design defensive equipment to detect these agents, to protect against them, and to decontaminate personnel and equipment.

Although the newly named U.S. Army Chemical Corps[14] had been reduced in size after the war, as had been much of the U.S. military, the Korean conflict ignited concern that U.S. forces might face CB weapons developed by Soviet and Chinese facilities. The Army built a production plant for GB-type nerve agents at Muscle Shoals, Alabama, in 1950, which would be producing agent by 1953. Stocks of chemical warfare agents and munitions were moved to an Army depot on Okinawa as a retaliatory capability prepared to respond to any adversarial first use of chemical weapons. Although the U.S. military did not use CW weapons during the conflict, it undertook significant efforts to execute smoke and obscurant operations and to use incendiary munitions. The Chemical Corps activated a new training center, moving their school from Edgewood Arsenal in Maryland to Fort McClellan, Alabama, in 1952.

Following the Korean conflict, the Chemical Corps lost its 4.2 inch mortars to the infantry, but it would retain its research and development role in respect to CB weapons. With the production of new nerve agents and corresponding new defense equipment, the Chemical Corps was exceedingly busy in the 1950s. Chief Chemical Officer Major General Egbert Bullene stated in 1953, "Today, thanks to Joe Stalin, we are back in business."[15] Primarily as a result of British research, the United States developed a more persistent nerve agent, called VX, by 1955. This thick, oily liquid could be aerosolized and disseminated on the battlefield to create a long-term hazard (lasting days to weeks) to unprotected personnel. The Soviet research community developed their own variant of VX as well. The V-class agents became called the "third generation" CW agents.

The United States had not developed biological weapons past its limited experience at Camp (later Fort) Detrick, so it initiated a new research and development effort that would lead to the production of biological weapons and to the stockpiling of weapons for a retaliatory capability.[16] The North Korean government claimed that U.S. pilots had bombed their forces with biological weapons, but these accusations were not credible at the time—the United States had no real military offensive BW capability in 1952—and these claims were proven false decades later. By the late 1960s, however, the United States did have a formidable BW stockpile. It had weaponized anthrax, botulinum toxin, and tularemia as lethal antipersonnel agents. Brucellosis, Q fever, staphylococcal enterotoxin type B (SEB), and Venezuelan equine encephalitis (VEE) virus represented its incapacitating antipersonnel agents. Three anticrop agents—rice blast, rye stem rust, and wheat stem rust—were developed and stockpiled ready for aerial spraying.[17] Investigations into the potential weaponization of anti-animal and other antipersonnel BW agents continued at Fort Detrick and Plum Island, if for no other reason than to ensure that the U.S. military could identify whether an adversary was using these agents and to develop medical countermeasures against them.

The two superpowers had CW stockpiles in Europe and Asia in preparation for what many thought would be a third world war. If U.S. forces had no chemical weapons and were attacked by Soviet chemical weapons, it was reasoned, the United States would have to retaliate with tactical nuclear weapons, which might start an escalation to strategic nuclear exchanges.[18] Far better to keep the conflict below the nuclear threshold. In response to this line of logic, the U.S. Army, Air Force, and Navy developed chemical weapons, including aerial bombs and spray tanks, unguided rockets, artillery shells, land mines, and guided missile warheads for their respective airplanes, artillery systems, and ships, ensuring they all had the ability to retaliate in kind to anticipated Soviet chemical weapon use.

These new weapon systems and new agents also drove the need for better understanding of how they worked on the open battlefield. In 1961, Defense Secretary Robert McNamara initiated a number of defense projects, one of which, titled Project 112, focused on open-air trials of chemical and biological warfare agents and simulants. The Army opened Deseret Test Center in Utah, next to Dugway Proving Ground, to support the execution of these tests, which also were carried out on the open seas, in the tropics, and in an arctic environment.

The Vietnam Conflict

The conflict in Vietnam brought a new type of conflict to the U.S. forces, one in which conventional styles of warfare were pitted against an untraditional adversary. Although the U.S. government decided against the use of unconventional munitions to fight the Vietcong and North Vietnamese, the Chemical Corps did develop colored smoke grenades, improve its riot-control agents, and develop herbicides that supported combat operations. The United States initially began Operation Ranch Hand, the name of the defoliant operation in Vietnam, at the request of the South Vietnamese government, to destroy the rice farms that were sustaining the Vietcong forces. U.S. forces soon discovered the value of spraying herbicides around their bases, limiting the ability of enemy forces to sneak up to them. Similarly, eliminating the foliage at riverbanks and where the enemy operated reduced the chance of ambushes and resulted in lower casualty rates for the U.S. military.

There had been no previous testing of the potential long-term effects of herbicides on exposed persons, either for civilian use in the United States or, certainly, for the large quantities used for military operations in Vietnam. The same chemicals had been used in much smaller quantities on U.S. lawns, and few had noted any severe effects described by veterans years after the conflict. There was no independent federal oversight in this area, since this use took place prior to the establishment of the Environmental Protection Agency (EPA). These herbicides were suspected of causing a number of illnesses in exposed soldiers and civilians in the area, but many symptoms did not show up until years later. After initially denying benefits to U.S. veterans, the U.S. government acknowledged that exposure to herbicides was related to wartime injuries and that service members should be compensated for exposure to these herbicides.

The increased presence of U.S. forces in Vietnam, starting around 1965, correlated with increased use of riot-control agents and brought strong rebukes by other nations and arms control proponents. Reporters noted that U.S. military advisors had begun to carry tear gas grenades and protective masks for self-defense. U.S. troops used riot-control agents to flush out enemy forces in tunnels and to create a harassing and nauseating effect on personnel and animals traveling on enemy supply routes. Many critics attacked this use of tear gas as a violation of the 1925 Geneva Protocol. The U.S. government strongly disagreed that employing tear gas was a treaty violation but held that even if it were a violation, the government was still not bound to an international treaty it had never ratified. The Chemical Corps was heavily into the research for chemical incapacitants (other than riot-control agents), which would become another source of controversy for the military. Agent BZ, the only incapacitating agent standardized by the Army, did not show any military operational value, since it took two to three hours to affect troops and was visible as a cloud during its dissemination.

While this debate raged, the Soviet-trained and equipped Egyptian Air Force was dropping chemical-filled bombs on Yemini royalists embroiled in their civil war. Despite clear evidence of chemical warfare, very little was done in the way of reprimanding Egypt or investigating the Soviet Union's role in arming and training the Egyptian Air Force. U.S. military strategists dismissed the use of chemical weapons as an aberration and not relevant to future conflicts with the Warsaw Pact. To this day, Egypt has continued to deny its involvement in chemical warfare during the Yemeni civil war.

Changing Perceptions: 1968–1976

Increasing environmental awareness, the publicized use of riot-control agents and herbicides in Vietnam, and the Nixon administration's arms control agenda drove an increased effort to prohibit CB warfare and to disarm the major superpowers. Between 1968 and 1972, a series of events occurred in the United States that drove the CB weapons program out of business. In March 1968, the Army was accused of causing the deaths of more than 6,000 sheep on ranches near Dugway Proving Ground, Utah. Attention focused on an open-air test of VX nerve agent in which the chemical was dispersed from an F-4 jet's spray tank at a test range thirty miles from the ranches. Despite the lack of any concrete or forensics evidence pointing to the proving ground's testing, Army leadership decided to settle the ranchers' monetary losses without admitting liability.[19]

The political and media uproar resulting from this event continued for more than a year and led to increased scrutiny of the U.S. government's CB warfare programs. In early May 1969, several congressmen and mayors protested the Army's plans to dispose of aging munitions by sinking retired Liberty ships full of chemical munitions more than 200 miles off the East Coast. Although there had been (and continues to be) no evidence of any ill effects resulting from the ocean dumping, the Army stopped this disposal practice and, in line with independent scientific recommendations, made plans to incinerate its obsolete and leaking munitions.

The United Nations commissioned a special report on CB warfare, releasing it in July 1969. This report stressed the danger of nations' engaging in CB weapons development, not merely to noncombatants but also to the nations' own military forces. That same month, a reported nerve agent leak at an Army depot in Okinawa increased the media focus on the Army's chemical weapons policy. Again, although the exposed personnel reported no long-term ill effects, the mere fact that the U.S. government had chemical weapons overseas, ready for employment, was disturbing to many. The Japanese government had had no idea that the weapons were there, let alone the American public.

President Richard Nixon called for a review of the government's CB warfare program in light of arms control proposals and military plans and policies. This review led to his announcement on November 25, 1969, that the U.S. government would renounce its offensive biological warfare program, would reaffirm the "no first use" policy for chemical warfare, and would stop producing CW agents until the new binary CW agents (binary agents consist of two parts that do not come together until they are used) were available. In 1972, the U.S. government signed the BWC, which would enter into force in 1975. By 1973, the United States had destroyed all of its stockpiled BW agents and toxins. In 1975, the U.S. Senate ratified the Geneva Protocol. These policy changes stopped the offensive BW program and stalled the U.S. military's attempts to modernize its chemical weapons.

These events also indirectly led to the Army's proposed disestablishment of the Chemical Corps in January 1973,[20] until the

Arab-Israeli War reignited the Army's desire to develop and retain defensive CB capabilities. The Israeli Army had captured Egyptian forces that had Soviet-designed chemical defense equipment, including portable collective protection shelters, chemical-agent detectors, decontamination kits, and medical countermeasures. This seemed to indicate that the Soviet Union was still very interested in CB warfare. If the Soviets were supplying their allies with this equipment, what were they preparing to do in Europe against U.S. forces? Ken Alibek, a noted former Soviet bioweapons researcher, revealed in his book *Biohazard* that the Soviets had suspected that Nixon's declaration was merely an attempt to drive the U.S. BW program under covert cover, so they had redoubled their efforts. One indication of the Soviet's offensive BW program was the accidental release of anthrax at Sverdlovsk in April 1979; hundreds were killed in this incident, which President Boris Yeltsin admitted in 1992 had been the result of a malfunction at a Soviet military BW production plant.[21]

The Army decided to stop its disestablishment of the Chemical Corps in 1976 and to reopen the Chemical School at Fort McClellan in 1979, in part due to its concern that it could not afford to neglect a strong CB defense capability. Unfortunately, the Army's disestablishment efforts had left the Chemical Corps at least a decade behind the rest of the world in the development and acquisition of CB defense equipment, a delay that could have been very costly when the Army had to respond to Iraqi forces invading Kuwait in 1990. Military forces were better trained and equipped in the late 1980s than in the 1970s, but they nevertheless had to deploy without a number of new CB defense items that were just coming out of research and development. As the Army reestablished its Chemical Corps, it also began to reexamine modernizing its offensive CW weapons.

Disarming the Superpowers

The United Kingdom and France had publicly declared their CB weapons stockpiles and had taken steps to eliminate them in the 1950s, but until the two major superpowers agreed to a new arms control program, the threat of chemical warfare would continue. International negotiations had started in the late 1960s, when the U.S. government initiated new talks focusing on chemical weapons disarmament with the Soviet Union in 1977. Following years of failed attempts to craft a new arms control agreement with the Soviets and after reports of Soviet chemical warfare in Afghanistan, the U.S. military moved to modernize its chemical weapons capability. This decision was very controversial, for it was seen by many as contrary to the spirit of international arms control. The U.S. government's position was that the development of a modern retaliatory capability and the pursuit of an arms control agreement were not mutually exclusive options. After years of debate, Congress approved President Ronald Reagan's requests to produce binary chemical munitions in 1985, and the first 155 mm binary artillery projectiles started to come off the production line at Pine Bluff Arsenal, Arkansas, that year. This production effort brought the Soviet Union to the table for serious negotiations, which resulted in the decision to halt the U.S. binary chemical munitions program in July 1990. The U.S. Army removed its chemical weapons from Germany in September 1990, storing them at Johnston Island (800 miles southwest of Hawaii) until they could be destroyed.

In January 1993, 130 countries signed the Chemical Weapons Convention treaty in Paris. This treaty prohibited its signatories from developing, producing, storing, or transferring chemical weapons and included a ban on using chemical weapons or assisting others to develop chemical weapons. It also called for the destruction of existing chemical weapons and production facilities, and it called for its signatories to refrain from the use of riot-control agents as a form of warfare. This treaty had a vigorous declaration procedure and inspection regime, which would be overseen by the Organization for the Prohibition of Chemical Weapons (OPCW), stationed in The Hague, Netherlands. The treaty entered into force after the sixty-fifth country ratified the language, on April 29, 1997. (The United States ratified the CWC on April 25, 1997.) To date, 175 countries have signed and 145 countries have ratified the treaty.

The United States initiated the destruction of its older chemical weapons in 1985, initially to make room for the new binary chemical weapons but later (after 1990) to meet their treaty obligations under the CWC. The disposal program deadline was set at 2007 to align with the CWC's deadline of disposing of all stocks within ten years. There exists a great deal of controversy about the use of incineration to destroy these munitions, but no one has been injured as a result of the U.S. military's storage or disposal operations. Because of this controversy on how the United States should dispose of its 31,400 tons of chemical weapons, there is little hope that the elimination of the U.S. chemical stockpile will be completed prior to 2007. Russia's planned disposal of 40,000 tons of chemical weapons is not on schedule for similar political and environmental concerns, but also, more importantly, for economic reasons (lacking the necessary funds to destroy these weapons). Although the U.S. government has assisted the Russian government in developing a program to dispose of these weapons, there is little chance that they will be completed on time. The CWC treaty has an allowance for a five-year extension to its deadline, which both nations will no doubt seek.

Continued Proliferation

As the superpowers destroy their CB weapons, a number of smaller countries have shown an interest in building them. We will investigate this more in chapter 3, but just as an example, consider the Iran-Iraq War of 1983–1988. Both sides developed and employed chemical weapons, and there was little censure from the major powers other than the initiation of export-control regulations in an attempt to slow down the flow of chemical precursors and equipment to these countries. Certainly, the United States faced its greatest credible threat from CB weapons since the Cold War during the 1990–1991 Persian Gulf War. Although Iraq did not employ its CB weapons against the U.S. military, Iraq demonstrated the emerging threat that any country with ballistic missiles and a CB weapons program could present to its neighbors, threatening both military forces and the civilian populace. Other countries in the Middle East have sophisticated weapons programs, as do North Korea and other Asian nations.

Despite the label of immorality that CB weapons have inherited, many countries continue to develop these capabilities, which has been made somewhat easier by the development and global marketing of dual-use technologies (equipment and material used for both military and civilian purposes), by the sharing of intellectual property around the world, and by more-widespread college education. Although arms control advocates like to call CB weapons a "poor man's atomic bomb," this moniker is inappropriate. China, India, Pakistan, and Israel are four countries that have nuclear weapons, yet all are also suspected of developing or of having the potential to develop CB weapons.

Iran, Iraq, Libya, and North Korea are also suspected of wanting nuclear, biological, and chemical (NBC) weapons. Primarily, it is thought that these countries seek unconventional weapons as a deterrent against their aggressive neighbors' stockpiles or as a threat to their weaker neighbors. In addition, marketing CB weapons technology could be a great potential moneymaker on the Third World market.

Although since the 1970s terrorists across the world have considered and threatened the use of CB weapons, there was only one case of BW terrorism in the United States prior to 2000. Similarly, the notion of CW terrorism was seen as a hollow threat prior to the Tokyo subway incident in March 1995. The Aum Shinrikyo cult manufactured its own sarin and even some BW agents in their preparations for what they thought was an upcoming worldwide apocalypse. In March 1995, members of the cult, which is credited with a number of CW incidents in Japan, released a sarin mixture at a dozen locations in the Tokyo subway. The number of casualties from this one event is often mistakenly stated as more than 5,000 civilians, However, this number refers to the large number of panicked citizens (the "worried well") who flooded the hospitals, thinking they had been exposed to nerve agents because they were on the subway trains about the time of the attacks. Twelve Japanese citizens died, and more than 900 people developed noticeable symptoms of nerve agent poisoning, including 135 emergency responders.[22]

The recent assault from four anthrax-laced letters, killing five people and affecting hundreds, has reinforced the desire to develop capabilities to protect U.S. citizens from CB terrorist attacks. The outbreak of thousands of anthrax hoaxes across the nation resulted in millions of dollars in wasted resources, as emergency responders scrambled to assess what they later discovered to be sugar, flour, or crushed white candies. Such hoaxes are not only a U.S. concern; countries all over the world have experienced (and continue to experience) similar anthrax hoaxes and have had to respond to panicked emergency calls about "suspicious white powders."

Conclusions

This is a very quick highlight of the history of chemical and biological warfare. The twentieth century has seen a rapid evolution of CB warfare from its humble beginnings in industrial enterprises to become an influential weapon of war. Over this period of time, it has received more than its fair share of myths and exaggerations, political hype, and public hysteria. The idea that the use of chemical and biological weapons could be a completely rational and not an immoral act amounts to heresy of a sort. Isaac Asimov once stated, "If a scientific heresy is ignored or denounced by the general public, there is a chance it may be right. If a scientific heresy is emotionally supported by the general public, it is almost certainly wrong," and in the same article, "It is not so much that I have confidence in scientists being right, but that I have so much in nonscientists being wrong. . . . It is those who support ideas for emotional reasons only who can't change."[23]

What Asimov may have been pointing out is that a lack of education on specific subjects causes people to make judgments that may be emotionally rather than intellectually based and as a result, to misunderstand the issues. Certainly this corollary applies to CB warfare. It takes a broader frame of reference to understand why militaries and terrorists seek out CB weapons. The mistake many people make is to focus on how CB weapons work and how they kill rather than looking at this issue in the broader context of armed conflict and politics. Whereas people focus on the lethality of a single drop of CW agent or a gram of BW agent, they rarely focus on how a single bayonet or a single round of full-metal-jacketed ammunition can kill an individual. Think about the ammunition in a sporting goods store and do the math; if each bullet can kill one individual, how many deaths are possible from one store's inventory? Of course, no one views handgun and rifle ammunition as "weapons of mass destruction," but similarly, it is just as fanciful to think about CB warfare agents as mass casualty weapons merely based on their lethality. One has to frame their use on the battlefield, which takes into consideration the weather, the weapon systems, and their intended target's training and preparedness.

To understand the real potential and shortfalls of CB weapons requires a broader perspective. The researcher should not merely read books about CB weapons (such as this one) but also investigate how military units operated on past battlefields and how they operate on current ones, how nations negotiate on arms control treaties (not just on CB warfare but on other topics as well), and how terrorists operate to push their agendas. It is with this broader education that one can really understand the role that CB weapons have played in our history and understand that these weapons, despite their larger-than-life image as "weapons of mass destruction," are at once less doomsday weapons and in a large measure just another tool of war. There are many issues that will remain unclear to the reader after concluding with this book: How did the military discover and design these specific weapons? Why is it that arms control treaties have failed to stop the proliferation of CB weapons? Are there instances where nations would be justified in using CB weapons, such as Churchill's urging that preparations be made to use mustard agent against potential German invaders in World War II? Is the threat of terrorist use of CB warfare agents a real and current danger to the United States?

This book is merely a first step. Understanding the nature of CB warfare is necessary to learn the nomenclatures, the issues, and the events where the use of CB weapons has been considered. After this education, the researcher must continue and examine the broader tapestry of how nations, militaries, and politicians exercise war and attempt to control its outcome. Then one can truly understand how the arms control treaties in this area have succeeded or failed, why nations continue to invest resources in building offensive CB warfare capabilities, how military forces seek to counter the use of these weapons, and exactly how much the general public should worry about the future of CB warfare.

Notes

1. The military definitions are derived from Joint Publication 1-02, *DOD Dictionary of Military and Associated Terms,* December 19, 2001 (online; available: http://www.dtic.mil/doctrine/jel/doddict/; accessed November 2002).

2. Captain A. T. Mahan, the famous naval strategist, was a U.S. delegate to these talks. His rationale for why the United States should not sign was "1. That no shell emitting such gases is as yet in practical use, or has undergone adequate experiment; consequently, a vote taken now would be taken in ignorance of the facts as to whether the results would be of a decisive character, or whether injury in excess of that necessary to attain the end of warfare, the immediate disabling of the enemy, would be inflicted. 2. That the reproach of cruelty and perfidy, addressed against these supposed shells, was equally uttered formerly against firearms and torpedoes, both of which are now employed without scruple. Until we knew the effects of such asphyxiating shells, there was no

saying whether they would be more or less merciful than missiles now permitted. 3. That it was illogical, and not demonstrably humane, to be tender about asphyxiating men with gas, when all were prepared to admit that it was allowable to blow the bottom out of an ironclad at midnight, throwing four or five hundred into the sea, to be choked by water, with scarcely the remotest chance of escape. If, and when, a shell emitting asphyxiating gases alone has been successfully produced, then, and not before, men will be able to vote intelligently on the subject"; "The Peace Conference at the Hague 1899: Report of Captain Mahan to the United States Commission to the International Conference at the Hague, on Disarmament, etc., with Reference to Navies," Avalon Project at Yale Law School (on-line; available: http://www.yale.edu/lawweb/avalon/lawofwar/hague99/hag99-06.htm; accessed April 3, 2003).

3. W. Michael Reisman and Chris T. Antoniou, *The Laws of War: A Comprehensive Collection of Primary Documents on International Laws Governing Armed Conflict* (New York: Vantage Books, 1994), 47, 57.

4. Jeffery K. Smart, *History of Chemical and Biological Warfare: An American Perspective* (Aberdeen Proving Ground, MD: U.S. Army, 1997), 14. This section of Smart's book is also chapter 2 of Frederick Sidel, Ernest Takafuji, and David Franz, eds., *Medical Aspects of Chemical and Biological Warfare* (Washington, DC: Office of the Surgeon General, 1997).

5. Rudolph Hanglian, *The Gas Attack at Ypres: A Study in Military History* (Edgewood Arsenal, MD: U.S. Army, 1940), 2–3.

6. Ibid., 167–169.

7. According to one source, the use of cylinders rather than artillery projectiles was not an attempt to circumvent international law. It was simple pragmatism: Because the agent was a nonpersistent industrial chemical, artillery shells could not place enough of the gas on target to affect personnel. Only a large number of cylinders could carry the quantities necessary to cause a noticeable impact over a large area.

8. John J. Pershing, *Final Report of General John J. Pershing, Commander-in-Chief American Expeditionary Forces* (Washington, DC: Government Printing Office, 1920), 77.

9. Martin Van Creveld, *The Art of War: War and Military Thought* (London: Cassell, 2000), 162–168.

10. Robert Harris and Jeremy Paxman, *A Higher Form of Killing: The Secret Story of Chemical and Biological Warfare* (New York: Hill and Wang, 1982), 53–54.

11. One of the best sources for the Chemical Warfare Service's work during World War II is the Center of Military History's three-volume collection in its green-hardback "U.S. Army in World War II" collection. The volumes are Leo P. Brophy and George J. B. Fisher, *The Chemical Warfare Service: Organizing for War* (Washington, DC: Office of the Chief of Military History, 1959); Leo P. Brophy, Wyndham D. Miles, and Rexmond Cochrane, *The Chemical Warfare Service: From Laboratory to Field* (Washington, DC: Office of the Chief of Military History, 1966); and

Brookes E. Kleber and Dale Birdsell, *The Chemical Warfare Service: Chemicals in Combat* (Washington, DC: Office of the Chief of Military History, 1966).

12. These specialized Army units included chemical mortar battalions that used their high-explosive munitions to support combat troops (since no chemical weapons were employed), smoke-generator battalions and companies, depot companies that stored and maintained the chemical defense equipment, processing companies that prepared impregnated chemical protective clothing, decontamination companies, chemical staff in the theater, army group and army headquarters elements, and laboratory companies for technical intelligence assessments. There were also chemical service units supporting the Army Air Force, specifically in the storage and handling of incendiary bombs.

13. Smart, *History of Chemical and Biological Warfare*, 45.

14. Congress redesignated the Chemical Warfare Service as the Chemical Corps on August 2, 1946.

15. Smart, *History of Chemical and Biological Warfare*, 48.

16. Norman M. Covert, *Cutting Edge: A History of Fort Detrick, Maryland, 1943–1993* (Fort Detrick, MD: Public Affairs Office, 1994).

17. George W. Christopher, Theodore J. Cieslak, Julie A. Pavlin, and Edward M. Eitzen, "Biological Warfare: A Historical Perspective," *The Journal of the American Medical Association,* August 6, 1997, 414.

18. As a short explanation, the military considers three levels of war: tactical, operational, and strategic. The tactical level of war includes planning for battles and engagements that focus on the arrangement and maneuvering of military combat elements to achieve combat objectives. In short, this level is the front-line actions to achieve near-term and immediate battlefield objectives. The operational level of war involves those plans to conduct and sustain tactical operations to accomplish strategic objectives within a particular theater of operation. The strategic level of war addresses the accomplishment of national and multinational military objectives and initiatives. With regard to nuclear weapons, military experts would state that tactical nuclear weapons would be those used to disrupt enemy military forces on the battlefield, whereas operational nuclear weapons would be those that targeted command and control headquarters, large logistics bases in the rear area, and air bases and seaports. Strategic nuclear weapons, of course, are those that target an adversary's major metropolitan cities and military bases to destroy the nation's infrastructure.

19. Albert. J. Mauroni, *America's Struggle with Chemical-Biological Warfare* (Westport, CT: Praeger, 2000), 29–43.

20. General Creighton Abrams, the chief of staff of the Army, was remolding the Army after the Vietnam conflict and proposed consolidating the special weapons function of the Chemical Corps into the Ordnance Corps. In January 1973, he announced that the Chemical Corps was disestablished. Congress had to make the final decision, since

the formation of the Chemical Corps had been approved by that body in 1946. The House of Representatives did not approve the disestablishment, instead returning the issue to the secretary of the Army for his decision. By then, General Abrams had died, and the results of the Arab-Israeli War demonstrated that the Soviet Union was still thinking about CB warfare.

21. Ken Alibek, with Stephen Handelman, *Biohazard: The Chilling True Story of the Largest Covert Biological Weapons Program in the World. Told from Inside by the Man Who Ran It* (New York: Random House, 1999), 234; and Edward M. Spiers, *Chemical and Biological Weapons: A Study of Proliferation* (New York: St. Martin's Press, 1994), 37.

22. F. R. Sidell, S. R. Lillibridge, S. S. Leffingwell, and J. A. Liddle, "A Report by a U.S. Medical Team on the Casualties from the Tokyo Subway Incident." Unpublished manuscript.

23. Isaac Asimov, "Asimov's Corollary," in the essay "Quasar, Quasar, Burning Bright," in *Quasar, Quasar, Burning Bright* (Garden City, NY: Doubleday, 1978).

2

Issues and Controversies

There is no end to the issues and controversies related to chemical and biological warfare. This is in part due to a natural distaste some people have when discussing a form of warfare that essentially treats humans like insects, to be exterminated by invisible, odorless gases, and in part due to misunderstanding or misinformation on how military forces employ these weapons. Even within the military, the offensive use of CB weapons has always been controversial, for it is not seen as an "honorable" form of combat. Some controversies are born from a lack of understanding or deliberate exaggeration of what CB weapons can and cannot do in the open environment. And when misinformation is combined with a dash of advocacy science and the fear that the government is not looking out for the public's best interests, the stories about CB weapons grow.

Countries and nonstate groups continue to develop these weapons, and, since this represents a current threat, it is important that the public as well as the military understand what they can and cannot do. Military forces use poison gases because they do kill people, and like other weapon systems, military forces train to use them because one can achieve predictable and measurable effects. There are two sides to each of these following discussions:

27

the dry, historical review of government actions and often a judgmental view of the appropriateness of these actions. It is incumbent upon the reader to further research each side to better understand how these issues developed and where the controversy lies. Do not take any presented issue at its face value (not even these below); do the research to understand that the issues are not as simple as they may appear.

The U.S. Offensive CB Warfare Program

Current and former administration officials and military officers such as General Norman Schwarzkopf have expressed their dismay that potential adversaries of the United States have CB weapons programs that could be employed against U.S. military forces or U.S. citizens.[1] In particular, these officials often view CB warfare as a form of combat that only rogue states and terrorists would employ, especially given the CWC and other arms control treaties. It may be somewhat surprising to some, then, to discover that the United States itself had a significant stockpile of these same weapons and that as recently as the late 1980s, it was attempting to replace aging stocks with modern binary chemical munitions. What was the rationale behind arming U.S. forces with these supposedly immoral weapons that only "cowardly" nations would use?

President Franklin Roosevelt developed the first policy on the offensive use of chemical weapons in 1941, warning the Axis powers that the United States would retaliate with chemical weapons if attacked by enemies using chemical weapons.[2] Because in 1941 the United States had only a very small stockpile of chemical weapons and no production capability to back up that warning, it embarked on a rapid buildup of research facilities, proving grounds, and weapons production to ensure the armed forces could carry out this mission. Many analysts believe that this retaliatory capability was a major factor preventing Germany from using its CW agents against the Allies.

President Harry Truman continued the "no first use" policy when discussions took place on the role of CB weapons in the Korean conflict. Determined to keep the conflict "limited," he directed the military not to use chemical weapons unless attacked in kind. The high casualties resulting from the Korean conflict caused some to consider a change in CB warfare policy. In 1956, the senior military leadership proposed establishing a new national security policy that would allow commanders to use CB weapons if there was a military advantage to be gained, rather than waiting for the other side to attack first with its CB weapons and then retaliating. This policy was discarded by President Nixon, who reaffirmed the "no first use, retaliate in kind" national policy for the employment of chemical weapons.

Through the 1960s and 1970s, this policy—of retaining chemical weapons to deter other nations from using them against the United States and to retaliate if deterrence failed—remained the primary rationale for maintaining an active offensive CW program. The concern was what the U.S. response would be if the Soviet Union or its allies used CB weapons against U.S. forces. If U.S. military forces could not respond similarly, the United States could only retaliate with tactical nuclear weapons, which could escalate to strategic exchanges. This rationale drove the Army, Air Force, and Navy to produce and test new CB weapons for their aircraft and artillery systems, thus developing a tactical response to adversarial CB weapons use.

The countering argument, against maintaining an active offensive CW program, has been that as long as the United States maintains a chemical weapons stockpile, other nations will want to develop their own CB weapons capability to ensure a level field of combat, thereby increasing the proliferation of CB weapons across the globe. If the United States has chemical weapons, then why shouldn't other countries? Also, a government gains a certain cachet, if nothing else to impress its own people, by having an unconventional weapons capability equivalent to a superpower's. There are some critics who believe that the United States should not even produce small amounts of CB warfare agents to test defensive equipment (which is currently permitted under international treaties), since this could encourage potential adversaries to continue research into more exotic agents that could bypass current detectors and protective ensembles.

There has always been concern that the U.S. military cannot develop and test CB weapons without inadvertently harming civilians or the military personnel involved in the tests. Some suspect the open-air tests of simulants over metropolitan cities in the 1950s and 1960s to have contributed to the poor health or even death of unprotected persons.[3] Controversy over testing conducted at Dugway Proving Ground has continued since the incident in 1968 when a CW agent was alleged to have killed a number of sheep. Even if the nerve agent did not kill the sheep at that time, there have been concerns that the local community might have been exposed to low levels of CW agents (more on this discussion below). How would one know? The agents were colorless and odorless, and the government did not tell the community when the tests took place or what agents were used. Such fears have led to speculation that unexplained illnesses within a community near or involved in a CB weapons study, even if the study involved only simulants, may have been caused by the testing.

Herbicides and Tear Gas

Unlike the European nations, the United States does not include herbicides or riot-control agents among chemical warfare agents. Before 1975, the U.S. military did define these as chemical munitions. The difference is that munitions filled with nerve and blister agents were "toxic chemical agent munitions," and the others, such as those filled with herbicides or riot-control agents, were merely munitions that dispensed a chemical substance instead of high explosives. On the other hand, riot-control agents came from similar military laboratories, filled similar munitions shells, were employed by military specialists, and fit the CWC definition as chemicals that could "cause death, temporary incapacitation or permanent harm to humans." This point of debate has had more to do with arms control policy than with how such materials were used by military forces.

The main difference to military operators was that, as a practical matter, the U.S. military did not employ herbicides or riot-control agents to kill or permanently incapacitate their intended targets. These chemical agents, in particular, have been employed to save military and noncombatant lives. U.S. forces used riot-control agents to prevent enemy adversaries—particularly unconventional troops in urban settings—from using noncombatants as shields, to break up unruly crowds, or to control prisoners of war who were attempting to escape. Herbicides were used to clear out potential ambush areas and to deny the enemy the ability to creep up on troop emplacements. The fact that these applications used chemicals did not equate, to the U.S. government at least, to the military use of toxic chemicals.

This issue arose to the level of public scrutiny during the Vietnam conflict, when reporters noted that U.S. military advisors were carrying tear gas grenades and protective masks for self-defense into the field. As the level of military involvement increased, so did the use of riot-control agents. The U.S. military used powered generators to pump riot-control agents into Vietcong tunnels and dropped riot-control agents onto enemy supply routes. These acts were viewed as offensive measures rather than defensive measures, since it appeared that U.S. forces were using a chemical gas to force persons from their tunnels in order to be captured or shot. As such, critics saw this as violating the Geneva Protocol.

Critics pointed out that the "first use" of tear gases could escalate to military forces' using lethal chemical warfare gases instead of merely temporary incapacitants. The Department of Defense noted that it was inconsistent to consider riot-control agents as chemical warfare agents when used by the military while, at the same time, many nations' police forces used the same riot-control agents routinely. One would think that a chemical warfare agent remained a chemical warfare agent without consideration of who was using it. Although the U.S. government still holds that herbicides and riot-control agents are not CW agents, the military does require presidential approval to employ them during wartime conflicts, even in defensive roles. During the Persian Gulf War, military police were granted permission to employ riot-control agents for the purposes of controlling enemy prisoners of war.

The use of the herbicide Agent Orange is similar in that the U.S. and South Vietnamese governments were not targeting people with herbicides. The South Vietnamese government requested U.S. support in denying rice crops to the enemy. This effort grew from an anticrop campaign to a deforestation operation when troops realized they could eliminate cover for enemy soldiers who were seeking to ambush patrols leaving their fire bases and boats maneuvering on the rivers. Agent Orange and other herbicides and defoliants were used in such great quantities that their impact on crops and forests was felt for decades. And it was suspected that the dioxin created in the mixing of Agent Orange could have affected U.S. military personnel and Vietnamese across the countryside. Was this deliberate chemical warfare or just unintentional collateral damage? This question is not asked in order to excuse the government for the harmful effects of dioxin; rather, it illustrates that the use of herbicides, in and of itself, is not and was not intended as chemical warfare.

Human Volunteer Testing

Certainly one of the most controversial topics is the use of human volunteers for testing CB warfare agents. During World War II, the United States and Britain called for soldier volunteers to be exposed to mustard agent and lewisite, both while unprotected and while wearing protective masks and clothing. The intent of these trials was to better understand the effects of vesicants on exposed persons and to develop better protective measures against potential enemy use. For a long while, it was common practice for chemical warfare specialists to receive a pinpoint of mustard agent on their arm so they could observe firsthand the effects of the agent and so they would be able to identify blister agents used on the battlefield. (This practice was discontinued when it was discovered that exposure to mustard agent only increased the person's sensitivity to later exposures.) At least in the United States and Britain, human volunteers were never exposed to lethal CB warfare agents or to high concentrations that would imperil their lives.

The discovery of tests conducted by the Japanese and Germans on human subjects drove the development of the Nuremberg Code in 1947, instituting strict guidelines on the role of humans in experimentation.[4] In 1953, the U.S. military redesigned its guidelines on human volunteer testing based on this code, which specifically addressed the testing of chemical, biological, and radiological agents. Officially, all CB warfare projects were to be approved by the secretary of the army, but this was not always followed according to the letter of the law. For instance, between 1959 and 1975, the Army had a blanket approval for testing nonlethal incapacitating agents on human volunteers.[5]

One of the best-known cases of this was Operation Whitecoat, which involved Army soldiers who were Seventh-day Adventists, conscientious objectors who joined the Army as noncombatants. These men were deliberately exposed to controlled releases of Q fever and tularemia at Fort Detrick (to develop vaccines) and at Dugway Proving Ground (to simulate the effects of a battlefield release). Although this may seem controversial, the volunteers were fully informed of the nature of the tests and were told that none of the agents were lethal. All agreed to the tests, and all of them fully recovered following the tests.[6] Following congressional hearings on the subject in 1975, the military canceled all CB weapons testing on human volunteers. Congress called for (and continues to require) the annual reporting of any Department of Defense experiments or studies involving human subjects for testing CB agents. There have been no human volunteer tests since 1975.

Open-Air Testing

Closely related to this issue is the open-air testing of CB agents and simulants by the Army and Navy in the late 1950s and through the 1960s. The military wanted to find out to what extent weaponized agents covered large areas. Because they could not use actual BW agents, they used zinc cadmium sulfide, which fluoresces under ultraviolet light, to simulate biological particles. This chemical was sprayed over the countryside by aircraft so that its coverage could be determined. The Army also used *Bacillus subtilis*, also called *Bacillus globigii* (BG), to simulate the release of anthrax and *Serratia marcescens* to simulate tularemia releases. The Army felt that the low levels that eventually came to earth would create little or no hazard to the environment or to people. What was controversial was that no studies had been conducted to determine the potential hazard to the general public. Some, such as those with respiratory problems, the old, or the very young, may have been at risk from exposure to these simulants. More controversy was stirred up because the public was not alerted to these tests; had they been alerted, they could have taken precautions. Of course, from a security perspective, that alert could have tipped off the Soviet Union to the nature of these tests.

The Army continues to use BG to simulate anthrax releases to test their biological detectors. In April 2002, the Army released a cloud of clay dust, powdered egg white, ethanol, and irradiated BG spores off the Florida Keys to determine if a military radar system, modified with a software algorithm, could detect a cloud of potential CB agents. The test parameters were developed with participation from state and federal health agencies, including the Environmental Protection Agency, the Federal Aviation Administration, the National Weather Service, the U.S. Fish and Wildlife Service, the Florida Keys National Marine Sanctuary, and others. The Army did alert the public well in advance of the tests, and a few people worried that somehow they could get sick from the exposure.[7] Following the Florida tests, no one reported any ill effects.

The toxic chemical weapons tests conducted by the military in the 1960s and early 1970s have recently attracted more attention. Open-air exercises using small amounts of toxic chemical agents were conducted for training purposes at Aberdeen Proving Ground (Maryland), Fort McClellan (Alabama), and Dugway Proving Ground (Utah) for years without incident prior to 1972. These exercises involved small quantities of CW agent that probably dispersed very quickly without imperiling unprotected civilians within or outside of the base. The military held larger exercises using toxic chemical agents at Fort Greeley (Alabama), Deseret Test Center (Utah), and Oahu (Hawaii), in addition to spraying exercises in the Pacific, in an effort to test and refine delivery systems that would dispense CW agents.

One of the more recently publicized series of exercises is Project Shipboard Hazard and Defense (SHAD), in which the military was trying to determine the vulnerability of U.S. warships to attacks with CB warfare agents and the potential risk to U.S. forces posed by these agents. Although military personnel were involved in the tests, they were not the subjects of these tests; the purpose was not to determine the effects of CW agents on humans but to determine the protective measures required on ships. More than thirty years later, the former military personnel involved in Project SHAD question whether their current health problems may have resulted from these tests. Although no one suffered any illnesses or reported medical problems at the time of the tests, there is a lack of knowledge about the potential health effects of low-level exposure combined with years of other health hazards in the environment. Proving that this possible exposure did or did not result in adverse health effects at this late date is next to impossible, but it remains a volatile issue as politicians assure veterans that their health costs will be covered.

The 1968 Dugway Proving Ground Incident

On March 15, 1968, local ranchers approached Dugway Proving Ground scientists to solicit their help in identifying a mysterious malady. A few thousand sheep had been afflicted with a strange disease, unable to rise to their feet and drooping their necks. The sheep had not responded to any medications, and an investigation was soon initiated. Attention soon focused on the open-air nerve agent trials conducted at Dugway, more than thirty miles from the ranches, and in particular, on an F-4 jet that had been testing a spray generator dispersing VX agent on the proving ground. When it was discovered that the sheep had ingested an organophosphate of unknown origin, the governor of Utah quickly blamed the U.S. Army and demanded redress.

The Army's seeming complicity was compounded by its policy of not commenting on the conduct of CB weapon systems at its primary proving ground, which should be unsurprising as this incident came at the height of the Cold War. No one wanted to release to the press what would have amounted to national security information. In their defense, the Dugway personnel had previously conducted 170 nerve agent spray trials without incident, not including the hundreds of other weapons tests conducted there. Through test cards and a tracer in the VX, they could account for nearly 98 percent of the agent dispersed during that trial. What that meant was that if the sheep had been sickened by the VX, then less than 2 percent, or five gallons, of VX had floated more than thirty miles, over a mountain range, onto the fields where the sheep fed. Although scientists and engineers considered this downwind hazard travel to be improbable by meteorological principles and although state and federal investigators had found no physical evidence, that was what the governor (who was up for reelection that year) and others were claiming.[8]

The Army leadership in Washington was briefed on the incident, and although they were unconvinced that it was VX that injured the sheep, they decided to pay the ranchers for the loss of their uninsured herds. The intent was to make the problem go away so the politicians would be happy and the Army could resume its tests at Dugway. That was not the message received by the media, which saw this as a tacit admission of guilt and as an attempt to dodge responsibility for what was perceived as an out-of-control CB warfare program. The initial 2,500 injured sheep became a claim for 4,400 disabled sheep put down by ranchers, plus another 1,900 that were potentially exposed (and therefore not marketable), which the press rounded out to "more than 6,000 sheep killed by nerve gas."[9]

But there is also a much simpler possible explanation: Suspicion remains that local ranchers may have sprayed their crops with an illegal organophosphate pesticide, which drifted a few miles to the sheep's feeding grounds, and that when the sheep ate the sprayed grass, they became sick with symptoms similar to those of nerve agent poisoning. The ranchers panicked and blamed the Army, a position that the politicians were quick to support in an election year. In any case, when it appeared that the Army would give them a blank check, the ranchers started shooting and burying the sheep before the Army, state, and federal investigators completed their examinations into the cause of death.

The furor over the incident caused Congress to cancel the military's open-air CB weapons testing and severely constrained the attempts to initiate the binary chemical weapons program. But without the ability to test and explode weapons on a test range, there is no credible way to tell how these weapons disperse their contents and therefore how to develop effective defenses against them. The Department of Defense's investigation of the 1991 Khamisiyah depot explosion is one example of failure to understand how modern CB weapons work (more below on the Khamisiyah incident). Nearly every CW incident since 1968, including Agent Orange, human volunteer tests associated with the CB warfare program, the chemical demilitarization program, and Gulf War illness, has been tied to the Army's handling of the 1968 incident at Dugway Proving Ground.

President Nixon's 1969 BW Program Declaration

In his pronouncement unilaterally ending the U.S. offensive BW program on November 25, 1969, President Nixon declared, "These steps should go a long way towards outlawing weapons whose use has been repugnant to the conscience of mankind. . . . Mankind already carries in its own hands the seeds of its own destruction. By the examples that we set today, we hope to contribute to an atmosphere of peace and understanding between all nations."[10] The irony is that the Soviet Union's response to this speech was to redouble its efforts to maintain its offensive BW program, and other nations were not persuaded to cease their efforts; rather, they continued developing their own offensive BW programs. Did President Nixon really believe this was an immoral weapon "repugnant to the conscience of mankind," or was this a political move designed to capitalize on his popularity early in his first term? Why exactly did Nixon sign a unilateral disarmament executive order?

There were certainly grounds for the president to order a review of the government's CB warfare program in June 1969. The Dugway Proving Ground incident was still fresh in everyone's mind, as was Operation CHASE (Cut Holes and Sink 'Em), a program to dispose of conventional and chemical munitions at sea. Information disclosed by the press had revealed that the U.S. military had overseas chemical munitions stockpiles in Europe and on Okinawa. The United Nations had initiated its own academic review of CB warfare in January, with its final report released in July. The UN report noted that "[w]ere these weapons ever to be used on a large scale in war, no one can predict how enduring the effects would be, and how they would affect the structure of society and the environment in which we live."[11] This dramatic statement, developed by fourteen scientists and without consideration of military utility, made a splash in the international headlines and had to be responded to.

President Nixon had directed a review of the U.S. government's CB warfare policy and issues in May, and on November 25, 1969, he announced the complete abandonment of an entire class of weaponry that had been in development for nearly thirty years, an unprecedented action. Nixon's own records do not give much information on why he decided to change existing policy. Some have speculated that Nixon dropped the BW program strictly as a political move to divert attention from Vietnam, but in 1969, his standing in the polls was very high, and the mass demonstrations against the conflict were yet to occur. One possible explanation is that he was trying to score a quick win against a Democratic-majority Congress in his first term, and he chose to do this through an aggressive arms control agenda, which included topics such as the Anti-Ballistic Missile Treaty and the Nuclear Non-Proliferation Treaty (NPT). Nixon knew that once he proposed the elimination of the BW stockpile, the Democratic leadership could ill afford to not support this action.[12]

The National Security Council had sponsored the review of U.S. policy on CB warfare, examining the Department of Defense's stated policy and actual practices in developing lethal CB agents, incapacitating CB agents, herbicides, riot-control agents, and anticrop agents.[13] The study recommended against further investments in the BW program but supported modernizing the CW program. The view was that maintaining an offensive BW agent stockpile was not necessarily the best deterrence option, that the agents were uncontrollable, and that the BW program was not worth the potential military effectiveness the agents delivered. Also, if the United States stopped its offensive BW program, there would be less incentive for other nations to continue a program, thus allowing the United States to retain its technological lead.[14]

This conclusion was not supported by the program's past performance. At that point, the U.S. Army had been researching biological weapons for more than twenty-five years and chemical weapons for more than fifty years. The military understood these agents' effects on personnel, they had developed efficient and effective delivery systems, and they had carefully tested and measured the effects. A weapon of war is not useful if the commander cannot predict the results of employing it, and the Army had done its testing well. Its main BW agents, anthrax, tularemia, botulinum toxin, and SEB toxin, were nonreplicating antipersonnel agents that could be controlled without worrying about epidemic outbreaks. Although infectious antipersonnel BW agents were studied, the United States did not plan to weaponize them (unlike the Soviet Union). President Nixon's decision was a calculated political move, not the moral decision many have painted it.

The Binary Chemical Weapons Program

The U.S. military's quest for modern chemical weapons started in the late 1950s as a result of the Navy's seeking chemical munitions that could be safely stored on carriers. The concept of binary munitions—which combined two precursor chemicals that react during flight to release a lethal CW agent on impact—was seen as an answer to that issue. The Army also saw this as a good modernization effort to replace its unitary chemical weapons, since binary weapons would be safer to store in peacetime, safer to transport in wartime, and safer to dispose of when they were obsolete. Research continued through the 1960s and into the 1970s, slowing down in the mid-1970s due to congressional limitations on the Army's offensive CW program following President Nixon's 1972 reaffirmation of "no first use."

With the resumption of an active Chemical Corps in 1976, the Army decided to push for a modern chemical weapons retaliatory capability, noting that its unitary munitions were aging (the last chemical munitions had been produced nearly a decade earlier) and that it needed weapon systems that were compatible with new weapon platforms. The Carter administration initially rejected the Army's requests, focusing on arms control talks with the Soviet Union. When it appeared that these talks were not bearing fruit and that the Soviets were increasing their CB warfare capabilities, the administration agreed to include a budget request for a binary chemical weapons program in its last budget submission to Congress. At the last moment, President Jimmy Carter pulled the program out of the budget, leaving it to the Reagan administration to make the case for binary chemical weapons.

The Reagan administration supported Army requests to fund the production of a binary chemical munitions plant, outlining its initiative as eliminating the chemical warfare threat in a two-part process. It would support the development of a verifiable chemical weapons treaty while deterring the use of chemical weapons against the United States by revitalizing the U.S. military's retaliatory CW capability. Congress authorized the construction of a binary weapons plant at Pine Bluff Arsenal without authorizing any actual production of binary weapons. The Army continued research and development of a 155 mm and an 8 inch artillery projectile, a Multiple Launch Rocket System (MLRS) warhead, and the Navy's Bigeye bomb.

The level of debate over the development of binary weapons increased dramatically, with critics accusing the Chemical Corps of supporting a binary weapons program only to secure its recent revival and accusing the Army of not supporting the international arms control talks. Scientists debated the efficacy of the binary munitions, with some arguing that it was hard to justify a new class of nerve agent munitions that were untested and that had not been evaluated against the unitary design. Since the open-air test ban was still in place, the Army was validating these munitions designs using simulant-filled projectiles and bombs at its proving grounds. This led to suggestions that the binaries might be inferior to the weapons they were replacing, since it was postulated that the mixing components might not create a 100 percent lethal mix prior to its dissemination over its target.

Other critics decried the entire concept of developing modern chemical weapons, noting that the U.S. efforts could encourage other nations to invest in their own chemical weapons programs. Thus, this line of reasoning went, the binary program was actually increasing the threat of chemical warfare to U.S. military personnel, rather than decreasing the threat by its retaliatory mission. Congress called for the president to form a commission to review the U.S. military's chemical warfare posture and to make a recommendation as to whether or not the United States should produce binary chemical weapons.

The Chemical Warfare Review Commission released its report in April 1985. The report concluded that only a small fraction (less than 20 percent) of existing CW weapons had any military value and that the bulk was militarily useless and should be destroyed. The commission thought that, given the growing Soviet threat, the modernization of the stockpile would be more likely to encourage negotiations for a multilateral, verifiable ban on chemical weapons and that it was not realistic to expect defensive measures alone to offset the advantages the Soviets would gain from chemical attack. This led to their conclusion that the proposed binary program would provide an adequate capability to meet the military's needs and was necessary. This report, endorsed by the administration, led Congress to release funds in 1985 to start production of the 155 mm artillery projectiles at Pine Bluff.

The countering view from the arms control proponents was that the best policy to prevent chemical warfare was international chemical disarmament. If, to show its sincerity, the United States had to unilaterally disarm before the Soviet Union did, this should have been the course of action rather than proliferating the threat. The binary program was seen by the arms control community as an obstacle showing that the United States was less willing to negotiate the fine points of a treaty banning all chemical weapons. Certainly, the 1970s had seen progress in nuclear arms talks, the Biological Weapons Convention, and other similar international treaties. One of the obstacles to the arms control talks was the need for a verification process to ensure that once a nation started disarming, it remained disarmed. With the large number of chemical weapons in existence, the technical points of exactly how inspectors would enter a country, inspect a site, challenge a government's records, and report its findings became the subject of loud and long debates.

Another challenge was determining what future role the unitary chemical munitions would play, now that the binary chemical munitions were being proposed. Congress passed legislation in November 1985 directing that for every binary munition produced, the Army would have to destroy a unitary munition. This led to the creation of the Army's chemical demilitarization program to destroy the 31,400 tons of chemical agents and munitions at the eight stockpile sites in the United States and the one at Johnston Island.

In 1987, the binary munitions facility at Pine Bluff started producing one of the two components of the 155 mm binary projectiles, ending a nineteen-year dry spell in chemical weapons production in the United States. The commercial firm that was to make the second component of the projectiles ran into production problems, preventing the formal completion of the effort. The Navy's Bigeye bomb had encountered a number of problems during operational tests, which had delayed the start of its production. The Army canceled its requirement for 8 inch binary chemical munitions, having started to phase the 8 inch artillery system out of the inventory, and focused on its MLRS warhead design. Congress continued to debate the program's goals against the ongoing CWC talks in Geneva, calling for several General Accounting Office reports to monitor the binary weapons program.

In 1990, the United States and Soviet Union agreed on a framework to accelerate the treaty discussions, and in June, they signed a bilateral destruction agreement that committed the two countries to begin disposing of their chemical weapons to bring their stockpiles down to 5,000 tons of agent by 2002. Part of the negotiations required the United States to cease its binary weapons program. Against the advice of the military, the first Bush administration agreed and directed the Army to stop all acquisition and test efforts in July. Thus the military's program never really reached its goal of modernizing its retaliatory capability, but many argue that without the program, the Soviet Union would have never come to the table to seriously negotiate in the first place.

The U.S. Chemical Demilitarization Program

President Ronald Reagan called for the resumption of the binary chemical weapons program early in his first term, and in 1985 Congress authorized the funding of that program contingent upon the disposal of the aging unitary chemical munitions, nearly 31,400 tons at nine sites. Could it be done safely, without harming the environment and without endangering the health of the demilitarization workers or local populace? The Army thought it could, having researched and executed various ways of disposing of chemical weapons for more than four decades. Congress had prohibited dumping the munitions in the ocean, and burial and open-pit burning were not options. The Army had examined chemical neutralization, but that technology had significant drawbacks and inefficiencies. So the Army chose incineration as the optimal technology to dispose of these weapons. The National Research Council agreed with this assessment, and the Office of the Secretary of Defense approved the decision.

Although the Army's tests showed they could successfully build and operate an incineration facility that would dispose of 99.9999 percent of the CW agent and its associated materials, this program met with fierce resistance from a small number of national critics and at least two of the nine communities near the sites. In part, this resistance was due to the perception that the public had not been involved in the Army's decision-making process. While the first plant was being constructed at Johnston Island, more than 800 miles west of Hawaii, Congress took on an increased role in directing the Army to conduct specific studies, to limit their options in executing the program, and to increase the participation of the public in its program. In the early 1990s, Congress directed the Army to examine alternative technologies to dispose of a portion of the stockpile. To the program's critics, this meant processes that would not use high-temperature technologies or open-air emissions.

Initial estimates of the total cost of the program over its life cycle was $1.7 billion for a nine-year program (1985–1994). This estimate was based on engineers' analyses and projections; it was not until the first disposal facility was built on Johnston Atoll that the Army could make a more refined estimate, in 1993, of $8.6 billion. This life-cycle cost estimate increased to $15 billion in 2000 and could reach $24 billion by 2012. The program's completion date has slipped from 1994 to 2004 to 2007, and it may be extended to 2012. Although this may seem like poor management, the fact is that the Army is running a disposal program that the Office of the Secretary of Defense oversees and Congress directs. Over the program's life span, Congress has directed additional studies of alternative technologies, the funding of emergency response programs for ten states, and the disposal of chemical weapons and material not in the stockpiles (discovered buried in the ground at old federal testing sites). These cost increases have been very similar to those of the Environmental Protection Agency's Superfund program. (The costs for the Superfund program, initially thought to be a $4 billion effort, are expected to reach $28 billion for 1,250 sites.)

Critics have accused the Army of inefficiency, of lying about the safety of the disposal process, and of inadequately investigating alternative technologies. The Army has stressed its safety and risk-management records, which has resulted in the successful operation of two disposal sites without any harmful exposures to workers or local citizens. The General Accounting Office has agreed that cost and program slippages have occurred, but it notes that Congress's requirements and state Environmental Protection Agency offices were just as much to blame for these slips as the Army's management. The Environmental Protection Agency, the Centers for Disease Control and Prevention (CDC), and the Department of Health and Human Services found that the Army's process was not only about as clean and safe as it could possibly be but was also much more efficient than commercial or private incinerators. The National Research Council agreed that most alternative technologies have too many unknowns to be certified as better than incineration and could be employed at only two of the nine stockpile sites.

The Army steadfastly maintains its program meets the congressional direction that it provide "maximum protection" to the environment, the demilitarization workers, and the public. Many residents around the stockpile sites have accepted the Army's program, although its critics continue to point to occupational safety concerns and reports of leaks as evidence that the Army has not chosen the right technology to dispose of these weapons and materials. Yet as late as 2002, the National Research Council identified the current incineration technology to be used at four of the eight U.S. facilities as the safe and effective way to go, far outweighing the risk to the environment and public that would result from continuing to store the chemical munitions for years waiting for the perfect disposal technology to come along.

CB Warfare Agent Exposure after the Persian Gulf War

When President George H. W. Bush authorized military operations in response to Iraq's invasion of Kuwait, many in the Department of Defense were convinced that Iraq would use its CB weapons against U.S. forces. Iraq had clearly demonstrated a CW capability against Iranian forces between 1983 and 1988, meeting the Iranian human-wave attacks with chemical weapons and conventional military forces.[15] What was not known was whether Iraq had the capability to wage biological warfare, which had not been demonstrated against Iran. Iraq was suspected of developing BW agents, but the United States had no idea how sophisticated or mature that capability might be in 1990.

This military campaign is discussed more in chapter 7. The Department of Defense came under attack from veterans' groups and from the press immediately upon its initial claim that CB weapons were not used in the war and that U.S. forces had not been exposed to CB agents. Given the large numbers of Iraqi chemical weapons discovered after the war, the poor training of U.S. forces, their lack of confidence in their defensive equipment, and the U.S. population's own lack of faith in the government's investigations, it is not hard to understand these suspicions. The controversy over whether troops were exposed to CB warfare agents prior to or during offensive actions against Iraq has more or less been discounted by very thorough studies conducted years later. The controversy that remains is whether military forces were exposed to CW agents as a result of explosive ordnance demolition operations that occurred in March 1991.

As U.S. forces cleared the battlefield, the Army destroyed vast stores of Iraqi weapons and ammunition. One of these weapons sites was the Khamisiyah ammunition depot, south of An Nasiriyah in southern Iraq. This depot was a huge collection of warehouses containing tons of conventional ammunition, everything from rifle ammunition to explosives to artillery projectiles. Both explosives experts and NBC specialists inspected the warehouses and failed to find anything other than conventional ammunition. In the course of destroying thirty-eight warehouses of ammunition on March 4, 1991, Army engineers unwittingly blew up several stacks of 122 mm rockets filled with the nerve agents sarin and cyclosarin. Less than a week later, they blew up stacks of 122 mm rockets in a nearby pit, rockets that were later determined to have been filled with nerve agents. Although no one was visibly harmed by the explosion or any apparent CW agent releases, later studies began to examine the possibility that U.S. forces had been exposed to less-than-lethal levels of nerve agents, released either by bombing Iraqi production and storage sites or by destroying these ammunition dumps.

In November 1995, Dr. Bernard Rotsker was appointed as the special assistant to the deputy secretary of defense for Gulf War illnesses. His office spent several years and millions of dollars investigating claims of CB weapons exposure, studying medical analyses of returning veterans and funding follow-on investigations and studies to discover the source of postwar illnesses. Although his office has concluded that there was no evidence conclusively showing CW exposure, the studies estimate that upwards of 100,000 personnel may have been exposed to low levels of nerve agents without their knowledge because of the Khamisiyah depot and pit explosions. The Gulf War Illness Office deliberately made this assessment overly conservative in an attempt to ensure that anyone who may have been exposed in 1991, no matter how insignificantly, would be warned and could take steps to address his or her medical condition.[16]

As their low-level exposure limit, the people modeling the hazard's parameters used the general population limit measure used by the Army to protect people from occupational exposure to sarin nerve agent: 0.013 milligrams per minute per cubic meter (mg-min/m^3). This measure is much lower than the recommended occupational exposure level for civilians who work in the chemical stockpile sites (0.04 mg-min/m^3), much lower than the incapacitating dose level of 2–3 mg-min/m^3, and significantly lower than the lethal dose necessary to kill an adult human (75–100 mg-min/m^3). Three chemical dispersion models and two weather models were used to predict who downwind might have been exposed even to this very low level of nerve agent, and all troops who might have been in that prediction area in any part of a three-day period were counted and later notified. To be on the safe side, the modelers deliberately overestimated the purity of the Iraqi agent and did not consider the fact that the nonpersistent nerve agent had been dispersed in the afternoon in a desert environment. (The nerve agent probably would have not lasted three hours, let alone three days, in the heat.) Because of these safe-sided assumptions, the actual number of people who might have been exposed to sarin is probably much, much lower than the estimate of 100,000. But the press, not appreciating the details behind the calculations, now reports the incident as one in which more than 100,000 military personnel were exposed—not "may have been exposed"—to nerve agents. The 100,000 number has a life of its own, much like the 6,000 sheep "killed" by nerve agent in 1968.

Several organizations still contend that CB warfare agents could have caused Gulf War illnesses, yet the lack of evidence from thousands of medical and chemical specialists who were in the conflict and the many medical studies conducted since 1995 do not support these allegations. All the medical reports and investigations have failed to discover a linkage between potential CB weapons exposure and veterans' illnesses. The conundrum is that no one will be able to clearly disprove that U.S. forces may have been exposed, since it is extremely difficult to study the effects of low levels of chemical agents combined with other battlefield conditions on people under controlled laboratory procedures. The best that can be accomplished is animal testing, which will always leave some level of doubt no matter how the conclusions come out.

Developing Medical Countermeasures against Biological Warfare Agents

One of the controversial aspects of the Persian Gulf conflict was the use of medical countermeasures for chemical and biological agent exposure. This included the use of pyridostigmine bromide (PB) tablets as a pretreatment and diazepam as a post-treatment for nerve agent exposure, and botulinum toxoid (to counter botulinum toxin) and anthrax vaccine as BW agent pretreatments. As already mentioned, the Department of Defense was convinced that Iraq would initiate CB warfare against U.S. forces once the offensive began. The lack of sensitive, near-real-time biological detection equipment meant it could take U.S. forces days to recognize that they had been exposed to anthrax or botulinum toxin. Inhalation anthrax, in particular, is very deadly: It is fatal to more than 90 percent of untreated personnel, and once signs and symptoms are visible (usually starting at forty-eight hours), medical treatment is useless. No other BW agent has this level of lethality and fast-acting effects. Combined with its ability to last for weeks or months in the environment and its ability to be spread over large areas, it is the megaton weapon in the BW arsenal.

The U.S. government had an anthrax vaccine that had received Food and Drug Administration approval in 1970. This vaccine is a point of great controversy, since critics note that it was never tested against airborne-delivered, laboratory-developed "weapons-grade" anthrax. However, this same vaccine has been safely and routinely administered to at-risk wool mill workers, veterinarians, laboratory workers, livestock handlers, and military personnel. Some people suffer side effects, but the overwhelming majority of side effects disappear after two days. About one in 200,000 persons suffer more serious side effects.[17]

What was perhaps even more controversial was the use of the botulinum toxoid, PB tablets, and diazepam autoinjectors (an anticonvulsant). These three drugs were not tested for their safety or efficacy in countering CB warfare agents prior to their use in the Gulf conflict. There were early tests that suggested the drugs would work, and there were related medical cases that suggested they were safe for administering to humans. There were no medical alternatives to using these medicines if troops were exposed to nerve agents or botulinum toxin, and the results of not using them were clear: Lots of U.S. military personnel could die. The decision to use these products was carried out under an Investigational New Drug (IND) application, which would permit the use of the drugs under the condition that the troops volunteered and understood the risk of taking them.

Whether U.S. personnel were apprised of the risks or whether they really volunteered is also a point of controversy. There was a war going on, and the implications of not taking the drugs if Iraq used CB weapons was pretty well understood. Some critics have accused the U.S. military of using military personnel as "guinea pigs" in medical experimentation, which is contrary to public laws and would be considered immoral. The idea that someone could give drugs to more than 500,000 personnel in a fluid wartime environment and hope to learn something is frankly ludicrous, but nevertheless there are those who persist in that argument.

In the 1990s, the Department of Defense and the Food and Drug Administration reexamined the challenge of developing medical countermeasures against CB warfare agents. After all, in the Gulf conflict they had only had the anthrax vaccine, and they felt they needed new vaccines for smallpox, plague, cholera, and other BW threats. They tried to work out procedures for how the U.S. government should approve pretreatments, antidotes, and post-treatments for exposure to weaponized CB warfare agents when they could not test the drugs for efficacy and safety as one did for commercial drugs. Between 1999 and 2001, the Food and Drug Administration developed protocols for using animal lab tests and other medical analyses to develop a basis for approving the release of these drugs.

There are not many pharmaceutical firms that want to make vaccines for BW agents. Due to the threat of lawsuits, the insurance required, and the small quantities of vaccines produced (the military being the sole purchaser), making these BW vaccines is not profitable. This is not a problem unique to BW vaccines; many vaccine manufacturers that were started in the 1970s are going out of business instead of modernizing their equipment due to the stringent Food and Drug Administration approval process. The controversies over developing and administering vaccines in general, let alone for BW agents, has caused the market to stop production, creating a challenge that still has not been solved. The recent decision by the Department of Health and Human Services to build a national vaccine stockpile for responding to BW terrorism has reinitiated the pharmaceutical firms' interest. Knowing that adversarial countries are developing BW agents, how do we ensure that U.S. forces and the population in general can be medically treated if they are exposed while unprotected?

Protection from Terrorist Use of CB Weapons

When the Aum Shinrikyo cult used sarin to attack Japanese civilians in the Tokyo subway in March 1995, it caused concern that terrorists could do the same in the United States. The Oklahoma City bombing, the Atlanta Olympics pipe-bomb incident, and attacks on churches and family health clinics only highlighted the fact that the U.S. populace was vulnerable. The incident in Japan led the U.S. government to revamp its Federal Response Plan, adding a section on terrorism response, and Congress directed the Department of Defense to start a Domestic Preparedness Program to develop emergency-responder capabilities in case of terrorist use of CB agents. This training program for emergency responders (police, firefighters, medics, hazmat teams, and so on) was to take place in 120 major cities across the country. More than 100 cities received federal training courses and training equipment from the Department of Defense between 1997 and 1999, with the Department of Justice taking over responsibility for the program in October 1999.

The National Guard promoted the development of small federal response teams as a resource for state governors to call upon in the event of a terrorist attack, for it was felt that federal response units, such as the Army's Technical Escort Unit or the Marine Corps' Chemical Biological Incident Response Force, would arrive too late to offer any valuable assistance. These teams, initially called Rapid Assessment and Initial Detection (RAID) teams and now called Weapons of Mass Destruction Civil Support Teams (WMD CSTs), were originally meant to be one per Federal Emergency Management Agency region, or ten total. This number grew (by congressional direction) to seventeen and then to twenty-two, and now thirty-two WMD CSTs are authorized. Recent (2003) congressional language has called for the creation of another twenty-three teams, for a total of fifty-five across the United States and its territories.

Critics have attacked the government's CB terrorism response program as a waste of money, arguing that too many federal agencies and industry consultants had gotten the money instead of the state and local responders. The program certainly does not ensure that every citizen will be protected, and smaller cities that were not among the original 120 cities complained that they needed the equipment and training as well. Although the level of interest increased, after five years, the prophecies of "It's not a matter of if but when terrorists will use chemical weapons" seemed to be growing stale. That was until the four anthrax-filled envelopes made their arrival in October 2001.

The threat of biological terrorism has created a new challenge. It is safe to say that even the BW experts were surprised by the high quality of the anthrax sent and its ability to disperse along the mail delivery routes. Although these letters could have been the work of an adversarial nation, the FBI suspected a lone individual with knowledge of the U.S. offensive BW program, based on the small quantities and the mail's targets (the Senate building, NBC's headquarters in New York City, and the *National Enquirer*'s headquarters in Florida). Although many people were potentially exposed to the anthrax and had to receive ciprofloxacin (an antibiotic), only five people died as a result of the letters. The perhaps unintended cross-contamination of other letters in the mail system created a panic across the nation, a panic that resulted in unscrupulous individuals peddling military masks and training manuals, not to mention surgical masks and glove box devices to ensure one could safely open one's mail at home.

The question of what the U.S. government should do in response to the potential for BW attacks by terrorists is receiving a great deal of attention. Some have suggested that everyone in the United States should have a gas mask and be vaccinated in preparation for another BW terrorist attack. Others have gone so far as to suggest that air purifiers and fans should be installed in office buildings and homes to minimize the chance of exposure. These ideas are more placebos than panaceas, since one would require a biological detector to warn of biological organisms and there would be no warning of exposure until days later, when people started getting sick.

BW terrorism requires more of a public health response than does CW terrorism, which calls for a hazardous materials cleanup that is easier to address and monitor. Investing in the public health system and developing a national medical surveillance system may prove more valuable than masks and filters that people do not know how or when to use. An increased intelligence effort to identify what terrorist groups and nations are investing in CB warfare agents seems reasonable if the intent is to stop terrorists before they use these agents.

Treating the populace before or after a suspected BW attack remains a topic of great debate. The Department of Defense developed vaccines for use on a population of relatively healthy eighteen-to-sixty-five-year-olds who are constantly monitored by medical personnel. These medical countermeasures were not developed or tested for children under eighteen or for older populations, since those populations are not represented in the military forces. The Food and Drug Administration approved the use of ciprofloxacin to treat civilians exposed to anthrax as an off-label use (that is, although the drug was not specifically designated for such use, use was permitted due to the high probability it would be effective), but the use of military-grade vaccines to treat the general population remains a controversial issue.

Another concern is the potential for terrorist attacks against the nation's crops and livestock. Imagine a terrorist group bringing foot-and-mouth disease to Texas cattle ranches or disseminating a wheat stem rust or corn blight virus across Kansas. The effects of these attacks would be catastrophic to the industry and would considerably shake the U.S. public's confidence in the government's ability to protect its food sources.

The U.S. government will invest millions, perhaps billions, of dollars to ensure there is a response capability against CB terrorism. Although the United States may be vulnerable to CB terrorist attacks, the question remains: Is this really the most critical threat facing the populace? Many analysts feel that high explosives and conventional weapons will remain the most probable terrorist threat in the years ahead.[18] Although our emergency responders need to be prepared for mass casualty events caused by CB warfare agents, the common citizens on the street should not be constantly thinking they are always in danger from this threat. There have been far more lives lost to crime and conventional terrorism, and that trend does not appear to be going away soon.

Notes

1. See conversations on chemical weapons in H. Norman Schwarzkopf's autobiography *It Doesn't Take a Hero* (New York: Linda Grey Bantam Books, 1992), 356, 389–390, 416, 419, 439, 451–452.

2. Senate Committee on Labor and Public Welfare, *Chemical and Biological Weapons: Some Possible Approaches for Lessening the Threat and Danger* (Washington, DC: Government Printing Office, 1969), 47.

3. Leonard A. Cole, *Clouds of Secrecy: The Army's Germ Warfare Tests over Populated Areas* (Totowa, NJ: Rowman and Littlefield, 1988).

4. See the "Nuremberg Code Directives for Human Experimentation," available on the National Institutes of Health's Office of Human Subjects Research web site (available: http://ohsr.od.nih.gov/nuremberg.php3; accessed February 14, 2003).

5. Constance M. Pechura and David P. Rall, *Veterans at Risk: The Health Effects of Mustard and Lewisite* (Washington, DC: National Academy of Sciences, 1993), 378–80.

6. See ABC News coverage of this topic on the Internet: "Brave Volunteers: Human Guinea Pigs Paved the Way for U.S. Biological Warfare," December 23, 2001 (available: http://abcnews.go.com/sections/wnt/DailyNews/Biowar_volunteers011223.html; accessed February 14, 2003).

7. CNN, "Army to Conduct Mock Aerial Chem-Bio Attack," April 13, 2002 (on-line; available: http://www.cnn.com/2002/US/04/12/gen.mock.attack/; accessed November 2002).

8. Albert J. Mauroni, *America's Struggle with Chemical-Biological Warfare* (Westport, CT: Praeger, 2000), 34–41.

9. For example, Brent Israelsen, "This Is the Place for Waste," *Salt Lake Tribune*, September 8, 2002 (on-line; available: http://sltrib.com/2002/09082002/utah/769513.htm); Mark Thompson, "When Fear makes Sense," *Time*, July 7, 1997.

10. "Nixon Renounces Germ Weapons, Orders Destruction of Stocks: Restricts Use of Chemical Arms," *New York Times*, November 26, 1969, 1.

11. Kathleen Teltsch, "Thant Urges Halt on Germ Weapons," *Washington Post*, July 3, 1969, A1.

12. Mauroni, *America's Struggle with Chemical-Biological Warfare*, 49–51.

13. The memorandum initiating this study was "U.S. Policy on Chemical and Biological Warfare and Agents," National Security Study Memorandum 59, May 28, 1969. The memorandum was signed by Henry Kissinger.

14. Interdepartmental Political-Military Group, "Report to the National Security Council: U.S. Policy on Chemical and Biological Warfare Agents," November 10, 1969. Also see the analysis conducted by the National Security Archive (on-line; available: http://www.gwu.edu/~nsarchiv/NSAEBB/NSAEBB58/; accessed April 3, 2003).

15. Anthony H. Cordesman and Abraham R. Wagner, *The Lessons of Modern War*, vol. 2, *The Iran-Iraq War* (Boulder, CO: Westview Press, 1990).

16. Albert J. Mauroni, *Chemical-Biological Defense: U.S. Military Policies and Decisions in the Gulf War* (Westport, CT: Praeger, 1998), 151–167.

17. See the Department of Defense site discussing anthrax vaccine, "AVIP: Anthrax Vaccine Immunization Program" (on-line; available: http://www.anthrax.osd.mil/; accessed February 14, 2003).

18. Jonathan Tucker, ed., *Toxic Terror: Assessing Terrorist Use of Chemical and Biological Weapons* (Cambridge: MIT Press, 2000).

3

Why Countries Develop Chemical and Biological Weapons

The first chapter reviewed the reasons the United States had developed an offensive CB warfare program: largely to develop a credible retaliatory capability to dissuade its opponents (primarily the former Soviet Union) from attacking its forces with the same weapons. The Soviet Union and the United States have not been the only two nations to develop chemical or biological weapons. More than twenty nations (depending on whose list one refers to) are suspected of having chemical or biological weapons programs or both, despite protestations by arms control advocates and other critics that CB weapons are immoral and ultimately inefficient. Why nations seek these weapons is not as simple as wanting to own a "poor man's atomic bomb," since nations owning nuclear weapons are suspected of also developing CB weapons. Obviously, there are other reasons that drive nations to acquire CB weapons.

Probably the most understandable rationale for a nation to develop CB weapons as an offensive capability is as a response to the discovery that its neighbor is developing these weapons, especially if that neighbor has a history of religious or ethnic differences or of aggressiveness. Take Pakistan and India, for instance: Although both have nuclear weapons capability, India has admitted to procuring chemical weapons, and Pakistan is suspected of having its own program (but has not admitted such). Since nuclear weapons represent a very final solution, if the two nations clash, they may seek to use CB weapons as a combat multiplier, each hoping to tip victory in a military conflict to its side without resorting to nuclear options. North and South Korea are another example of such traditional conflict, as are China and Taiwan, Iran and Iraq, Egypt and Israel; all are suspected of having CB weapons programs of some degree and magnitude.

Another reason may be to create or bolster a sense of national pride in being able to develop military capabilities that rank with those of the superpowers. There is also the practical reason: Military adventures can be very expensive if they continue too long, and CB weapons can considerably reduce an opponent's ability to defend itself. The ability to employ ballistic missiles capped with CB warheads allows a nation to threaten military forces from hundreds of miles away with little or no risk to its own forces. CB weapons can even cause the superpowers to hesitate to rush into a nation's neighborhood. For example, Iraq was able to stall the United States for six months with the mere threat of CB weapons use, forcing the U.S. and coalition forces to rush huge stocks of CB defense equipment into the theater prior to liberating Kuwait.

There are a number of lists of nations suspected of having CB weapons, based on official sources or on an author's research at that time. Usually they will use terms such as "confirmed," pretty self-explanatory; "probable," the nation has shown enough interest that it appears to have scientists developing agents and engineers developing weapon systems, but it has not used them in combat recently; and "possible," the nation has the technology to make such weapons, its scientists may have written a few papers on the topic, and it has a motive to promote a CB warfare program. The mere fact of having the technical capabilities (industries that can produce toxic chemicals in large amounts and research into pathogens and toxins) does not mean a country is developing an offensive CB warfare program, but combined with other factors, it may be an indication of intent.

The only nations that have "confirmed" chemical and biological weapons programs have been Russia, the United States, and Iraq. India and South Korea have admitted to having chemical weapons stocks but have declared their intent to destroy them under the CWC. China, Iran, and South Africa have stated they once had chemical weapons but destroyed all their stocks prior to signing the CWC. The former member states of the Soviet Union had some CB weapon stocks; they either returned these stocks to Russia or asked the United States for assistance in destroying them. Although no nation admits to having an active biological weapons program, it is suspected that a number of nations do, treaties and statements to the contrary.

An examination of most countries' programs reveals a predictable pattern in the development of CB weapons: A country starts with chemical weapons and moves to biological weapons second. Chemical weapons are relatively safer to handle and easier to develop, assuming that the host nation already has the technology and resources to develop industrial chemicals in mass quantities. After researching and developing specific CW agents, the next step is to weaponize the agents and to test the delivery systems in the field. Most modern nations can easily develop mustard agents and nerve agents, for there is plenty of scientific literature on their structures and formulation. After gaining this experience, a nation may feel emboldened to take the next step, to researching, developing, and producing BW agents. If they pattern their programs after the former U.S. offensive BW program, they start with the low-casualty-causing agents, such as the pathogens that cause brucellosis and tularemia, before going on to such "big guns" as anthrax, plague, and smallpox.

Although there may be many motivations for nations to develop CB weapons, there is still a great deal of question as to what chain of logic drives a nation's leadership to desire an offensive CB warfare capability in the first place. In a thesis prepared for the Joint Military Intelligence College, Lieutenant John Dahm postulated that there may be an analytical framework to the decision-making process that a nation undertakes in the acquisition and employment of CB weapons.[1] He believes that national decisionmakers have to develop a certain mentality that will lend itself to integrating the concept of employing CB weapons into their national political and military thinking. This mentality requires being pushed to the point of rejecting international norms prohibiting CB warfare and overcoming any natural psychological aversions to CB warfare use, thus bridging a "psychological threshold." For example, does the political leadership willingly choose to develop CB weapons because of a desire to gain international recognition of the nation's military credibility or to threaten its neighbors, or does the leadership feel forced by circumstances into using this technology by its neighbors' CB weapons program? Once the leadership accepts the need for an offensive CB warfare program, the military leadership needs to identify what threats or requirements could be addressed with CB weapons, where CB weapons would address a particular battlefield application better than conventional or nuclear munitions. The key decision points may include the military leadership's seeing that use of CB weapons will succeed where use of conventional munitions have failed, potential political costs, enemy vulnerabilities, and terrain and weather conditions. There may be a desire to use CB weapons early in a conflict to gain a quick victory, or a wish to hold back the use of these weapons to stave off defeat and to ensure regime survival. Once they have identified these requirements, they have crossed the "operational threshold" and begun a serious pursuit of a CB weapons program. This leads into the science, engineering, and development of military weapons and the initiation of the military training required to turn that nation's intent to develop CB weapons into a true military capability.

Because of intelligence concerns and a desire on the part of most countries to maintain secrecy about their offensive CB warfare program, it may be difficult to analytically examine each country through this framework, but it is an interesting thesis to use. The number of nations seeking CB weapons has steadily increased since World War II, and few have ended their programs. It may be instructive to examine why these nations are interested in developing what have been called horrible, immoral, and ineffective weapons, and when nations make the transition from having the capability to build a CB program to having the intent to wage CB warfare. The following discussions have been derived from various references identified in chapter 9.[2]

Europe

At the beginning of World War I, no nation was actively seeking a chemical warfare capability. The decision to investigate gas munitions came as a result of the deadlock caused by trench warfare. As the two sides hunkered down, progress in gaining ground became very difficult and very expensive in terms of human lives, resources, and time. When the German army employed chlorine gas at Ypres in April 1915, it gained only a few miles against the Allied forces, but that was much more than other campaigns had so far achieved. Although the Germans retained a technological lead over the British and French throughout the war, all three nations invested heavily in this new form of warfare. At this point in history, chemical weapons were not considered "weapons of mass destruction," but they did play a significant role as tactical weapons. Specifically, chemical munitions allowed one side to demoralize its enemy by forcing them into uncomfortable protective masks for hours, to disrupt hostile artillery batteries, and to diminish enemy infantry's capabilities prior to the infantry advance.[3]

Once it was demonstrated that gas warfare could have an impact on a particular battle (promising to break the deadlock of trench warfare), the British, French, and German armies began to identify what agents they would employ (phosgene, cyanogen chloride, and so on) and how they would employ them (cylinders, projectiles, or artillery shells) on the battlefield. Industries in all countries manufactured thousands of tons of chemical agents, and the use of gas became a standard practice in battles. The British Army formed a Special Brigade within its Royal Engineers branch as its technical and operational specialists, in addition to employing artillery-delivered gas munitions. The German Army also called on its engineer brigades to deliver gas at specific points on the battlefield.

Although the initial troops came from the engineers, the American Expeditionary Force quickly developed a Gas Service to focus its efforts. Because the Americans had entered the war late and had not developed any chemical weapons, they relied on loans of British Stokes mortars and Livens projectors and French 75 mm artillery as chemical weapon delivery systems. The British loaned masks to the U.S. Army and trained many of their forces going into battle. Of interest is the fact that many U.S. commanders did not necessarily want to execute gas attacks, in part because they felt that using gas in an attack would increase the odds that the Germans would retaliate with gas against them. This might be interpreted as the U.S. forces' failing to cross what Dahm called the operational threshold. The Germans used gas against U.S. positions anyway, whether the Americans withheld their gas or retaliated. The British, French, and Germans, having been deadlocked in a deadly and vicious seesaw battle for years, had fewer illusions. They were willing to use these weapons to gain any combat advantage that would gain territory and avoid the losses and devastation seen so far.

Following the war, many critics downplayed the military significance of gas warfare, claiming it had never lived up to its creators' expectations. In part, this was true. Gas attacks on their own had not changed the war's outcome, but for that matter, neither had the tank or military aircraft, also born in World War I. Gas demoralized the troops upon which it descended, allowing the attackers to gain some tactical advantage. By delivering gas against enemy artillery batteries, one could reduce the number of barrages and gain some local superiority in firepower. These advantages were often not enough if the enemy was too evenly matched in the number of troops and given the intricate, interlocking trench designs. It did, however, allow the Germans to repulse Russian attacks in the east and to assist Austrian forces in breaking the Italian forces in the mountain passes at Caporetto.[4]

Following the end of World War I, Italy and Japan encouraged the fear of chemical warfare proliferation by their pioneering use of CB weapons. Italy was facing Ethiopian forces who were fighting on their own terrain, using the mountains and desert to their advantage and threatening to delay the Italian conquest of that nation. The Italian forces used mustard bombs against the Ethiopians in the mountains and in the rear areas, disrupting the supply columns of donkeys and barefoot men. Conventional munitions would not have caused the sudden collapse of resistance as quickly as the mustard bombs did; some analysts estimate that it reduced a multiyear campaign into eighteen months. Despite pleas to the League of Nations for assistance, the Ethiopian forces received no relief. Although Italy had the capability and training to use these same chemical weapons against the Allies, it never did, perhaps because of the fear of retaliation that President Roosevelt promised if the Axis powers were to use chemical weapons against U.S. forces. (See below for Japan.)

In World War II, Britain, France, and the United States all armed themselves with CB weapons in the fear that Germany, Japan, and Italy would instigate CB warfare against the Allies, but it never happened. Instead, these stocks were moved from theater to theater as potential retaliatory weapons. Although some believe that Hitler's gas warfare experience in World War I was the reason why he never pushed nerve agents into the war, that view is overly simplistic. As Dahm pointed out, a nation's leadership and military force need to be pushed over the operational threshold to use these weapons. For both Germany and Japan, conventional forces were adequate to gain victories in their respective theaters for some time. Tactical operations and logistics priorities weighed against the CW option. Germany in particular had no desire to slow down its blitzkrieg with the use of chemical weapons and the accompanying need for protective masks and suits to protect themselves against retaliatory strikes. Germany's military leadership had fought in the previous war, and they recognized that initiating chemical warfare could bog down their blitzkrieg tactics, which they could not afford. And once the Allies gained air superiority, the German leadership recognized that their cities would be at risk from enemy gas attacks if they were to use CW agents against the invading forces and so chose to refrain, despite being against the ropes.

Following World War II, the United Kingdom and France did continue their research into CW agents, especially with the discovery of nerve agents. In the 1950s, both nations abandoned the development of chemical weapons, perhaps in part because of their experiences in the world wars and in part due to the cost of developing a new set of weapons.[5] They continue strong CB defense programs to this date. All the European countries and the United States have signed and ratified the BWC and CWC. The United States, having an ample budget and competing with the Soviet Union in a CB weapons arms race, continued to develop a retaliatory capability, but its military and political leadership never really believed in using CB weapons in a true offensive capability. The Soviet Union, also a signatory of the BWC and CWC, had different motivations.

The Former Soviet Union and Russia Today

Russia had suffered greatly in World War I, with more deaths from gas weapons than all the other countries combined and more gas casualties than Germany and France combined. Developing a chemical warfare program was not just a desired capability; it was a necessity if the Soviet Union was to fight another war. Part of the increase in capability came as a result of German scientists' using Russian facilities and resources in the mid-1920s. Although the Germans were primarily interested in retaining their world-class industrial chemical status, the Soviets gained knowledge as well. This alliance did not last long. The Germans were more open about their mobilization for war in the 1930s, and they soon abandoned their Soviet colleagues to openly continue their research in Germany. At the beginning of World War II, the Soviet military had a healthy ongoing offensive CB warfare research effort and a considerable defensive capability. This capability was soon wiped out by the early successes of the Germans in 1941. Although the research efforts could be relocated, the defensive equipment and troops were lost.

There is some speculation that the Soviet Union did employ tularemia against the German military operating in southern Russia in the summer of 1942. Large numbers of German troops suddenly came down with the disease, so many that their campaign temporarily came to a halt. Unfortunately, more than 100,000 Russian soldiers and civilians also contracted the disease. This unprecedented spike in tularemia casualties was not likely to have occurred naturally.[6] The impetus for the Soviet Union to develop a CB weapons capability was very clear: For the second time in the twentieth century, it was fighting for the Motherland and losing millions of soldiers and civilians. Conventional weapons were barely enough to stem the tide this time, and even that only because of liberal supplies of weapon systems and equipment from the United States.

Following World War II and on into the Cold War, the Soviet Union worried that the United States was surpassing it in CB warfare capability. In 1956, the Soviet defense minister, Marshal Georgy Zhukov, commented that the Soviet Union had to be able to fight in future wars that included the use of "weapons of mass destruction." Although many analysts chose to interpret that as the Soviet Union's intent to develop these weapons, from the Soviet side, it was an expression of their concern that CB weapons would be used against them and thus of the need to balance the scales. This concern led to a very robust science and engineering effort at dozens of facilities across the country.

Interestingly enough, the Soviet scientists developed many of the same biological weapons and delivery systems as the United States had, and they conducted similar large-area tests between 1960 and 1980. Unlike the United States, they did not limit themselves to weaponizing noninfectious lethal agents, exploring agents such as smallpox, Marburg virus, and others.[7] When President Nixon made his announcement in November 1969 officially canceling the U.S. offensive BW program, the Soviet leadership did not believe the United States would be so foolish as to halt research on such an effective weapon system. They felt assured that the United States would not abandon the results of millions of dollars in past investments and that the hundreds of civilian researchers would not just stop working. The U.S. offensive BW program had, in their minds, just gone underground.[8]

The Soviet production would reach the capability to produce and store literally thousands of tons of BW agents per year. The program was huge, and it was not limited to developing "weapons of mass destruction." Soviet-supplied ricin was used in the assassination of Georgi Markov, a Bulgarian defector in London, in September 1978. In April 1979, at Sverdlovsk, a worker did not replace a large filter correctly at a BW production facility, resulting in the release of pulmonary anthrax spores that killed more than 100 civilians in the town. The incident was initially dismissed as gastrointestinal anthrax; it was not until 1992 that the Russian government admitted that the "gastrointestinal anthrax" incident had been an anthrax production plant accident.

When the Soviets invaded Afghanistan, they brought a large contingent of their chemical warfare specialists into the country. U.S. government reports allege that the Soviet military forces used chemical weapons between 1979 and 1986 against mujahideen rebels, using first mustard and nerve agents and then graduating to "yellow rain"—trichothecene mycotoxins, or T-2 toxin—and other experimental CB warfare agents.[9] Again, because conventional munitions were not sufficiently slowing the Afghan rebel action, the Soviet military turned to chemical weapons as being more effective. In 1986, reports of Soviet CW attacks dropped off, perhaps because the attacks were not seen as being all that effective against the well-hidden rebel forces. The Soviets had also shifted to mass bombings with incendiaries, submunitions, and other better-designed bombs that may have been more effective than CB weapons.[10]

Following the breakup of the Soviet Union, President Yeltsin officially called for the end of his country's offensive BW research program. The U.S. Cooperative Threat Reduction program is intended to help Russia and former Soviet Union member nations disarm their nuclear, biological, and chemical warfare production factories and associated weapon systems. Some people are still concerned that the thousands of unemployed researchers might be tempted to assist smaller nations to develop their offensive CB warfare programs, thus proliferating the threat across the world. Although this may be a reasonable concern, certainly many countries are able to research and develop these agents on their own today, given that the technology and knowledge required to build these facilities are no longer state-of-the-art.

As a note on the side, it should be said that the former Warsaw Pact allies benefited from their association with the Soviet Union's offensive CB warfare program. Romania, Bulgaria, and the former states of Czechoslovakia and Yugoslavia all either had their own means of manufacturing chemical weapons or had Soviet chemical munitions in their countries. Although these countries no longer have active programs, they had the knowledge and capabilities to develop these weapons, and they had motivations much like Russia's. In fact, the Czech Republic now works closely with the United States, the United Kingdom, and the Netherlands on chemical defense research issues.

East Asia

In East Asia, a number of countries have traditionally been at conflict for decades, if not centuries. Prior to Japan's military ambitions in World War II, China had clashed with Vietnam, Korea, and Japan. Thailand, Singapore, Malaysia, and Indonesia have all had their clashes, internally and externally. These powers have developed their respective military capabilities with a careful eye on each other. Part of that history has included the development of CB weapons.

Japan's early efforts investigating biological warfare are well documented; history has noted not only its research and experimentation in Manchuria in the 1930s and 1940s but also its failure to develop biological weapons and use them effectively.[11] By the late 1930s, the Japanese were producing CW agents and weapons and had initiated a BW research program in Manchuria under the name Unit 731. The Japanese researched several biological warfare agents and used prisoners of war as research subjects, eventually weaponizing some BW agents for use against Chinese cities. Japan's ability to use chemical weapons against the Chinese military, though effective, was not necessary to aid Japan's military successes. Between 1937 and 1942, Japanese forces employed riot-control agents, phosgene, hydrogen cyanide, and mustard agents in tactical battles against the Chinese military. Although the Japanese regarded chemical weapons as legitimate battlefield weapons in World War II (they had not signed the

Geneva Protocol), the use of chemical weapons was not the major factor in winning these battles.[12] In the face of steady U.S. military victories and the slow collapse of their forces, the Japanese military hurled kamikaze pilots into combat, but not CB weapons. The threat of American retaliation against Japanese cities, already seen with incendiary munitions, may have held the Japanese government from authorizing CB weapons attacks against Allied forces. Although both the Americans and Soviets sought out the Japanese researchers and their efforts, what they found was somewhat less than anticipated and did not do much to advance the superpowers' efforts. Since World War II, Japan, like Germany, has not invested in any offensive CB warfare program. The Japanese have increased their defensive capabilities, notably since the Aum Shinrikyo incident in 1995. Japan has signed both the BWC and CWC.

The Korean conflict did not include any CB warfare, despite claims from China and North Korea to the contrary. Here again, however, is a case where the countries involved—North Korea, South Korea, and China—see that the use of conventional munitions alone may be insufficient to advance their desired military goals. North Korea is believed to have been developing an offensive CB capability since the 1960s, and it has the capability to produce and weaponize these agents in large quantities through its indigenous chemical industry. North Korea can deliver these agents through artillery systems or via aircraft, but the real concern is whether it has mated its CB warfare capability with its ballistic missile program. Ballistic missiles, developed in part from old Soviet technology and research assistance, pose a real threat not merely to North Korea's neighbors but to U.S. forces in the theater. Although North Korea has acceded to the BWC, it has not signed the CWC.

North Korea's motivation to invest in an offensive CB warfare program can be tied directly to its perspective that the United States is the aggressor against smaller countries, and to its feeling that it requires a significant capability to prevent the United States from interfering with its interests. Since the U.S. military has nuclear weapons and has demonstrated the will to use them, the North Korean government sees unconventional weapons as the key to counter that threat.[13] The Iran-Iraq War demonstrated the utility of chemical weapons, causing a renewal of interest in developing an indigenous production capability. North Korea's military regularly trains in chemical defense operations, being told they should expect South Korea and the United States to employ chemical weapons against them. Chemical agents—estimated at 2,500 to 5,000 tons—added to the country's ballistic missile program give the North Koreans what they feel is a tactical edge against a well-trained and well-equipped South Korean military and the U.S. forces in the theater.

The continuing threat of a North Korean "first attack" intended to reunite the two Koreas is a threat not merely to the South Korean populace and to U.S. forces but also to Japan, which supports U.S. military efforts in the area. The growing range of North Korea's ballistic missiles puts Japanese cities and U.S. military forces in Japan at risk. North Korea has also sold ballistic missiles and related technology to Pakistan and other countries as a source of hard currency, increasing the potential use of CW-tipped ballistic missiles throughout the world.

In addition to its nuclear weapons program, China is believed to have begun developing a chemical weapons program in the 1950s, and it has the industrial infrastructure and technical expertise to have begun a biological weapons program. China's military also patterns itself after the Soviet model, with similar artillery, rockets, aircraft, and ballistic missiles that can deliver CB warfare agents. Its industry and military forces have grown to rival the industrialized powers of the West. The United States believes that China's declarations of never pursuing a biological weapons program are "inaccurate and incomplete" and that it does have a moderate arsenal of traditional CW agents.[14] China has, nonetheless, signed and ratified the CWC and acceded to the BWC.

China's programs and motivations to develop an offensive CB warfare program are not as clear as North Korea's or as other nations'. It is certainly not seeking a "poor man's atomic bomb," given that it has a mature nuclear weapons capability. One reason that China may be at least investigating CB warfare agents is that it may feel that Taiwan has developed CB warfare agents of its own, and that it needs a defensive and retaliatory capability (a position much like the U.S. position with respect to the Soviet Union in the 1980s).

Taiwan makes some military analysts' lists as a nation that has the potential to have developed CB weapons. Certainly it has the technology, a strong manufacturing capability, and the motivation. Since the nationalist Chinese army retreated to this island, Taiwan has been under the watchful eyes of the People's Republic of China. If the mainland Chinese military decided to invade

Taiwan, the small island would not be able to resist with conventional munitions alone and without U.S. assistance. There have been persistent reports since 1989 that Taiwan has, at the least, manufactured CW agents for researching defensive measures. The government has denied having an offensive BW program, but it does admit to having a robust CB defense program.[15] Although the leadership may be considering offensive CB warfare measures, it is unlikely that its military has been able to train to use these weapons (given the size of the island). Taiwan has ratified the BWC but not the CWC because of its nonnation status in the United Nations.

Vietnam makes the Congressional Research Services (CRS) list of countries possessing chemical weapons capabilities primarily because of its past association as a suspected testing ground for Soviet CB weapons such as the T-2 mycotoxin, mustard agent, and nerve agents employed against H'Mong tribespeople and Laotians in the 1970s.[16] It is not believed that Vietnam's military has retained an active offensive CB warfare program. Vietnam has acceded to the BWC and ratified the CWC since then. Myanmar (formerly known as Burma), Indonesia, and Thailand all make the CRS list as well, but mostly because of the possibility that they may still have old stocks abandoned by the British forces during World War II. All three have signed the BWC and CWC.

South Asia

Both India and Pakistan have invested in chemical weapons programs at the least, and they are believed to have investigated biological weapons to some extent. The exact year that these countries started their programs is unclear, but it probably would have been in the 1960s or 1970s at the latest. Both have signed and ratified the BWC and CWC; India in particular declared that it had an offensive chemical weapons capability that it would demilitarize. Pakistan has not declared any chemical weapons stocks and it continues to develop its chemical industries in areas that could be useful for developing chemical weapons. The continued instability in the region, caused in a large part by disagreement over control of the Kashmir region, has kept tempers hot.

Both countries have the technology and inherent resources to develop offensive CB weapons, but both claim to have focused on defensive programs only. Both sides have a great deal of investment in advanced military equipment, including ballistic missiles and nuclear weapons. There is probably little chance that they will put down their nuclear arms in the near term; the desire to retain those weapons as a hedge against full-scale war may be the reason why these nations have agreed to abandon offensive CB weapons. Both have significant conventional forces, but neither can afford to neglect researching what the other may be planning to employ. The hard-liners in both governments will probably ensure that these two countries remain at high military alert for the foreseeable future.

It is probably easier to understand why Pakistan would invest in offensive CB weapons, for its infantry forces are outnumbered five to one and outgunned three to one in tanks and artillery when compared against Indian forces. Although nuclear weapons may be Pakistan's last line of retaliation in the event of a full-scale invasion, nuclear weapons do not help in the numerous smaller conflicts that continue to occur between the two nations. Pakistan may see CB weapons as the way to counter the larger Indian forces, much as Iraq held off superior Iranian numbers in their conflict. India's concerns about a growing Chinese influence in the region, added to the existing friction over the Kashmir region, were probably its justifications for initiating an offensive CB warfare program. India has a mature scientific and industrial capability that could support research and development of its own offensive weapons, if need be. It was the first of the two to declare that it did have a dedicated CW production capability and that it would disarm, a declaration that might have been in recognition that its conventional superiority in the area negates the need for an offensive CB warfare program, although India continues its defensive CB program.

It is of some interest to note that the cases of Pakistan and India again demonstrate that CB weapons are not merely "poor man's atomic weapons," since neither country is relying on CB weapons as a surrogate for nuclear weapons. CB weapons have a clear and distinct use between conventional and nuclear weapons for these (and other) countries. The label "poor man's atomic weapons" is more of an arms control community attempt to believe that countries seek CB weapons for the same reasons that they seek nuclear weapons.

Middle East and Africa

The Middle East has been and remains the hottest region for potential CB warfare conflicts. This may not be a surprise to most military analysts and even to the general public, considering the number of conflicts going back decades in this region. Israel has signed but not ratified the CWC, has not acceded to the BWC, and does not participate in the Nuclear Non-Proliferation Treaty (NPT). It is suspected of having an offensive chemical and biological weapons program, and it may have used nerve agents in an attempted assassination of a Hamas leader in 1997.[17] Given its CB warfare capabilities, combined with its nuclear weapons program and its ballistic missiles, Israel is a country that in its efforts to be secure from invasion by its neighbors has developed a very sophisticated unconventional weapons program.

Like Pakistan, Iraq, and Taiwan, Israel developed these capabilities because it can be outnumbered and outgunned by its Arab neighbors, as has been the case several times in the past. Although Israel's military may have superior technology and highly trained military personnel, not to mention the support of the United States, the sheer volume of military forces invading from the north, east, and south could overwhelm the Israeli military despite its superior conventional weapon systems. Needless to say, Israel's neighbors are developing their own offensive CB warfare capabilities in response, which in turn, spurs on the Israeli efforts to develop at least a retaliatory capability. Because of these threats, Israel has a very highly organized homeland security organization that distributes protective masks, medical countermeasures, and shelter-in-place kits to its citizens.

Egypt's CW program came to light when Egypt was involved in the 1962–1970 Yemeni civil war, supporting the republican forces against the royalists. It is believed that the Soviet Union supplied nerve and mustard bombs to Egyptian forces, causing more than a thousand casualties when Soviet-supplied Egyptian bombers dropped chemical bombs on Yemeni royalist forces. In the 1973 Arab-Israeli War, Israeli forces captured Egyptian soldiers with protective masks and chemical antidotes and Soviet-supplied armored vehicles with collective protection equipment.

It is believed that Egypt, in particular, has continued to upgrade its CB warfare capabilities because it sees that attaining nuclear weapons is not feasible. It therefore has both rationales and incentives for continuing its research and development efforts in this area. The rationales include its assessment that Israel has a mature offensive CB warfare capability; that other Arab countries in the Middle East are seeking these weapons and there needs to be a balance of power; that Egypt should continue to be a leader, strategically and militarily, in this region; that CB weapons have a significant strategic and military value and contribution; and that Egypt has the technical capability to sustain and enhance this unconventional capability. It continues to refrain from signing the CWC.[18] Egypt has the potential to develop CB warheads for its ballistic missiles, although it is unclear whether it is actively seeking this capability.

Egypt denies having an offensive CB warfare program today, and it has acceded to the BWC but refuses to sign the CWC as long as Israel has not participated in the NPT. Iraq, Libya, and Syria have followed suit. Military analysts believe these nations may have developed CB weapons programs to counter Israel's suspected offensive CB warfare and nuclear programs, especially seeing that they cannot develop nuclear weapons—yet. In addition, given an area where every state is developing CB weapons, no state wants to be the one in this volatile region without them.

Syria has signed but not ratified the BWC, and it also refuses to sign the CWC. Syria is believed to have the most sophisticated CW program in the region, one that started in 1973 with Egypt sharing its chemical weapons as Syria's ally in the Arab-Israeli War. After 1982, Syria was seen as increasing its NBC weapons training. Its military has similar equipment as the Soviet Union and is believed to have tested ballistic missiles with CW warheads. Its chemical capability includes Scud and Frog missiles in addition to cluster bombs and modified incendiary munitions. Although it has an impressive arsenal, it is probably the only Arab nation that has an offensive CB warfare program but has not used CB weapons in a military conflict.

Syria has an indigenous chemical precursor capability, a strong industrial infrastructure, and at least three CW production facilities. Although Syria has the infrastructure to support an offensive BW program, there is no clear evidence that it has done anything other than limited research.[19] However, some sources believe the Syrians have been seeking to develop a BW capability since at least 1988.[20] Although President George W. Bush did not include Syria in his "axis of evil" of Iraq, Iran, and North Korea, it certainly ranks as a country that has both "weapons of mass destruction" programs and connections to terrorists.

Iraq and Iran used chemical weapons against each other in the first Gulf War between 1983 and 1988. This conflict is described in more detail in chapter 7. Iraq began developing its CW program in the 1970s using European materials and equipment, and by the 1980s, it had a fairly substantial program. Starting with mustard bombs and graduating to nerve agents, Iraqi military forces were able to beat back Iranian human-wave attacks that were threatening to overwhelm them in the south. Again, the main motivation for the use of these weapons was that conventional munitions were not sufficient against the larger enemy numbers. Although Iran tried to develop an offensive CW capability later in the war, it was never as successful as Iraq had been, given its lack of a modern chemical industry and the necessary technology to develop these weapons. Both sides had ballistic missiles, but neither had developed chemical warheads during their conflict.[21]

Iraq has used its chemical weapons in combat and to terrorize its own populace, but it has not demonstrated any operational biological warfare capability. That does not mean it was not developing an offensive capability. When the United States prepared to attack Iraqi forces in the spring of 1991, there was a great deal of concern about whether Iraq would use CB weapons to counter the coalition forces. Six months of training and stockpiling CB defense equipment gave coalition forces some confidence that they would at least survive any Iraqi attacks. Air superiority, a heavy offensive against suspected production and storage sites, and strong attacks against Iraqi artillery and air systems also limited the chance of Iraqi CB warfare attacks. Fortunately, it appeared that Saddam Hussein had used his CB warfare capability as more of a bluff, and U.S. forces returned without having been engaged in CB warfare.[22]

Since the Gulf War, Iraq has resisted the efforts of international arms control experts to identify and eliminate its offensive CB warfare program. The United Nations Special Commission (UNSCOM) tried to penetrate Iraq's special weapons programs for seven years, with only limited success.[23] UNSCOM did clarify what Iraq had developed in the way of offensive CB weapons, but it seemed that Iraq was holding back information on current stocks. UNSCOM did install automated monitoring systems at known facilities, but without being maintained, these systems eventually ceased to operate. Between 1998 and 2000, Iraq refused to allow UN inspectors into Iraq, leading President George W.

Bush to threaten to take offensive action if Iraq did not allow the return of UN inspectors and live up to the terms of the 1991 cease-fire agreement that specified it would eliminate all of its unconventional weapons.

Iran's efforts to develop offensive CB weapons started during the Iran-Iraq War, largely in an attempt to retaliate against Iraq's first use of such weapons. Although analysts believe that Iran employed chemical weapons against Iraq (although without much effect), it has never admitted to such. Iran has claimed that it no longer has an offensive CB warfare program, and it has ratified both the CWC and BWC. Military analysts believe its program could still be active, given its history of conflict with its neighbors. Iran receives a good deal of support from Russia and China, including production technology and expertise in chemical and biological manufacturing that could be used to create an advanced and self-sufficient military capability. If Iran continues to build up its industry and expertise, it could resume its offensive CB warfare programs, which is one reason that President Bush included the nation on his "axis of evil" watchlist.

South Africa was developing chemical and biological weapons in the 1980s and into the early 1990s, a program that was not exposed until 1998. In the early 1940s, South Africa had manufactured mustard agent for the British military in anticipation of its use in World War II. Following the war, the government dumped these stocks at sea. Despite having signed and ratified the BWC, the South African government began research on developing CB weapons in the 1970s. With civil wars erupting around it and feeling an increasing sense of isolation, the government began a partnership with Israel on armaments development, which may have included CB weapons technology.[24] Following the change of governments in 1994, South Africa disestablished its offensive CB warfare program, in part as a result of increasing pressure from the governments of the United States and the United Kingdom. South Africa has also signed the CWC, as have more than forty other African nations.

South Africa is another example of a country that built nuclear weapons in addition to CB weapons. South African forces did not employ CB warfare agents against guerrillas or its neighbors, since it has a very well trained and equipped conventional force that was able to accomplish its missions without relying on CB weapons. This example does reflect how the government can see a political justification to start such a research and development program, but the program remains more of a political weapon than a military one. The cases of South Africa, Iraq, and Iran also demonstrate the difficulties of stopping a nation from developing its CB warfare programs. Although arms control treaties and watchdog organizations exist, and the major powers may pressure countries to stop offensive CB warfare programs, it is difficult to stop a country from developing a covert CB warfare program, especially if it does not rely on external sources for the chemicals and biological material to manufacture these weapons.

A number of other Middle Eastern and African countries remain on the list of nations suspected of having such weapons. In 1987, it was reported that Libya had used chemical weapons (obtained from Iran) against Chad, with less than successful results. For many years, the U.S. government was more worried about Libya's offensive CB warfare program than about those of other countries in the Middle East, although now it seems that the intelligence estimate was mistaken. Libya was suspected of developing a chemical weapons program at Rabta and most recently, in its hardened underground facility at Tarhuna. This effort is believed to have been suspended, largely because the country lacks a scientific or technical base to advance past the laboratory stage. Its continued reliance on foreign sources for supplies allows the major powers to limit the precursors required for CB weapons. Libya once pursued the development of nuclear weapons and ballistic missiles, but this interest seems to have died off. Libya has signed the BWC but not the CWC.

Ethiopia and Sudan are suspected of developing, or at least of being interested in developing, chemical weapons capabilities, programs that are in part supported by Iraq. Both states have internal conflicts with rebels and guerrillas, fights their conventional forces have been unable to contain. Iraq's connections with Sudan led to the U.S. government's cruise missile attack on a suspected chemical weapons production facility in August 1998. Saudi Arabia came under suspicion when it purchased fifty CSS-2 ballistic missiles from China. These missiles are inaccurate and of little value if used with conventional warheads, but if they are equipped with chemical warheads, they would do just fine on the battlefield.[25]

The Western Hemisphere

Cuba is perhaps the only country in the Western Hemisphere that is still thought by the U.S. government to be interested in an offensive CB warfare program. Although Brazil and Argentina have had their conflicts and interests in nuclear weapons, there was no evidence of any interest in CB weapons, although they both have the technology and infrastructure to develop such weapons. During the height of the Cold War, Cuba no doubt benefited from education and funding from its Soviet colleagues in developing its military capabilities. Ken Alibek relates in his book that the Soviet Union supported the development of biotechnology research in 1981, research that led to a very sophisticated genetics engineering laboratory, one that might be used for BW research. Although the United States government remains convinced that Cuba has an active BW program, it is actually Cuba that has accused the United States of BW attacks against its agricultural industries over the years.[26] Whether Cuba has this capability or not, it is not known to have used CB weapons in any military operation. Cuba is a signatory of both the BWC and CWC.

Canada has had a role in offensive CB warfare research, one that is not as well known as the U.S. or U.K. efforts. Between 1937 and 1947, Canadian researchers supported both major powers in the development of anthrax as a weaponized agent. Open-air and laboratory CB weapons tests were conducted at a military research station near Medicine Hat, Alberta. Canada had developed small stocks of mustard and nerve agents, which had all been destroyed by 1990. The overwhelming majority of Canada's research was in support of the development of defensive measures. To that end, Canada joined with Britain and the United States in a tripartite agreement to share information and research on CB defense efforts.[27] In the 1980s, Australia joined this group, creating the ABCA (American-British-Canadian-Australian) Quadripartite group.

Notes

1. John M. Dahm, *Mentality, Perception, Bugs, and Gas: South Africa's Chemical and Biological Warfare Program* (Washington, DC: Joint Military Intelligence College, 2000).

2. An excellent source is the Monterey Institute of International Studies' Chemical and Biological Weapons Resource Page (on-line; available: http://www.cns.miis.edu/research/cbw/possess.htm; accessed March 2003).

3. Albert Palazoo, *Seeking Victory on the Western Front: The British Army and Chemical Warfare in World War I* (Lincoln: University of Nebraska Press, 2000), 72.

4. Martin Gilbert, *The First World War: A Complete History* (New York: Henry Holt, 1994), 346–447, 351, 369.

5. Robert Harris and Jeremy Paxman, *A Higher Form of Killing: The Secret Story of Chemical and Biological Warfare* (New York: Hill and Wang, 1982), 179. This book also includes a very detailed discussion of the British CW program during World War II.

6. Ken Alibek, with Stephen Handelman, *Biohazard: The Chilling True Story of the Largest Covert Biological Weapons Program in the World. Told from Inside by the Man Who Ran It* (New York: Random House, 1999), 29–30.

7. Ibid., 42–43.

8. Ibid., 234–235.

9. Whether the Soviets experimented with T-2 toxin, or "yellow rain," as CW agent in Laos is still somewhat under question. For the counterargument, read Grant Evans, *The Yellow Rainmakers: Are Chemical Weapons Being Used in Southeast Asia?* (New York: Verso, 1983).

10. Anthony H. Cordesman and Abraham R. Wagner, *The Lessons of Modern War,* vol. 3, *The Afghan and Falklands Conflicts* (Boulder, CO: Westview Press, 1990), 214–218.

11. Peter Williams and David Wallace, *Unit 731: Japan's Secret Biological Warfare in World War II* (London: Hodder and Stoughton, 1989).

12. Eric Croddy, with Clarisa Perez-Armendariz and John Hart, *Chemical and Biological Warfare: A Comprehensive Survey for the Concerned Citizen* (New York: Copernicus Books, 2002), 154–155. The Japanese government developed about 8,000 tons of CW agents during World War II, as compared to the U.S. production of 146,000 tons.

13. Peter R. Lavoy, Scott D. Sagan, and James J. Wirtz, eds., *Planning the Unthinkable: How New Powers Will Use Nuclear, Biological, and Chemical Weapons* (Ithaca, NY: Cornell University Press, 2000), 183.

14. William Cohen, *Proliferation: Threat and Response* (Washington, DC: Department of Defense, 2001), 15.

15. See Federation of American Scientists, "Chemical Weapons" (on-line; available: http://www.fas.org/nuke/guide/taiwan/cw/index.html; accessed February 14, 2003).

16. Robert Shuey, *Nuclear, Biological, and Chemical Weapons and Missiles: The Current Situation and Trends* (Washington, DC: Congressional Research Services, 2001).

17. Barton Gellman, "For Many Israelis, Assassination Is Only as Bad as Its Execution," *Washington Post,* October 12, 1997, A1. Two

Mossad agents were captured in Jordan on September 25, 1997, after failing to assassinate Khaled Meshal, the chief of the militant Islamic group Hamas's political bureau in Amman, Jordan. There were no discernible comments by the press or the U.S. government as to the Israeli agents' possible use of CW agents as their weapon.

18. See Dany Shoham, "The Evolution of Chemical and Biological Weapons in Egypt" Ariel Center for Policy Research (on-line; available: http://www.acpr.org.il/publications/policy-papers/pp046-xs.html; accessed March 2003).

19. See "Syria Overview" on the Nuclear Threat Initiative web site for Syria's suspected capabilities (available: http://www.nti.org/e_research/e1_syria_1.html; accessed February 14, 2003).

20. Anthony H. Cordesman and Abraham R. Wagner, *The Lessons of Modern War*, vol. 1, *The Arab-Israeli Conflicts, 1973–1989* (Boulder, CO: Westview Press, 1990), 282.

21. Anthony H. Cordesman and Abraham R. Wagner, *The Lessons of Modern War*, vol. 2, *The Iran-Iraq War* (Boulder, CO: Westview Press, 1990).

22. Albert J. Mauroni, *Chemical-Biological Defense: U.S. Military Policies and Decisions in the Gulf War* (Westport, CT: Praeger, 1998).

23. An excellent description of this effort is Scott Ritter's *Endgame: Solving the Iraq Problem Once and for All* (New York: Simon and Schuster, 1999).

24. Steven Burgess and Helen Purkitt, *The Rollback of South Africa's Chemical and Biological Warfare Program* (Maxwell AFB, AL: USAF Counterproliferation Center, 2001), 1–6.

25. E. J. Hogendoorn, "A Chemical Weapons Atlas," *Bulletin of the Atomic Scientists*, September/October 1997 (on-line; available: http://www.thebulletin.org/issues/1997/so97/so97hogendoom.html; accessed April 3, 2003).

26. Alibek with Handelman, *Biohazard*, 273–275.

27. Perhaps the only book that documents Canada's role in the U.S. military's CB warfare program is John Bryden's *Deadly Allies: Canada's Secret War, 1937–1947* (Toronto: McClelland and Stewart, 1989).

4

CB Warfare Chronology

This chapter presents a time line of chemical and biological warfare throughout the world, focusing primarily on the period from the dawn of the twentieth century to the present. There are certainly roots to CB warfare (CBW) that predate the twentieth century, but such warfare was more the exception than the rule. Although science had supported the development of weapon systems in the past, it was the maturity of chemical sciences and engineering in mass production industries in the twentieth century that allowed CB warfare to become a true branch of the military arts. A review of this history will help set the stage for discussions of how nations have dealt with CB warfare events.

Early History (1000 B.C.?–A.D. 1899)

Incidents of CB warfare are woven throughout many conflicts of history, from the Chinese to the Greeks to European military forces. Whenever there has been conflict, there have been those developing new ways to defeat their adversaries. For the most part, attempts to weaponize chemicals or biologicals during this period were relatively crude and were not part of a sustained mil-

75

itary effort to develop a true CB warfare capability. Instead, they are instances of military forces using their own intuition and improvisation to weaken or break the morale of the enemy, rather than the development of a new method of warfare. These methods included poisoning wells, using toxic smokes, and catapulting corpses into walled cities. It was not until the nineteenth century that chemistry began to come into its own as a true science, replacing alchemy, leading people to theorize what this branch of science could do to support military operations.

Birth of Modern Chemical Warfare (1915–1946)

Although many might credit Fritz Haber with being the father of modern chemical warfare, certainly the topic was under review by many nations prior to 1915. Both British and French scientists examined various chemicals for use as tear gases to irritate and demoralize opposing forces. The French use of tear gas projectiles in 1914 was a justification for the Germans to investigate chemical warfare options. The Germans were significantly more advanced in chemistry than their European cousins, in part due to a strong dye industry. Other German scientists had developed artillery projectiles filled with chemicals in 1914, which were employed against the British in October and the Russians in November, without any visible effects. It was Haber who suggested the concept of creating a toxic cloud using not artillery shells but a line of gas cylinders, which was more effective as a wide-area weapon and would help reduce a dependence on high explosives for delivery. This led to the first successful gas attack at Ypres in April 1915, when 168 tons of chlorine gas were used against unprepared Allied forces.

The use of chemical weapons quickly escalated on both sides, until practically half of all artillery shells were chemical-filled projectiles. Although the British and French decried such attacks as immoral and barbaric, they were quick to develop and use the same weapons throughout the rest of the war. Erich Maria Remarque's excellent novel *All Quiet on the Western Front* mentions the impact of British gas attacks against the Germans, for instance. After the war, European forces tried to implement treaties that would limit certain forms of warfare seen in the Great War, including chemical warfare. This led to the Geneva Protocol of 1925, which called for no first use of chemical weapons but did not ban production and storage of gas weapons for the purpose of retaliation in kind.

Military theorists envisioned a major role for strategic bombers loaded with gas weapons in the future of warfare, leading all nations to continue their research efforts into both offensive and defensive chemical warfare. At the advent of World War II, this led to the mass manufacture of civilian gas masks in addition to military masks and suits, detectors, and decontaminants. The massive U.S. industrial complex quickly built up a military CB warfare infrastructure in anticipation of Axis use. For the reasons mentioned earlier in this book, these attacks never came. Following the war, the discovery of Germany's nerve agents ensured that the United States, its Western allies, and the Soviet Union would continue their research and development.

Cold War Era (1947–1990)

The development of biological weapons during World War II added another aspect to the chemical warfare community, since these weapons also were an application of scientific products against human physiology. The U.S. Army's Chemical Corps also began to take part in nuclear weapons development, with a focus on studying radiological contamination, on the grounds that they were the technical specialists when it came to scientific products of war. The Korean conflict, with fears that the Soviet Union and its allies were preparing to use CB weapons against U.S. forces, revitalized the CB warfare infrastructure. With the two superpowers facing off against each other, the term "weapons of mass destruction" came into vogue, lumping the new nuclear weapons with their significantly less destructive cousins, chemical and biological weapons.

The Cold War era was the high point of the U.S. and Soviet CB warfare programs. The era was marked by a massive research and development effort to turn the new nerve agents and biological weapons into tactical weapons for the military. The two superpowers' offensive programs were remarkably similar, focusing on many of the same weapons and delivery systems and on testing those systems to determine their large-area coverage capabilities. For the first twenty years of the Cold War era (1947–

1967), the development, testing, and evaluation of various CB warfare agents remained primarily in the domain of the two superpowers, who stockpiled the successful ones in preparation for future conflicts. However, other nations were starting their investigations into developing this capability.

By 1968, the military forces in both countries had a sophisticated and robust CB warfare capability. At first, these weapons were not seen as so-called weapons of mass destruction as much as they were seen as a halfway step between conventional and nuclear weapons. But increasingly, arms control talks in the 1960s viewed these unconventional weapons as just as deadly as if not worse than nuclear weapons. Since the two superpowers were not going to give up their nuclear arms, arms control groups focused on reducing or eliminating CB weapons. Although the two superpowers participated in these multilateral talks, it was clear that neither one trusted the other. The key obstacle in these discussions was the point of verification, which would require a nation to permit inspections of its facilities and stockpile sites to assure other nations that it was in compliance with the respective treaties.

Proliferation of CB Weapons (1968 to the Present)

Rather than discussing biological and chemical weapons together in arms control talks, it was seen as easier to separate them, in part because no one had used biological weapons against any major power, whereas several nations either had used or possessed stores of chemical weapons stockpiles. This led to the development of the Biological Weapons Convention, which had no verification component to the treaty. President Nixon's 1969 announcement that the United States was unilaterally disestablishing its offensive BW program was made in the good faith that other nations would follow suit. Instead, the Soviet Union, believing that the United States had simply moved its offensive BW program underground, redoubled its efforts. The United States decided to resume modernization of its CW stockpile in the late 1970s, in part due to concerns that the Soviet Union had continued its offensive program to the point that U.S. military forces would be at a significant disadvantage in any conflict. This decision led to the resumption of the binary chemical weapons program, whose research had been halted in 1972.

Increasingly, other nations began developing their own offensive CB warfare programs, often based on the Soviet and U.S. programs. With increases in education and industrial capability across the globe, any nation could develop the basic tools to research and develop a CB warfare capability. The international trade in bulk chemicals and the industrial nations' building facilities overseas and selling dual-use (military or commercial) equipment to smaller nations willing to buy their services meant that these nations could produce their own stockpiles. With continued conflicts across the globe, nations had the incentive to build a CB warfare program before their adversaries did. The basic template remained the same: First they developed and tested chemical weapons, then they developed and tested biological weapons. Although only a few conflicts have seen the use of CB weapons, the potential for future CB warfare conflicts continues while these countries retain their CB weapons stockpiles.

The advent of new technologies, such as ballistic missiles, cruise missiles, and unmanned aerial vehicles (UAVs), has increased the ability of many nations to develop and deploy their CB warfare capabilities against major forces without significantly imperiling their own forces. These delivery systems could use either conventional high-explosive or CB warfare agent payloads. Many countries today do not aspire to become superpowers holding 30,000–40,000 tons of stockpiled material. A smaller stockpile of a few hundred or a few thousand tons of CW agents will do fine, if managed and delivered to the right place on the battlefield at the right time. These facts make it difficult to monitor and inspect nations suspected of violations of arms control treaties.

The ability of nonstate actors (whether terrorist groups, freedom fighters, irregular militias, death squads, and so on) to develop rudimentary CB warfare skills has become increasingly greater. If terrorist groups have the resolve to move from conventional weapons to unconventional ones, they can buy specialists and the required equipment. Many groups can get away with bluffs and hoaxes, or they can experiment with small amounts of homemade toxins to threaten particular targets. Aum Shinrikyo's use of sarin in Tokyo has been seen by military experts and think tanks as more of an aberration than an indication of the future, yet it has frightened enough politicians to make them start thinking seriously about the potential of future terrorist attacks.

CBW Time Line

1000 B.C.   Chinese armies use arsenic smoke in battle.

600 B.C.   Assyrians contaminate enemy water supplies with rye ergot. This fungus produces a hallucinogen similar to LSD.

429–424 B.C.   Spartans and their allies use toxic smoke (from burn ing wax and sulfur) and flame (pitch) against Athenian-allied cities during the Peloponnesian War.

187 B.C.   Inhabitants of Ambracia in Epirus use toxic smoke to drive off Romans undermining their walls.

A.D. 800–1300   Besieging armies in Europe and Asia catapult diseased corpses over city walls to weaken the defenders and force an early capitulation. European scholars develop alchemy, brought by the Arabs to Spain.

1347–1352   Twenty-five million people, nearly one-third of the population, die in Europe from bubonic plague. The disease is suspected to have come from trade ships traveling from China to Italy.

1675   The Treaty at Strassburg between the French and Germans outlaws the use of poisoned bullets. This is the first international agreement on prohibiting poisoned weapons.

1763   British soldiers give smallpox-infected blankets to Indians at Fort Pitt, Pennsylvania. This disease wipes out a large Indian population on the East Coast.

1855   During the Crimean War, Sir Lyon Playfair proposes to the British High Command that the military should use cacodyl cyanide–filled projectiles to break the Russian forces. The British military rejects the idea.

1863–1865   Union forces examine proposals to fill artillery shells with chlorine liquid and to mix hydrochloric and sulfuric acids to create a toxic cloud. Instead, the Union issues General Order no. 100, which states, "The use of poison in any manner, be it to poison wells, or food, or arms, is wholly excluded from modern warfare." Confederate forces, on the defensive, poison wells and ponds to deny water sources to the advancing Union forces.

1887 British, French, and German governments begin considering using tear gases for military purposes.

1899 The First Hague Convention with Respect to the Laws and Customs of War on Land is signed on July 29 forbidding "the use of projectiles the sole object of which is the diffusion of asphyxiating or deleterious gases." Twenty-seven nations sign, including France, Germany, Italy, Japan, Russia, and Great Britain. The United States does not sign the treaty.

1907 At the Second Hague Convention, the Declaration Concerning Asphyxiating Gases is signed on July 29, codifying the language of the First Hague Convention.

1915– The Germans successfully use 168 tons of chlorine
1916 against the Allied forces at Ypres on April 22 and use the gas five more times in April and May. The British retaliate at Loos on September 15 with 150 tons of chlorine, albeit less successfully. The Germans escalate to using phosgene at Ypres by the end of the year, and the British use phosgene against the Germans at Somme in June 1916.

1916 The Germans begin to use diphosgene in May. The French try hydrogen cyanide in July and cyanogen chloride in the fall. Both sides begin to mix agents and to experiment with camouflage materials to prevent quick identification.

1917 The Germans introduce mustard agent at Ypres on July 12. The British use mustard agent against the Germans in September 1918, but they rely more on phosgene as their main weapon. The U.S. Army establishes a Gas Service in the American Expeditionary Force, with its

1917, cont.	main laboratory at Edgewood Arsenal, Maryland. By the end of the war, it is estimated that more than 124,000 tons of chemicals have been employed by all the belligerent forces.
1918	On June 28, the War Department formally establishes, by executive order, the Army's Chemical Warfare Service, which is to assume full responsibility for all facilities and functions relating to toxic chemicals as of July 1, 1918.
1919	The Treaty of Versailles, signed on June 28, prohibits Germany from producing, importing, or using "asphyxiating, poisonous or other gases and all analogous liquids, materials, or devices."
1920	The U.S. Army decides to disestablish its Chemical Warfare Service and to move the responsibility for defense and retaliatory measures to the Corps of Engineers. Instead, Congress authorizes the permanent establishment of the U.S. Army Chemical Warfare Service on July 1.
1922	At the Washington Arms Conference, the U.S. delegation suggests language abolishing chemical warfare. Although the arms control treaty is ratified by the United States and other countries, it is not enacted due to French objections to language concerning the use of submarines in combat.
1925	The Geneva Protocol for the Prohibition of the Use in War of Asphyxiating, Poisonous or Other Gases, and of Bacteriological Methods of Warfare is signed on June 17. The protocol condemns the use of CB weapons except in response to first use by a belligerent state using CB weapons. The United States signs the protocol, as do twenty-eight other countries, but the Senate rejects the treaty.
1935– 1936	Italian forces in Ethiopia use mustard bombs and aerosol sprayers against Abyssinian guerrillas to protect their flanks and to attack the enemy rear areas.

Ethiopia appeals to the League of Nations, which imposes limited economic sanctions against Italy in an effort to stop the war.

1936–
1938

German scientists discover tabun and sarin, later type-classified as nerve agents GA and GB. Germany does not use these CW agents in its attacks against France or Russia, but the German government builds a few weapons factories to develop a retaliatory capability in the event that Allies use chemical weapons against Germany.

1937–
1942

Japanese forces in China begin to use CB weapons and tear gas grenades against poorly equipped and trained Chinese forces. China appeals to the League of Nations but receives no response.

1940–
1945

The United States produces more than 146,000 tons of CW agents as a potential retaliatory capability against the Germans and Japanese. The United States also produces thousands of portable laboratories; hundreds of thousands of detector kits, impregnated uniforms, and chemical protective masks for soldiers and civilians; and millions of gallons of decontaminants.

1941–
1945

Secretary of War Henry Stimson asks the National Academy of Sciences to appoint a Biological Warfare Committee in 1941. In February 1942, this committee recommends that the United States take steps to reduce its vulnerability to biological warfare, resulting in the creation of the War Research Service in August 1942. In April 1943, Camp Detrick, Maryland, is activated as the center for BW research.

1942

The British test weaponized anthrax on Gruinard Island, off the northwest coast of Scotland. The island is sealed off for nearly fifty years until it can be decontaminated to a level permitting unprotected civilians to come back.

1943

In December, a German air raid against the port of Bari in Italy damages the SS *John Harvey*, a U.S. ship carry-

1943, cont.	ing more than 100 tons of mustard-filled aerial bombs. This results in a large release of mustard agent into the port's waters, causing more than 600 military and civilian casualties. The harbor cleanup takes three weeks.
1944	German scientists discover soman, later type-classified as nerve agent GD. Soman is much more persistent and lethal than the earlier nerve agents.
	The United States builds a large-scale anthrax production plant at Vigo, Indiana, near Terre Haute. The military runs tests with biological simulants to ensure it can be safely operated. In the meanwhile, Camp Detrick produces weapons-grade anthrax at its pilot plant. An initial batch of 5,000 four-pound bombs are produced and sent to Britain.
1945	The U.S. Army develops plans to move chemical munitions to the Pacific in anticipation of a forced ground invasion of the Japanese islands. With the use of nuclear weapons against Hiroshima and Nagasaki, these plans are scrapped.
1946	The Army demobilizes the Chemical Warfare Service, which had grown from 2,000 specialists in 1940 to nearly 70,000 at the peak of World War II. Congress authorizes the formation of the Chemical Corps on August 2.
1947	Pfizer, Inc., purchases the Army's anthrax production plant at Vigo and converts it into a plant producing veterinary-grade antibiotics. The Vigo plant had never been used to produce anthrax, its intended role, during the war.
1948	The United States military standardizes G-nerve agents tabun and sarin for their arsenal and begins to develop new detectors and protective ensembles for the new agents. The M-9 protective mask is the first one of its kind to protect against both chemical and biological warfare agents.

1948–   The United Kingdom executes five major open-air
1955   CB weapons trials, all carried out at sea. The intent is
        to determine the potential operational impact of these
        weapons on the battlefield, specifically, how much
        area can be covered with specific weapon systems.

1950   The U.S. Navy sprays San Francisco, from two miles
        offshore, with *Serratia marcescens* (simulating tu-
        laremia) and *Bacillus subtilis* (simulating anthrax) to
        test the potential coverage of a covert BW attack
        against a major city.

1950–   The United States builds facilities at Muscle Shoals,
1953   Alabama, and Rocky Mountain Arsenal, Colorado, to
        produce GB nerve agent. A biological weapons pro-
        duction plant is initiated at Pine Bluff Arsenal,
        Arkansas, in 1951.

1952   The Army Chemical School moves from Edgewood
        Arsenal in Maryland to Fort McClellan, Alabama.

1952–   British scientists discover nerve agent VX, an agent
1953   more persistent and toxic than the G-series agents, and
        share this information with the United States.

1953   The U.S. military starts large-area coverage experi-
        ments with CBW agents and simulants in the United
        States and in the Pacific and other remote areas.

1954–   The U.S. Army exposes Seventh-day Adventist volun-
1973   teers to Q fever at Dugway Proving Ground. This is
        the beginning of Operation Whitecoat.

1956   Camp Detrick becomes Fort Detrick in February.

        Marshal Georgy Zhukov, the Soviet defense minister,
        tells the Twentieth Party Congress that future war will
        include "various means of mass destruction, such as
        atomic, thermonuclear, chemical and bacteriological
        weapons."

        U.S. military policy changes to require the military to
        be prepared to use CBW agents in a general war to

1956,   "enhance military effectiveness." The decision to use
cont.   CBW agents is still reserved for the president.

1957   The United States standardizes VX nerve agent for
           weaponization and builds a plant at Newport, Indiana,
           to produce the nerve agent in 1959. The Soviet Union
           develops a variant of VX for its own military purposes.

1960   International negotiations begin in Geneva to ban
           chemical weapons and to require the destruction of all
           chemical munitions stockpiles.

1962   In response to requests from the South Vietnamese gov-
           ernment, the U.S. government authorizes Operation
           Ranch Hand for anticrop operations (attacking Viet-
           cong rice fields). This operation grows to support major
           defoliation operations across the country in an effort to
           eliminate ambush sites around bases and along rivers.
           The main agents used are Agents Orange and Blue.

           The Army establishes Deseret Test Center at Fort
           Douglas, Utah, next to Dugway Proving Ground.
           Under the name Project 112, the center supports open-
           air CB weapons testing for all the military services de-
           veloping new delivery systems.

1963–   The U.S. Navy runs Project Shipboard Hazard and
1969   Defense (SHAD), part of Project 112, to evaluate CB
           weapons and defensive equipment. Both simulants
           and CBW agents are used without incident.

1965   U.S. advisors to South Vietnamese troops use tear gas
           grenades in Vietnam for self-protection. The use of tear
           gas grenades and CS powder, a riot-control agent, in-
           creases as more U.S. troops deploy to Vietnam. Critics
           accuse the United States of gas warfare in Vietnam.

1965–   The military uses BW simulants to test the potential
1966   spread of terrorist-employed BW agents at the Na-
           tional Airport Greyhound Terminal, in the Pentagon's
           air-handling system in Washington, D.C., and in the
           New York subways.

1967   Egyptian forces bomb Yemeni royalists with mustard and nerve agents, causing more than a thousand casualties during the Yemeni civil war. Soviet support is suspected.

1967–   Operation CHASE (Cut Holes and Sink 'Em), a pro-
1969   gram to dispose of conventional munitions at sea, accepts shipments of obsolete chemical munitions. Environmental and political concerns stop the ocean dumping, although no signs of any contamination or damage to the environment are noted from the dumps, which take place 250 miles from the U.S. shores.

1968   In March, local ranchers accuse Army testers at Dugway Proving Ground of injuring more than 6,000 sheep. The Army makes a financial settlement with the ranchers without admitting guilt. Congress calls for hearings that eventually result in the end of open-air CB weapons tests in the United States.

1969   On July 2, the United Nations releases a report from an international panel of scientists studying the danger of CB warfare. The report calls for the elimination of CB weapons stockpiles worldwide. It also concludes that there is no defense against CB weapons and no way of predicting the duration of effects on the environment.

     On July 8, twenty-three U.S. soldiers are exposed to low levels of sarin while repainting depot buildings on Okinawa but are back on duty in twenty-four hours. The resulting media blitz ten days later reveals the presence of U.S. chemical stocks overseas. By the end of the month, congressional representatives leak information to the press that there are CW stocks in West Germany as well.

     In July, the United Kingdom submits a draft convention to the national delegates at Geneva for the prohibition of the development, production, and stockpiling of biological and biological toxin weapons. In September, the Soviet Union submits a similar draft. These

1969, *cont.*	drafts become the framework for the Biological Weapons Convention.

President Richard Nixon renounces the offensive BW program and reaffirms the U.S. policy of "no first use" of CW weapons on November 25. In February 1970, he extends the ban to biological toxins.

1970	In April, the Department of Defense orders a temporary ban on the use of Agent Orange, in part due to the increasing political criticisms about potential impact on the Vietnamese people and on the country's environment. In October, Congress calls for a National Academy of Sciences study on the ecological and physiological effects of the defoliation program conducted in Vietnam.

1971– 1973	The U.S. military moves its chemical weapons from Okinawa to Johnston Island in the Pacific under Operation Red Hat. It destroys its stockpile of BW materials, changing the BW program to a biological defense research effort. The Soviets redouble their BW research efforts, suspecting the United States of continuing its work in secret.

1972	The Biological Weapons Convention is signed in Washington, London, and Moscow on April 10. Ratification by the Senate is delayed by its consideration of the Geneva Protocol of 1925 and by the question of whether herbicides and riot-control agents are to be considered as CW agents.

The Army appoints Colonel Sam Bass as the program manager for demilitarization of chemical materiel on October 11. His job includes disposal of aging and leaking munitions. In 1975, the post's title is changed to program manager for chemical demilitarization and installation remediation. The first project is the cleanup of Rocky Mountain Arsenal in Colorado.

1973	General Creighton Abrams, chief of staff of the Army, announces the disestablishment of the Army Chemical

Corps in January, with the intention of absorbing its personnel into the Ordnance Corps as "special weapons" handlers. The Chemical School closes at Fort McClellan, Alabama, and moves to Aberdeen Proving Ground, Maryland.

1973–
1975
Israeli and U.S. military analysts inspect Soviet armored vehicles with collective protection systems and Soviet detection and decontamination equipment captured during the Arab-Israeli Yom Kippur War. They are concerned that the Soviet military is planning to operate in CBW conditions in Europe.

1975
The Senate ratifies the Geneva Protocol of 1925 and the Biological Weapons Convention (BWC) on December 16, 1974. This allows President Gerald Ford to sign documents of ratification on January 22, subject to the provision that the United States can still retaliate with chemical weapons in response to an enemy's first use of chemical weapons. The BWC enters into force on March 26, 1975.

1976
The secretary of the army, Martin Hoffman, reverses the decision to disestablish the Chemical Corps, allowing the recruitment of chemical specialists for the first time in four years. The Chemical School reopens at Fort McClellan in 1979.

1978
In September, Bulgarian dissident Georgi Markov is assassinated in London with a pellet loaded with ricin and delivered by a spring-loaded umbrella. The use of ricin is not noted until a second assassination attempt on another Bulgarian dissident fails and the pellet is found.

1979
An unintentional release of airborne anthrax from the Soviet Institute of Microbiology and Virology at Sverdlovsk kills more than 100 civilians in the town. The Soviets blame gastrointestinal anthrax from spoiled meat. In 1992, President Yeltsin admits the event was an accident from a weapons production plant.

1980 The Conference on Disarmament's Ad Hoc Committee on Chemical Weapons continues negotiations on developing a Chemical Weapons Convention. More than forty nations are participating, but the focus is on the two superpowers, without whom an agreement is worthless. There are three major camps: the NATO allies, the Warsaw Pact, and the nonaligned states.

1981 In September, Secretary of State Alexander Haig accuses the Soviets of supporting CB warfare in Laos in the mid-to-late 1970s. This brings the issue of "yellow rain" to public attention.

1983– Iraqi forces use chemical weapons against Iranian
1988 forces during the Iran-Iraq War. Although Iran attempts to retaliate, it lacks the requisite technologies and training. After the Scud "war against the cities" ends, Iran sues for peace.

1984 In August and September, members of the Rajneeshee cult poison 751 residents of The Dalles, Oregon, with salmonella sprayed on salad bars in local restaurants. Their intent was to shape upcoming elections in their favor.

    The Australia Group, an international arms control group, is formed in response to Iraqi chemical weapons use. Its goal is to recommend export controls on precursors and equipment that could be used to develop CW munitions.

    The National Research Council endorses the Army's use of incineration as the best available technology for the disposal of chemical munitions and materials.

1985 Congress authorizes the U.S. Army to begin a national chemical disposal program to eliminate its aging stocks of unitary chemical weapons and to begin production of binary chemical weapons to modernize the U.S. retaliatory capability. These efforts are initiated under the Program Executive Office for Chemical Munitions, which oversees the program manager for chemical demilitarization and the program manager for binary munitions.

Iraq begins its offensive BW program. It had been working on a CW program since the mid-1970s. Although Iraq uses chemical weapons against Iran, it never develops a capability for biological warfare prior to the end of hostilities.

1987 The United States accuses Libya of using chemical weapons against Chad in August and ships 2,000 protective masks to Chad.

1988 Congress authorizes the Army to begin a Chemical Stockpile Emergency Preparedness Program (CSEPP) to improve emergency response at its eight chemical stockpiles and the surrounding communities.

1988–
1990 The U.S. government asks the West German government to explain why West German companies had assisted Libya in the production and equipping of a chemical weapons facility at Rabta. In 1990, the U.S. government calls for the Libyan government to destroy the facility. In March 1990, a fire erupts in the complex, destroying much of the facility and its materiels.

1989 The United States and the Soviet Union sign the Wyoming Memorandum of Understanding, agreeing to exchange information on each other's chemical weapons stockpiles in the interest of leading to arms control talks. A year later, the two countries sign a Bilateral Destruction Agreement that commits them to reducing their respective CW stockpiles to 5,000 tons each.

After two years of construction, the Johnston Atoll Chemical Agent Disposal System (JACADS) is ready for operation. Congress demands a vigorous operational verification testing prior to beginning full-scale operations.

1990	The U.K. Ministry of Defence returns Gruinard Island to the heirs of the previous owner. The island had been a testing ground for anthrax bombs in 1942.
	In June, the Army begins full-scale tests at its disposal facility on Johnston Island. The military moves all chemical weapons stored in Europe to Johnston Island between September and the end of November in Operation Steel Box.
1990–1991	Iraq invades Kuwait in August 1990. The United States leads a coalition to force Iraq out of Kuwait. Fearing that Iraq might use CB weapons, the coalition uses diplomacy and threats of retaliation and prepares to counter possible use of CB weapons with increased training and with CB defense equipment. The conflict ends without any offensive use of CB weapons. One soldier is treated for mustard burns received while inspecting an empty Iraqi ammunition bunker.
1991	In March, engineers from the Eighty-Second Airborne Division demolish Iraqi munitions at Khamisiyah depot. UNSCOM inspectors examine the remains in October and suggest that one of the thirty-eight bunkers blown up had contained chemical weapons. They also find several hundred mostly intact 122 mm rockets in a nearby pit and 6,000 intact 155 mm artillery shells filled with mustard agent.
	The Army transports World War II mustard-filled artillery projectiles from the Solomon Islands to Johnston Island for storage and eventual destruction.
1992	The U.S. government reveals that the total amount of chemical weapons in its stockpile is 31,400 agent-tons. The Russian government declares approximately 40,000 agent-tons in its stockpile and states that it has ended the former Soviet Union's offensive BW program.
	The FBI arrests two members of the Patriots Council in Minnesota for possession of ricin under the 1989 Biological Weapons Anti-Terrorism Act.

1993   The Chemical Weapons Convention is signed in Paris on January 13. The parties agree not to develop, produce, acquire, stockpile, or use chemical weapons; not to assist others in developing chemical weapons; and to destroy all existing stocks. It will enter into effect on April 29, 1997, 180 days after the sixty-fifth nation ratifies the treaty.

The U.S. Army starts the Non-Stockpile Chemical Materiel project under the program manager for chemical demilitarization. One of its first projects is to assist in the cleanup of Spring Valley in Washington, D.C., where chemical munitions were discovered in January, unearthed during a housing project.

In August, the U.S. Army's second disposal plant completes construction at Tooele Army Depot, Utah. As it begins a three-year testing phase, the Army certifies that the Johnston Island disposal facility is safe and ready to assume full-scale operations.

U.S. intelligence sources note the construction of a deeply buried facility at Tarhuna, about sixty-four kilometers southeast of Tripoli, Libya. Several western European companies are suspected of being involved in the construction there of a CW production facility.

1994   The Aum Shinrikyo cult attacks the living quarters of three judges in Masumoto, Japan, with a truck-mounted generator issuing a sarin aerosol cloud, killing seven and injuring several hundred. No one is arrested.

Congress passes a public law (P.L. 103-160) forcing the military services to consolidate their four separate CB defense research and development programs into one defense-wide program, with oversight from one single focal point under the assistant to the secretary of defense for nuclear and chemical and biological programs (ATSD[NCB]).

1995   In February, Larry Wayne Harris is arrested for ordering a strain of plague bacteria through the mail from American Type Culture Collection. At his trial, he claims the purchase was for "defensive research."

The Aum Shinrikyo cult plants eleven bags of sarin on three subway lines on March 20. Twelve civilians die, more than 900 are hospitalized with symptoms of nerve agent poisoning, and 4,000 "worried well" flood the hospitals believing they have been exposed while on the subway.

In July, the Iraqi government admits it had an offensive BW program, whose scale is confirmed after the discovery of Iraqi research documents and the defection of Saddam Hussein's son-in-law Hussein Kamal Al Majid. In February 1996, Hussein Kamal returns to Iraq, where he is assassinated.

1996   The Pentagon releases a statement that approximately 20,000 service members may have been exposed to low levels of nerve agents as a result of the Khamisiyah incident. This number is eventually raised to approximately 100,000 service members who may have been exposed.

Tooele Chemical Agent Disposal Facility (TOCDF) begins disposal operations. Deseret Chemical Depot, located at Tooele Army Depot, holds 46 percent of the Army's chemical weapons stocks.

1997   The Senate ratifies the Chemical Weapons Convention (CWC) on April 24. The CWC enters into force five days later. The Russian Federation ratifies the CWC in November. The Organization for the Prohibition of Chemical Weapons comes into being to enforce the treaty.

Unknown persons mail a petri dish filled with a red gelatin marked as "anthrax" to the B'nai B'rith in Washington, D.C., forcing more than 100 people to remain in quarantine while emergency responders work to contain the hazard. This was later discovered to have been a hoax.

In June, India acknowledges it has an offensive chemical weapons program and states that it will dispose of its chemical munitions under the CWC's auspices.

The Department of Defense initiates a domestic preparedness program, intended to train the emergency responders of 120 cities on the basics of responding to CB terrorist incidents. They start with Denver, where the G-8 summit is to meet and where Timothy McVeigh's trial is to be held that summer.

1998   In February, federal agents arrest Larry Wayne Harris on the suspicion that he has weapons-grade anthrax in his car. It turns out to be an anthrax vaccine sample with only dead organisms.

Tomahawk missiles destroy a suspected nerve agent production plant in Sudan. Although the Sudanese government claims the plant was a pharmaceutical factory, the U.S. government reveals its concerns that the factory was funded by Osama bin Laden for the purposes of developing chemical warfare agents.

The Defense Threat Reduction Agency is formed from a consolidation of DOD arms control and counterproliferation agencies and offices. The core of the reorganization is the Defense Special Weapons Agency, formerly the Defense Nuclear Agency.

The Department of Defense decides to vaccinate the entire military force against anthrax using a vaccine approved by the FDA in 1970. In 1999, the decision is made to extend vaccination to emergency-essential civilians and contractors operating in high-threat areas.

In June, CNN releases a news story accusing the U.S. military of using nerve agents in Vietnam under the name Operation Tailwind. The story is later discred-

1998,
cont.
ited by nearly all personnel involved in that operation and by the absence of any credible evidence.

In October, a wave of letters claiming to contain anthrax are sent to Planned Parenthood Centers and abortion clinics in Kentucky, Indiana, Ohio, and other states. The letters are revealed to have been a hoax.

Iraqi president Saddam Hussein refuses to cooperate with UNSCOM inspectors, who report that Iraq has not complied with UN disarmament accords. The UN inspectors leave Iraq.

1999
In February, a second wave of letters claiming to contain anthrax are sent to Planned Parenthood Centers and abortion clinics across the country. Again the letters are revealed to have been a hoax, but hoaxes begin to proliferate.

In April, President Bill Clinton announces that the United States will not destroy its remaining stocks of smallpox, despite the World Health Organization's recommendation.

In September, the Army Chemical School moves from Fort McClellan to Fort Leonard Wood, Missouri.

2000
The Johnston Atoll Chemical Agent Disposal System (JACADS) begins closure operations in November, after destroying more than 4 million pounds of chemical agents and more than 400,000 munitions.

In October, Army civilian workers discover six M139 bomblets suspected of holding sarin in a scrap yard at Rocky Mountain Arsenal. The Army develops an elaborate explosive destruction system to destroy them within a contained facility.

2001
In May, four more sarin bomblets are found at Rocky Mountain Arsenal. The Army's system destroys all ten without risk of exposure to anyone.

In June, the Department of Health and Human Services (HHS) Advisory Committee on Immunization Practices recommends that emergency response workers be vaccinated against smallpox to prepare for a possible bioterrorism attack and to respond to a possible attack involving smallpox.

In October, four letters containing anthrax are discovered, two to Democratic leaders in the Senate, one to the American Media, Inc., in Boca Raton, Florida, and one to Tom Brokaw at New York's NBC Studios. FBI officials suspect that an American with biotechnology experience, perhaps gained at a military lab, is responsible. Five victims die, six are treated for inhalation anthrax and recover, eleven are treated for cutaneous anthrax, and scores of postal workers and congressional staffers begin medical treatments.

2002   In January, the Senate Hart building in Washington, D.C., is declared clean of anthrax spores. In October, the cost of cleaning the building and preparing it for occupation again is announced to be more than $41 million. The Brentwood postal facility in Washington, D.C., and the American Media building in Florida continue to be cleaned.

The construction of the Aberdeen Chemical Agent Disposal Facility is completed. Aberdeen's facility will be the first one to use an "alternative technology," that is, a technology other than incineration, to dispose of more than 1,600 tons of mustard agent. The selected technology is neutralization with hot water, followed by treatment at a chemical waste facility.

In September, President George W. Bush accuses Iraq of maintaining an active CBW program before the UN General Assembly. Prime Minister Tony Blair of Britain, in a statement to the House of Commons, repeats this charge and offers a dossier of intelligence data on Iraq's CBW program.

2002,
cont.

In late September, the Department of Health and Human Services (HHS) releases an updated postevent "Smallpox Response Plan and Guidelines," which discusses the use of "ring vaccination" around outbreaks of smallpox caused by terrorist incidents.

The Russian military uses a chemical compound to knock out fifty Chechen terrorists holding several hundred people hostage in Moscow in November. More than 100 hostages die from the gas. The United States and other nations refrain from criticizing the Russian use of gas as an internal police action.

2003

In March, the U.S. and U.K. militaries, with multinational support, invade Iraq with the stated mission of removing the threat of weapons of mass destruction. Despite concerns of Iraqi use of CB weapons, especially in a regime-survival situation, no CB weapons are used.

In April, the undersecretary of defense for acquisition, technology, and logistics (USD[AT&L]) signs a memorandum announcing a new management structure for the DOD CB Defense Program. This includes a Joint Requirements Office in the Joint Staff and a Joint Program Executive Office under the Army.

5

CB Weapon Systems

There is a tendency for both laymen and military analysts to talk about chemical and biological weapons as if they are one and the same threat. The military analysts do not do this because they think chemical and biological warfare agents are the same in terms of lethality and effectiveness—they are not—but rather because they are both considered unconventional weapons and they have very similar employment means and similar capabilities. This lack of distinction is more of a problem when people use the term "weapons of mass destruction."[1] No one can mistake the destructive force of even tactical nuclear weapons, let alone of the big city-busters, yet politicians and arms control advocates seem to believe that chemical and biological weapons should be considered on the same level with nuclear weapons. This is a dangerous perception, one that continues to cloud the issue as to the true threat caused by chemical and biological weapons. For that reason, I will avoid the popular but overused term "weapons of mass destruction."

The reader may note that this book uses the terms "CB warfare" and "CB weapons" frequently, and this may seem at odds with the above statement seeking to distinguish chemical from biological weapons. Although they have different scientific properties and effects, they have similar employment properties. Chemical and biological weapons are two sides of the same coin, in that they both originate from the field of natural sciences and are both employed on the modern battlefield. Because chemical and biological weapons share a common scientific technology and use similar weapon systems to target people, there is a common defensive approach to facing these weapons. They harm humans and animals based on their inherent interactions with living matter (as opposed to explosives or piercing weapons), generally attacking through the respiratory tract and skin. They are delivered by similar weapon systems: artillery projectiles, aerial bombs, aerial and ground aerosol sprayers, ballistic missiles, even hand grenades, as well as through covert operations using small amounts of such agents against individual targets. Most chemical and biological agents are largely invisible to the naked eye and have little or no odor; they both can cause mass casualties relatively quickly if disseminated in large quantities over a large area. Chemical and biological weapons both provide an unconventional capability of demoralizing, diminishing, or destroying a military force that is unprepared for their effects.

The technical and physical properties of CW agents are very different from those of BW agents, which is important when a nation develops specific defenses for military personnel and civilians. CW agents are not natural to the environment, are relatively quick-acting, and cover a much smaller area than BW agents. This means, for instance, that a force needs a larger number of CW detectors to cover a certain area than it does BW detectors, and the detectors must work much more quickly. There are broad differences within the category of CW agents. Many people, discussing CW agents, fixate on the nerve agents—invisible, odorless, and lethal in a matter of seconds or minutes—but these are not the only chemical weapons available. Some nations still consider the use of phosgene and hydrogen cyanide, both of which have detectable odors and, unless present in large quantities, are not immediately lethal. Mustard agent is not lethal; it was chosen for its incapacitating qualities (although complications from exposure—that is, infection—can be lethal).

Similarly, the range of BW agents is very broad. People focus on anthrax or smallpox (or some new, engineered, superlethal, and infectious BW agent they saw in a movie) in their discussions of biological warfare, but most BW agents are much less lethal and yet still quite effective. Inhalation anthrax is certainly the megaton munition in the BW arsenal, with its hardiness, lack of visible signs, and almost certain lethality if left untreated. If an anthrax victim is not treated within forty-eight to seventy-two hours, medical treatment cannot help, and death is a foregone conclusion. Even smallpox, although very infectious, is survivable, being lethal to only 30 percent of untreated victims. Many viruses, bacteria, and rickettsia (causing such diseases as brucellosis, tularemia, and Q fever) may sicken a large population, but they have much lower lethality rates. Most BW agents require days or weeks to become infectious and are natural to the environment, and small amounts can cover large areas. The toxins (poisonous substances produced by biological organisms), of course, act more like their chemical cousins than their biological parents, which increases the diversity of potential BW agents. These significant differences between BW agents and CW agents call for different technical approaches in developing detectors, protective ensembles, and decontaminants, but the ultimate means by which military personnel execute chemical and biological defense are remarkably similar. The challenge is to identify the unique aspects of chemical versus biological agents and then to understand how to develop common defensive equipment and tactics for both.

Chemical Warfare Agents

There are a number of ways to categorize CW agents. One can categorize them by lethality, as either lethal or merely incapacitating agents, or by their effect on personnel: as choking, blister, blood, nerve, or irritant agent. Another way to categorize them is by how long they remain viable in the environment: There are nonpersistent, semipersistent, and persistent agents. There are other books that delve into the different scientific and physiological effects; this book's approach will be to examine the generations of CW agents, that is, what "wave" of development brought particular agents into the military stockpiles.

The first-generation agents were those developed during World War I and stockpiled into World War II. These were largely industrial chemicals. Some were toxic enough to kill those who inhaled the vapors, while others were merely irritants. The early gases included irritants, or tearing agents: benzyl bromide, bromoacetone, bromobenzyl cyanide, chloropicrin, chloroacetophenone, dichlormethyl ether, dibromomethyl ethyl ketone, ethyl iodoacetate, and xylyl bromide. These irritants can cause temporary blindness and inflame the respiratory system. They were meant not to incapacitate troops but to harass them and perhaps to increase the time it would take them to get a protective mask on. The choking agents, or asphyxiants, included chlorine, phosgene, and diphosgene. These gases are heavier than air, so they remain near ground level, filling foxholes and trenches. They inflict damage by reacting with water vapor in the lungs and forming hydrochloric acid, causing the body to react by flooding the lungs with fluids. Medical professionals call this pulmonary edema; soldiers called it "dry-land drowning." The blood agents inhibit the body's ability to transfer oxygen from the blood to muscles and organs. They include hydrogen cyanide and cyanogen chloride. Because of their high volatility, they had to be used in large quantities as a surprise attack, or else they would dissipate and concentrations would decrease to harassing rather than lethal levels.

The problem with these first-generation agents was that they were largely nonpersistent, volatile chemical gases. The chemicals' odors often tipped off the defense that they were being gassed, especially if the gases were used in large quantity. If the defense had masks and got them on in time, there were few to no casualties. Of course, in some cases, that is all the side employing the gases wanted to do: force the other side to have to don cumbersome masks, limiting their vision and reducing their effectiveness while the attackers came at the trenches. For success, one had to hope for the element of surprise or for untrained troops (or both). As troops increasingly used masks and became accustomed to these gases, continued research led to other CW agents, notably the vesicants, or blister agents.

Mustard agent was the best-known and most effective CW agent of the war, in part due to its delayed effects and to its effect on the skin, eyes, and lungs. It is often incorrectly referred to as "mustard gas," but it is actually a liquid that is aerosolized for employment against personnel. It caused about three-fourths of all U.S. gas casualties in the war, but phosgene caused most of the deaths. Although mustard agent can kill if an individual is exposed to large enough quantities, its value was more in disabling personnel. Originally, the United Kingdom and the United States could not determine how the Germans manufactured their mustard, so U.S. and British efforts could only produce what the

United States called the "Levinstein" mustard. This form had up to 30 percent impurities, but its effects were close enough to those of the purer agents for military operations. Following World War I and the capture of German documents, the Allied countries developed the technology to make distilled mustard agent similar to the Germans'. Nitrogen mustards, developed prior to World War II, have less persistence and less odor than the sulfur mustards and can be sprayed at lower temperatures, but they are not as harmful to the skin.

Other vesicants included ethyldichlorarsine, dibromethyl sulfide, and lewisite, which was developed just at the end of World War I. Lewisite, an arsenic-based compound, is as persistent as mustard agent, can be used in cold weather, and is immediately irritating to the unprotected eyes and skin. Its one drawback: It is not effective in wet weather because it readily reacts with water. The United States abandoned its production and storage of lewisite as a CW agent after World War II.

Table 5.1 gives the reader an idea of the toxicity of these first-generation agents. The unit used, milligrams per minute per cubic meter (mg-min/m^3), is a standard used to identify the toxicity of aerosols and vapors in their effects against humans. The measure used, LCt_{50}, is the lethal concentration for 50 percent of the population.

The second-generation CW agents include the G-series nerve agents: tabun, sarin, soman and cyclosarin.[2] These CW agents are actually liquids that can be aerosolized into the air, not gases like the first-generation agents, but they do have a significant vapor hazard. They have differing persistencies, with sarin being a relatively nonpersistent liquid and soman being the most persistent agent, but they all act the same. Once inhaled, they inhibit acetylcholinesterase in the body, which then cannot break down acetylcholine. This excess acetylcholine causes postsynaptic action potentials and activities in the organs—translated, that means the body's muscles start contracting and relaxing violently, leading to cardiac arrest and an inability to breathe. Early signs of low-level exposures can include miosis (pinpoint pupils), excessive tearing and salivation, headaches, nausea and cramping, shortness of breath, and loss of consciousness.

The real advances of the G-series nerve agents over the earlier agents are their lack of color and odor, persistence similar to that of water (not too quick but clearing within an hour), and extreme lethality in small quantities (see Table 5.2; LD_{50} is the dose

Table 5.1
Toxicity of First-Generation Chemical Warfare Agents

Agent	Military Abbreviation	LCt_{50} (mg-min/m³)
Chlorine	(none)	19,000
Phosgene	CG	3,200
Diphosgene	DP	3,000
Hydrogen cyanide	CA	2,500–5,000 (time dependent)
Cyanogen chloride	CK	11,000
Arsine	SA	5,000
Mustard	HD	1,500 (respiratory), 10,000 (skin)
Phosgene oxime	CX	3,200
Lewisite	L	1,200–1,500 (respiratory), 100,000 (skin)

Note: LCt_{50} is the lethal concentration for 50 percent of the population; mg-min/m³ = milligrams per minute per cubic meter.

for percutaneous effects, measured in milligrams for a 70-kilogram man). They are easily weaponized and can be aerosolized over large areas, or thickeners can be added to increase the time they remain on the ground. Ideally, they are used as inhalation hazards, but in large enough amounts, they can act through the skin. Although sarin acts more quickly through the respiratory system, soman, in particular, is twice as toxic, and its effects can become irreversible, requiring exposed personnel to take prompt medical countermeasures if they are to have any chance of survival. This reaction is called aging, in which the agent-enzyme complex forms a refractory complex that lowers or eliminates the effectiveness of the antidote. Aging occurs very quickly in cases of exposure to soman (two minutes) but does not occur that quickly in the majority of the other nerve agent exposure cases; for example, sarin ages in four to six hours and VX in approximately sixty hours, meaning there is ample time for continued medical treatment. Although these agents are definitely deadly, several researchers and military personnel have been exposed to low levels of nerve agents in the process of research or storage of chemical weapons and survived, with the proper medical care. (The term commonly used within the military and government civilian worker environment is being "bitten" by nerve agents.)

The second generation of incapacitants include the riot-control agent CS, or o-chlorobenzylidenemalononitrile (now you know why the military abbreviates these agents). Because chloroacetophenone (CN) is not as potent or as stable as some would like, researchers at Porton Down (England's chemical de-

Table 5.2
Toxicity of G-Series and V-Series Nerve Agents

Agent	Military Abbreviation	LCt_{50} (mg-min/m^3)/LD_{50} (mg)
Tabun	GA	400 (respiratory), 1,000 (skin)
Sarin	GB	100 (respiratory), 1,700 (skin)
Soman	GD	50 (respiratory), 350 (skin)
Cyclosarin	GF	No data—similar to GB
VX	VX	10 (respiratory), 6–10 (skin)

Note: LCt_{50} is the lethal concentration for 50 percent of the population; LD_{50} is the dose for percutaneous effects, measured in milligrams for a seventy-kilogram man; mg-min/m^3 = milligrams per minute per cubic meter.

fense center) developed CS powder in the 1950s. It could be disseminated as a solid or vaporized in a pyrotechnic grenade, increasing its potential hazard area. CS quickly became the riot-control agent of choice for the police forces of many nations, and it is still used today by the U.S. military for training purposes.

The third generation of CW agents includes the V-series nerve agents. Discovered in the 1950s, VX is a very persistent liquid whose lethal effects rely almost entirely on contact rather than on any vapor hazards. This makes it particularly useful for contaminating large tracts of land, such as air bases, seaports, or rear-area logistics dumps. Its variants include VE, VG, and VM, all of which share a common organophosphate chemical structure. These liquid agents are also colorless and odorless, and once absorbed through the skin, they have a much faster reaction time and require smaller doses to kill an exposed individual. VX, for example, is about ten times more lethal than GB. It does not, however, vaporize quickly and blister flesh as portrayed in the popular movie *The Rock*.

The military and the Central Intelligence Agency (CIA) investigated psychochemicals during the development of this "third generation." The one that was seen as having the most potential was agent BZ, or 3-quinuclidinyl benzilate. This agent is a solid in its natural state, but when exploded or dispersed into the air, it can be inhaled. About a half hour after exposure, it can cause a dreamlike hallucination state that could last for days, depending on the dosage. The United States decided it would not make a suitable CW agent, since it could take two to three hours to affect an individual, its effects were unpredictable, and BZ being disbursed could be seen as a large smoke cloud. This has not stopped other countries from developing this agent.

The fourth generation of chemical warfare agents were developed by the Soviet Union between the 1980s and 1990s. The *novichok* agents (*novichok* is Russian for "newcomer") are binary chemical warfare agents with toxicities similar to VX and with the aging effect of GD. More important, these agents are believed to be made from common industrial and agricultural chemicals that are not prohibited by the CWC Schedule of Chemicals.[3] One could argue that because these CW agents are not specifically prohibited, their use would not constitute a treaty violation. However, this interpretation obviously violates the spirit of the treaty.

Last, there are different forms of these agents that offer unique aspects of delivery. The nerve agents tabun and sarin can be thickened, by using polymers, to increase their persistency from minutes to hours. There are also dusty agents, in which mustard and nerve agents are applied to a solid carrier, such as silicon dioxide or talc. This aerosolization makes the agents travel further in the wind, and because the agents have properties similar to those of dust particles, they penetrate protective suits at their interfaces (between the gloves or mask and the suit or between the trousers and pants of an ensemble). The Germans investigated dusty mustard during World War II, and Iraq is suspected of using dusty mustard against Iranian military forces in the 1980s.

There are some in the United States and Europe who consider the threat of toxic industrial chemicals to be a potential hazard to deployed military personnel, especially in urban areas of the world, where terrorists or insurgents could easily obtain industrial chemicals. Certainly industrial chemicals such as ammonia, chlorine, phosgene, diborane, and sulfuric acid are more accessible than CW agents; indeed, tankers of these chemicals crisscross the country every day. Although the possibility that terrorists might use toxic industrial chemicals exists, the actual probability of military personnel being attacked with these chemicals is low. The reason industrial chemicals are not used as warfare agents anymore is that they are just not as toxic as the "classic" CW agents, not by several orders of magnitude. One would require thousands to tens of thousands of gallons to cause a real life-threatening event, and, as in the majority of hazardous material accidents, people can smell the danger and get out of the area prior to suffering any serious health threats.

Many countries (including the United States) are inching toward using CW experts in a health-protection role, employing them to assess industrial sites that could release a toxic industrial chemical if a terrorist were to sabotage the site or if an accident were to occur. Although there may be a certain amount of technical overlap between chemical warfare and hazardous-material handling, it should be stressed that the two areas are distinct: CW agents are employed to create an immediate, operational impact on the battlefield, whereas toxic industrial chemical incidents are more occupational hazards to one's expectations for a full and long life. They should not be confused as being the same threat.

Chemical Weapon Delivery Systems

Military forces desire a few basic features from chemical agents and their delivery systems. They must be able to disperse CW agent efficiently over a large area, and this dispersion must be predictable (to ensure that one's own forces do not run into the hazard). Commanders desire a degree of flexibility that will allow them to attack across the battlefield; that is to say, they want to attack front-line combat forces to reduce the enemy's strength, but they also want to attack the rear-area combat support forces, which supply and transport the combat forces. This leads to the large variety in CW delivery systems. There are mortar shells and howitzer and artillery projectiles for the close battle, land mines to make it more difficult for the enemy to negotiate terrain, aerial bombs and sprays to attack the rear-area forces, and ballistic missiles to attack ports, airfields, and cities deep inside an adversary's country.

It requires a great deal of CW agent to effectively attack a large area and cause a number of casualties—up to one metric ton per square kilometer to have good coverage. In general, there are two kinds of CW attacks: point and line source. Point attacks include those explosive releases from artillery shells, bombs, and mines (and to a degree, bulk-agent filled ballistic missiles—that is, when the warhead bursts open, the contents are released all at once). These normally contain "burster charges" surrounded by a CW agent; when the burster ruptures the munition, the liquid agent is released as a cloud of small droplets.

The limitation of these devices is that too much explosive used to open the shell at the right point and time could burn off the CW agent. Artillery shells typically hold less than ten pounds of agent, so a force must fire a large number of these to cause casualties. A few bombs can drop a couple hundred pounds of CW agent, covering a larger area with fewer munitions. A single ballistic missile can deliver a few hundred pounds of agent; a volley of ballistic missiles can effectively cover an air base, if properly targeted. Most nations prefer to weaponize chemical munitions for artillery systems; they are cheaper, easier to handle, and easier to train personnel to employ.

Bulk-release munitions disperse aerosols into the airstream created by the projectile, and base-ejection devices push agent out the rear of the projectile. Either of these releases causes the formation of a "line source" of CW agent, dispersing the droplets along the trajectory of the projectile. These technologies are a little more complicated and expensive. Although these two technologies are more effective in dispersing their payloads on target, many nations rely on the tried-and-true explosive release method. One loses some CW agent, but it is still effective, and it is less expensive, which counts when one must hurl hundreds of projectiles to affect a large area where enemy troops lurk.

Spray generators, whether mounted on aircraft, on boats, or on ground vehicles, are the most effective form of dissemination. Spray generators are more easily controlled than munitions and will generate a more uniform coverage of a large area. If the generator is manufactured to create the right size particles, the aerosol can drift a good distance before dropping to the ground or evaporating. If the particles are too big, they fall to the ground too soon; conversely, if they are too small, the aerosol cloud disperses too quickly and is ineffective. Another limitation to aircraft-delivered sprays is that the plane must operate slowly and in a straight line, which makes it vulnerable to enemy attack. The spray attack would be ideal for attacking poorly trained or unprepared personnel.

Which CW agent to use in these delivery systems depends on what the target is and what effect is desired. Land mines are meant to deny terrain to maneuvering forces, so the persistent agents such as mustard and VX are chosen for the fills. With artillery projectiles, usually the attacker wants quick results, so lethal agents are chosen, such as hydrogen cyanide or sarin. The larger artillery projectiles (8 inch guns, 115 mm and 122 mm rockets) might use mustard, VX, or thickened GD to contaminate areas behind enemy forces, threatening their ability to resupply or to reinforce a particular sector. Because aerial bombs and ballistic missiles often target the rear areas rather than the front lines, they will often be armed with persistent agents.

A quick note about ballistic missiles: The early Soviet and Iraqi Scud missiles were bulk-agent filled. This method is technically easy but inefficient. When the U.S. Army developed guided-missile warheads, they used agent-filled submunitions, where a few hundred bomblets in a warhead would come tumbling out and, at a certain altitude, crack open. This created a much more efficient dispersion pattern, covering a wider area of the target (but these were more expensive than the bulk-agent filled warheads). This 1960s technology is certainly feasible for most nations to engineer today.

Those liquid agents that volatilize into gases present a vapor hazard in addition to a contact hazard, but wind can spread this vapor hazard much further than the area under attack. Weapons planners can calculate the downwind hazard, based on the number of chemical munitions and the CW agents they hold to effectively cover the intended target, and predict a certain percentage of casualties. If the targeted personnel are trained and have defensive equipment, the casualties will be low. If the personnel are untrained or lack equipment, the casualties will be high. The weather is the final arbitrator in how effective a CW attack is. The wind speed is critical to effective coverage, making the difference between a puddle, a large hazard area, and a dust storm. Rain will affect the success of an attack (washing the liquids away), as will the heat of a summer sun (vaporizing the agent), or the depth of winter (freezing the agent).

Biological Warfare Agents

BW agents are not distinguished into generations, as their cousins on the chemical side are. Overwhelmingly, the currently most dangerous BW agents are those natural diseases found across the globe. Talk about "designer" BW agents or bioengineered agents have remained just that—talk—with the exception of the former Soviet Union's BW programs. In a decade or so, other nations may catch up to where the United States and Russia are now, and then it will be time to worry again about such BW agents. Until then, the natural diseases, culled out of nature using equipment that could be dual-use for pharmaceutical research (or even for brewing beer), seem to be the major threat. BW agents have been researched for specific effects against humans, animals, plants, and even materials. They can be divided into pathogens, living organisms, and toxins, which are chemical by-products of biological organisms. As with CW agents, one can also divide them into the two classes of lethal and incapacitating agents.

There are thousands of biological organisms in the world that have detrimental effects on people, but there is a relatively short list of the ones that usually show up in a nation's offensive BW program. The ideal BW agent should be hard to detect, consistent in its predicted effects on its targets, able to be produced in mass quantities, able to be disseminated over a large area, stable while in storage and in transportation, and with a short and predictable incubation period. Ideally, the target population should have little or no immunity, whereas the force using it should have its military and civilians inoculated.[4] These requirements reduce the list of possibilities to fewer than thirty or so prime candidates, which the CDC lists as restricted agents to control their handling and transportation.

We can break the pathogens down into classes of bacteria, viruses, rickettsia, and fungi. Bacteria are everywhere—in yogurt, in your stomach, in the air, water, and soil. They are complex, single-cell microorganisms that do not require living tissue to reproduce, and they are environmentally hardy. Rickettsia are rod-shaped bacteria that require a living host to reproduce. Viruses are much smaller microorganisms, not true cells, really just a small amount of genetic material carried in a protein shell. They require a living host to reproduce, are much more vulnerable to the environment, and are very selective about what hosts they harm as opposed to the hosts they merely infect.

Although it takes hundreds or thousands of bacteria to infect a person, it may take as few as one to ten viral organisms to infect that same person. On the other side, bacteria are often more sturdy than viruses, which die off quickly in the natural environment if not incubating in a host. Although bacterial infections can be combated with vaccines and antibiotics, viral infections often do not have specific vaccines or treatment therapies; all one can do is treat the victim's symptoms and wait for the virus to "burn out." Although many pathogens will incapacitate a healthy individual, only a few have a high mortality rate. Most pathogens have an incubation period of from days to a few weeks before the exposed individual shows symptoms. This delay time means two important things: First, BW agents have a limited tactical use but have a good strategic value for softening up an adversary's military or nation in advance of military operations (or as a last-ditch weapon). Second, BW detectors do not have to give the alarm within seconds, as long as there are medical countermeasures that can be used within a day or two.

Some potential antiplant BW agents include rice blight and corn blight (caused by bacteria); tobacco mosaic virus, potato virus, and sugar-beet curly top virus; and rice blast, rye stem rust, and wheat stem rust (caused by fungi). Anti-animal BW agents could include foot-and-mouth disease, glanders, psittacosis (against chickens), rinderpest (cattle plague), camel pox, and African swine fever.[5] One useful feature of these anti-animal and anticrop BW agents is that they could be weaponized against a specific cash crop or livestock of one's adversary, while ensuring that one's own crops and animals remain healthy.

Of course, most of the interest in BW agents focuses on the antipersonnel agents.[6] The lethal BW bacterial agents include inhalation anthrax, pneumonic plague, and tularemia. Lethal diseases caused by rickettsia include Rocky Mountain spotted fever and epidemic typhus. Untreated, these agents can cause high percentages of casualties, but none matches anthrax, with its short incubation period (one to five days) and almost certain lethality (more than 90 percent if untreated). Bubonic plague is the form of plague that devastated Europe, spread by the bites of fleas. The airborne variety, called pneumonic plague, can occur naturally as a secondary condition of bubonic plague and can be spread by being breathed out. The pneumonic plague was weaponized by the Soviet Union and the United States. It requires two to three days of incubation, and it can cause up to 35 percent mortality if untreated. Tularemia is not as lethal as these two, which makes it a prime learning agent for many countries starting out in this area. It is easily weaponized, and only ten to fifty particles are necessary to infect a human. Both tularemia and plague can be treated after symptoms appear. Not so anthrax—when anthrax patients show up at the hospital complaining of aches and pains, it is already too late. Anthrax and tularemia are not contagious, meaning there is no need for quarantine procedures, as is required with many viral infections.

The nonlethal BW bacterial agents include brucellosis, cholera, and dysentery. The one nonlethal BW rickettsia is *Coxiella burnetii*, also known as Q fever. All four can cause death in a small number of cases if untreated, but in the majority of cases, these diseases just make the victim extremely sick for a few days to weeks. Brucellosis is another primer agent for nations beginning an offensive BW program, for it is easily weaponized but not too lethal and requires anywhere from five to sixty days' incubation before its effects are seen. Cholera and dysentery are hard to weaponize, being more water-borne diseases than airborne ones, so people often refer to these as "potential" BW agents. Q fever is very infectious in low doses, can be transmitted by air, but is rarely lethal. It takes ten to forty days' incubation before any ill effects are seen.

The lethal BW viruses include smallpox and such viral hemorrhagic fevers as yellow fever, Lassa, Marburg, and Ebola. Although the last known naturally occurring case of smallpox was in Somalia in 1977, both the United States and the Soviet Union held on to stocks to ensure they could make the vaccine if "someone" were to use the BW agent. Concerns that other nations could have produced their own stocks have surfaced lately, causing a scramble to stockpile the vaccine. Although smallpox is less than 30 percent lethal, it is highly contagious and leaves many scars on its survivors. The only gleam of light in this dark scenario is that victims are usually not infectious until just before and during the time the scabs start showing (seven to ten days after exposure), thus warning other potential victims. Of the others, yellow fever is only transmitted by mosquitoes and has a fairly common vaccine, making it an unlikely (but still possible) BW candidate. The Soviet Union spent time investigating how to weaponize Marburg and Ebola viruses. As very infectious and lethal organisms, they could be potentially deadly if they could be transmitted by air instead of by aerosols or bodily fluids.

The nonlethal BW viruses include Venezuelan equine encephalitis (VEE), western equine encephalitis (WEE), and eastern equine encephalitis (EEE). These viruses can be transmitted by mosquitoes or by aerosols, are highly infectious, and are relatively inexpensive to acquire. VEE and WEE can cause chills, headaches, and high fevers for a few days, but they are rarely (less than 10 percent) lethal. EEE is the most lethal; it can cause between 30 and 60 percent mortality. Table 5.3 summarizes the major U.S. and Soviet BW programs, which look amazingly similar for having been developed by two adversarial nations not aware of each other's capabilities.

Toxins, because they are complex chemicals derived from biological organisms, are not contagious and cannot reproduce. Because they are not themselves living organisms, some nations (such as Russia) do not recognize them as true BW agents but,

Table 5.3
Major U.S. and Soviet Biological Warfare Programs

Biological Warfare Agent	Type	U.S. Program	Soviet Program
Anthrax	Bacteria, lethal	Yes	Yes
Tularemia	Bacteria, lethal	Yes	Yes
Brucellosis	Bacteria, incapacitant	Yes	Yes
Venezuelan equine encephalitis (VEE)	Virus, incapacitant	Yes	Yes
Q fever	Rickettsia, incapacitant	Yes	Yes
Botulinum toxin	Toxin, lethal	Yes	Yes
Staphylococcus enterotoxin type B (SEB)	Toxin, incapacitant	Yes	No
Glanders	Bacteria, lethal	No	Yes
Plague	Bacteria, lethal	No	Yes
Smallpox	Virus, lethal	No	Yes

rather, regard them as CW agents. The two most common toxins mentioned are staphylococcal enterotoxin type B (SEB), which is nonlethal, and botulinum toxin, which is lethal. SEB is very stable, gives an extremely toxic reaction in low doses, and can be aerosolized easily. Botulinum toxin, more commonly known for its presence in spoiled foods, can also be aerosolized and acts quickly (within twelve to twenty-four hours) once inside a person's system. Gram for gram, toxins are much more deadly than any chemical or biological weapon, but because they cannot be spread by infection or by evaporation, their utility on the battlefield is limited.

There are other toxins, such as the toxins from venomous creatures (snakes, frogs, puffer fish) and ricin toxin (from castor beans), but these are more appropriately viewed as assassination tools than as BW agents meant for the battlefield. Aflatoxin, found in Iraq's arsenal, is a naturally occurring mycotoxin (mycotoxins are produced by fungi, especially molds). Before the Gulf War, intelligence analysts did not include this as a "threat" agent, since it is not lethal, but it is a known carcinogen.[7] The Soviet Union was alleged to have employed a mycotoxin called T-2 toxin, or trichothecene, in Laos and Afghanistan. This was the "yellow rain" aerosol that received so much attention in the 1980s. Some feel that the former Soviet Union abandoned this toxin as a failed experiment, having other more effective biological weapons in its arsenal.

Biological Weapon Delivery Systems

A successful BW attack relies on at least four elements: the BW agent, the munition being used, the weather, and the delivery. Far from the popular concept that "anyone" can develop BW agents in their bathtub, the art of developing BW agents and the munitions is a carefully guarded secret. Even decades after the U.S. offensive BW program ended, there is not much published about how these weapons were developed or employed, for the fear that other developing nations might pick up some tips. It is certainly true that if a militia group wants to distill one gram of ricin out of a few bags of castor beans to attack a local citizen, they can do it. But manufacturing fifty kilograms of anthrax to take out a city is a major technical challenge. The key to weaponizing a BW agent is getting the BW agent to cluster in particles of the right size: one-micron to five-microns. Less than one micron, and the agent does not stay in a person's lungs. More than five microns, and it drops to the ground and threatens no one. Between one and five microns, the small particles act almost like a gas, passing over terrain for miles and potentially exposing a large number of unsuspecting people.

BW agents can be developed in either a liquid slurry or a dry powder, depending on the agent. Although explosive projectiles are the favorite delivery device for chemical munitions, they will not work for BW agents, usually killing most of the agent as the burster opens up the munition. Using liquid slurry in an explosive dissemination works slightly better, but still gives a very low yield. The Soviet method for compensating for this low yield was just to use lots of munitions with big payloads. The U.S. approach was to use gaseous energy, either from a nozzle or a rotor blade, to expel the agent from its projectiles or bomblets. This approach was far more efficient than explosive dissemination, but it is more technically demanding and more expensive.

The most efficient method of delivery is the spray generator, preferably under the wing of a high-performance jet. Both the United States and the Soviet Union developed spray generators, which, depending on the speed of the airplane carrying the generators, the liquid's physical properties, and the stability of the agent, could get efficiencies of between 30 and 75 percent. As with the CW agents, a long line source would increase the total area that could be covered. How much agent was needed depended on the BW agent employed, but as long as it was a pathogen, the numbers were in the single digits: two to eight kilograms per square kilometer. Toxins could require more, upwards of 100 kilograms per square kilometer.

Secretary of Defense William Cohen, talking on television on November 16, 1997, about the threat of BW terrorism, held up a five-pound bag of sugar and commented that a similar-size bag of anthrax could wipe out Washington, D.C. This was a slight exaggeration; it might take up to ten times that amount to effectively cover the city with a lethal dose of anthrax. Even then, less-than-ideal wind and weather conditions could defeat the delivery. What the secretary of defense was talking about was the lethal dose that would have to be carefully administered in minute quantities to every man, woman, and child in the city. Although his example was factual, he did not explain how the anthrax would be disseminated appropriately to get this highly efficient efficacy. Remember that not all of the anthrax that is spread over a city would be inhaled or ingested; much of it would eventually fall onto the ground, roofs, and streets and be washed away or destroyed by the sun's ultraviolet rays. The point of this example is not to belittle the suggestion that five pounds of anthrax is dangerous but to point out that creating a truly effective mass casualty weapon does take a good-size quantity of agent and skillful dissemination.

The ideal line source delivery system is a low-flying plane, and today's technology does not require a manned plane to conduct a long line source of BW agents. An unmanned aerial vehicle (UAV) or a cruise missile could be modified to spray its tanks in a straight line in front of enemy troops. In fact, this UAV or cruise missile could release its payload several miles from its target and still disperse an effective dose of BW agents, given the distance some can travel downwind (if the weather is right). There is the potential use of ground-mounted generators as well; during the Gulf War, there was a great deal of concern that Iraq had purchased agricultural sprayers from Italy and modified them for dispersing BW agents from trucks or small boats. Covert forces could carry backpack sprayers similar to those used for mosquito spraying and disseminate agent at night upwind of a target. It would not be as effective as an airplane-mounted sprayer, but it would produce the desired results.

All of these techniques are useless if the weather is not cooperating. On a sunny summer day, the winds would probably carry a released agent straight up and disperse it without causing any casualties. A sunny day also has a lot of UV radiation, which will start killing pathogen agents as soon as they are exposed, and wet weather will wash the agents away. The ideal conditions for the release of BW agents are in the early morning and late evening or on a day with overcast clouds. These windows of opportunity were key decision points for Air Force weapons planners when they targeted suspected Iraqi BW production and storage sites during the Persian Gulf conflict.

As a final note, some people are concerned about nations' ability to covertly develop BW agents in laboratories or pharmaceutical factories, and others worry about the chance that a lone terrorist could create a BW agent. Although in theory both these scenarios are feasible, the amount that can be made in such modest installations is small, and possible even then only if the manufacturers have the right equipment and education. A terrorist could use a small amount to cause great panic, but it would not be a "mass casualty" threat.

Military operations require a good supply of bulk agent to have a sustained effect on the adversary. The U.S. production plant at Pine Bluff Arsenal had fermenters that could make almost a ton of anthrax each year, a ton and a half of tularemia, a ton of brucellosis, about two tons of SEB toxin, and less than a ton of botulinum toxin. The Soviet Union had six production facilities, and each one was larger than Pine Bluff Arsenal's production plant. At one time, Soviet plants could make 4,500 tons of anthrax each year, 1,500 tons of tularemia, 1,500 tons of plague, 100 tons of smallpox, and 250 tons of Marburg virus.[8] That's a significant military capability.

CB Terrorism

There have been entire books written about terrorism and the potential for terrorists to employ CB weapons or materials. I will not attempt to duplicate what has already been discussed in these sources. The question to pose here is, when does a "weapon of mass destruction" stop being a weapon of mass destruction? The answer is, when they do not destroy any structures or cause mass casualties, such as when terrorists employ small amounts of chemical or biological warfare agents. These weapons of mass *disruption* are very effective as fear-inspiring tools against the masses.

Terrorist groups have been interested in CB warfare agents since at least the early 1970s, perhaps as they observed the mass media focus on CB warfare created as a result of multiple events (at the Rocky Mountain Arsenal in 2000, at Dugway Proving Ground in 1968, the use of Agent Orange and tear gas in Vietnam, the CHASE operation, the nerve agent leak at the Army depot in Okinawa, and so on). The goal of terrorists is to perpetrate violence against noncombatants in order to influence a broader audience (to paraphrase the U.S. State Department's definition). Certainly if a terrorist group were to use CB warfare agents against a civilian or military target, it would get into the national (and international) news. Certainly the technology to develop CB warfare materials is not out of reach of a university-educated individual funded by a wealthy sponsor. If this is the case, why have we not seen more cases of CB terrorism?

In a review of historical cases, Jonathan Tucker of the Monterey Institute of International Studies makes the point that politically motivated terrorists have not sought to use CB warfare agents for several reasons: their unfamiliarity with the required scientific technologies, the hazards and unpredictability of toxic agents, moral constraints, concerns that the use of CB weapons could alienate current or future financial sponsors, and concerns that CB weapons use could bring down a heavy retaliation from the affected government.[9] Terrorists can use conventional arms very simply and without much hazard; rifles, explosives, and knives work and the message still gets across.

This observation does not mean that simply because large numbers of civilians do not get hurt by CB terrorism, the governments of the world do not have to prepare to respond to potential CB terrorism events. The threat exists. But the question is, how credible is the risk, and how much should governments spend to prepare for it? There is a great deal of misinformation by so-called experts in the field, the result of which has been the over-quoted warning "It is not a matter of if, but when." It has been nearly twenty years since the Rajneeshees poisoned a salad bar in Oregon in 1984, and since then, the anthrax-tainted letters seen in the United States in 2001 have been the only case of successful CB terrorism. Based on the anthrax incident, the government is spending billions of dollars to prepare every town and state to be ready for the next attack. This is in addition to the development of a large and expensive national BW-vaccine stockpile, despite the difficulties the Department of Defense has had in executing an anthrax-vaccine program.

A far bigger problem than actual BW terrorism events has been the number of hoaxes that have occurred, from people phoning "anthrax warnings" to schools to people putting flour in an envelope to scare their office colleagues. The emergency response from state and federal agencies costs thousands of dollars each time, and there have been hundreds of hoaxes across the country, not to mention in other nations. These reactions are often based on the assumption that the responders need to be prepared to combat a worst-case scenario in case a given threat is not a hoax. The popular phrase is "It's not a question of if, but when. . . ." But the questions no one wants to answer are: How much will the response program cost? Who will implement the program? Who will be responsible for its oversight, and how and when is the public to know when the government has done enough?

Terrorists will probably keep using conventional attacks, because they work fine and get the results required. Ironically, some experts think that the recent awareness of terrorism and the resulting security measures to harden buildings (including the Jersey barriers forcing cars and trucks to keep at a distance) may drive terrorists toward CB weapons. It will probably remain true that if terrorists get CB weapons, the amounts they will employ will be small, enough to scare people and cause a huge response, but not enough to kill thousands. These CB terrorist attacks, if they come, will not occur outdoors where a small amount of agent will disperse quickly into the air. Rather, they will occur indoors, where an agent's effects will linger, as happened in the Hart building and the Brentwood post office.

As to where they will attack, terrorists do not plan different targets for conventional weapons than for unconventional ones. As we have seen in Israel, they attack shopping malls, sports events stadiums, bus stations, coffee shops—anywhere people cluster. They use letter bombs, small aerosol cans, poisoned darts, improvised bags of agent that leak into a subway car—any form of improvised delivery device, aiming not at mass casualties but at mass disruption. When a CB terrorist event hits the news, you can be sure that a few people have died but that thousands will think they were at risk because they were in the general vicinity of the event—what some experts are calling the "worried well." These "worried well" are the real part of the "mass disruption."

The bottom line here is that people who do not differentiate between battlefield use of CB warfare agents and terrorist employment of CB warfare agents are making a huge error in judgment. The misinformation and exaggerations about CB warfare agents leads to overreactions in dealing with this issue. These weapons are not ineffective or immoral weapons; they are not coward's weapons; nations use them because they kill people, and that is what is intended to happen in war. Nations invest in CB warfare agents because they give the using military force an edge on the battlefield. Terrorists may use CB warfare agents not because of their military effectiveness but because they know the people, being ignorant about their effects, are terrified of them.

Notes

1. The Department of Defense defines weapons of mass destruction as those weapons that are capable of a high order of destruction, of being used in such a manner as to destroy large numbers of people, or both. Weapons of mass destruction can be high explosives or nuclear, biological, chemical, or radiological weapons, but they do not include the means of transporting or propelling the weapon where those means are not part of the weapon. (Joint Publication 1-02, *DOD Dictionary of Military and Associated Terms*, April 12, 2001 [on-line; available: http://www.dtic.mil/doctrine/jel/doddict/; accessed November 2002]).

2. Cyclosarin, GF, was a nerve agent investigated and abandoned by the U.S. Army. It was thought that Iraq had stocks of GF nerve agent during the Gulf War.

3. Steven Willingham, "Military Role in U.S. Response to Terrorism Remains Unclear," *National Defense*, June 2000.

4. Malcolm Dando, *Biological Warfare in the 21st Century: Biotechnology and the Proliferation of Biological Weapons* (London: Brassey's, 1994), 33.

5. The U.S. Air Force stockpiled but did not weaponize rice blast, rye stem rust, and wheat stem rust. The U.S. military investigated but never stockpiled any anti-animal BW agents.

6. The CDC's list of selected BW agents that require handlers to have special guidance for transferring or receiving from one facility to another can be found on its web page "OHS—Interstate Shipment of Etiologic Agents" (on-line; available: http://www.cdc.gov/od/ohs/biosfty/shipregs.htm; accessed April 3, 2003).

7. Aflatoxin has respectable toxicity: The LD_{50} for aflatoxin B1, by mouth or injection, is about 1–3 mg/kg in experimental animals (personal communication from Eric Croddy).

8. This information was relayed by William Patrick, a renowned expert in offensive BW programs and former U.S. BW weaponeer.

9. Jonathan Tucker, ed., *Toxic Terror: Assessing Terrorist Use of Chemical and Biological Weapons* (Cambridge: MIT Press, 2000), 266.

6

Defenses against CB Weapons

ollowing World War I, General John Pershing, commanding general of the American Expeditionary Force, said, "Whether or not gas will be employed in future wars is a matter of conjecture, but the effect is so deadly *to the unprepared* that we can never afford to neglect the question [emphasis added]."[1] The fact is that CB warfare is a facet of combat operations that military personnel have to face. Because military forces are a pragmatic bunch, they have examined the challenge of trying to survive and sustain combat operations in a CB-contaminated environment. Although they do not like the idea and would rather fight conventionally, they can operate in CB-contaminated environments, given the right equipment and training.

There are a number of different perspectives on defending against the adversarial employment of CB weapons. It used to be that all one studied was how to protect against the threat of CB weapons used on the battlefield. This perspective has changed significantly, especially since a 5,000-pound bomb planted in a truck demolished the Khobar towers (near Dhahran, Saudi Arabia) in June 1996, killing nineteen U.S. military service members. Although terrorists' targeting of U.S. military personnel is not a new phenomenon, the concept of force protection of military and

121

civilian personnel at military installations has become increasingly important.[2] Even though terrorists have not used chemical or biological warfare agents against military installations, there is increasing concern that given the tighter security measures against conventional terrorist weapons (handguns, knives, and explosives), they may turn to weapons that can be used at a distance from their target.

The issue of homeland security has been a popular theme for many talking heads since September 11, 2001. The anthrax-laden letters have shown a third form of CB warfare: attacking U.S. citizens and public institutions directly. Although the Department of Defense (DOD) has been focused on CB defense within the aspects of traditional warfighting and force protection, they have also been involved with homeland security, the protection of noncombatant U.S. citizens and institutions, although not as the lead agency. Currently, the issue of homeland security against CB warfare agents has been seen as an issue for the Department of Health and Human Services (HHS) and the Environmental Protection Agency (EPA), with the DOD playing a supporting role in any responses to CB terrorism incidents.

We will examine each of these three mission areas—traditional battlefield warfare, the protection of military installations, and homeland security—in turn. Although the same CB hazards present themselves in each area, the response within each area is unique and requires discussion to ensure one does not make the mistake of assuming they require the same approach.

The Traditional Warfight

In a traditional force-on-force combat scenario, military forces expect the possibility of CB warfare, given that deterrence efforts may fail and they may be unable to destroy their adversary's storage sites and delivery systems. As a result, they are trained to look for early signs and symptoms of exposure to CB warfare agents. They have specialized equipment to detect and identify the hazards, to communicate a warning across the battlefield, to protect themselves from exposure, and ultimately to clean up any residual contamination. Before they are forced to use this equipment, however, there are other efforts taking place at the political and strategic levels that can reduce the threat of CB warfare to military forces.

There have always been arms control efforts, but the resulting treaties never seemed to stop the steady proliferation of countries that were researching and developing CB warfare programs. For the majority of the twentieth century, the threat of CB warfare agents during wartime had one response: to retaliate in kind (or with heavier weapons), threatening to expose the enemy's forces to the same debilitating and harassing agents to which one's own force was exposed. This is what some call "classic deterrence." Following the Persian Gulf conflict, the U.S. military began a re-examination of strategy on how they should attempt to deter, roll back, prevent, or reduce the threat of CB warfare. This was in a large measure due to the coalition's unsuccessful attempts to stop Iraqi mobile Scud launchers from firing ballistic missiles at their forces, missiles that had the potential to deliver CB warfare agents over a wide area.

Nonproliferation efforts are intended to influence countries either to give up their CB weapons or to not begin an offensive CB warfare program in the first place. This includes the use of the full range of political, economic, or informational or military tools to prevent proliferation of NBC weapons and missiles, reverse it diplomatically, or protect U.S. interests against an opponent armed with NBC weapons.[3] Most people associate nonproliferation with global arms control agreements and export controls to prevent the spread of technology and supplies to those nations that lack an internal capability to produce these weapons. This includes inspections, monitoring, verification, and enforcement support for arms control treaties.

These efforts can also include attempting to persuade nations not to develop these weapons; denying the materiel, technology, and expertise to nations seeking this capability; disarming nations that have the weapons with arms control efforts; and diplomatic pressure to punish those nations that proliferate the threat. Nonproliferation efforts include collecting and sharing intelligence with other nations, offering incentives or disincentives, and purchasing certain materials to prevent their transfer to potentially unfriendly nations.[4] For instance, in August 2002, the United States worked with Russia to move 100 pounds of highly enriched uranium from Yugoslavian nuclear reactors to Russia for disposal. The United States has also worked with the former Soviet Union states to clean up the former offensive CB weapons stockpile sites. There is a program to offer salaries to former Soviet Union weaponeers to keep them from selling their services to the highest bidders in countries trying to develop their own offensive CB warfare programs.

In the realm of CB warfare, the Geneva Protocol and the Biological Weapons Convention (BWC) have no verification protocol; in fact, they were deliberately designed not to infringe on a nation's inherent rights of eminent domain. The Soviet Union's negotiators fought hard to prevent including any references to uninvited inspections in the BWC's language, despite campaigns from the British and United States envoys to the contrary. The Australia Group similarly posts information on export controls but must rely on individual nations to enforce them. The Chemical Weapons Convention (CWC), on the other hand, does have significant verification protocols in overseeing chemical weapons disposal and verifying that its signatories follow the rules. The Organization for the Prohibition of Chemical Weapons (OPCW), an international group stationed in The Hague, executes this function. Although a nation can challenge one of the signatories on specific suspected sites of weapons production or storage, this has never happened. Rather, the OPCW has exhibited a more passive role of routinely inspecting declared stockpiles and ensuring their destruction.

Defense Secretary Les Aspin led an initiative in 1993 to develop a counterproliferation policy, which was intended to prevent or reduce the threat of an adversary using NBC weapons against the U.S. military. Counterproliferation efforts include activities that span the full range of U.S. government activities, including the use of military power to protect U.S. forces and interests; intelligence collection and analysis; and support to diplomacy, arms control, and export controls, with particular responsibility for assuring that U.S. forces and interests can be protected should they confront an adversary armed with NBC weapons.[5] Counterproliferation efforts have been defined as the DOD's effort to limit NBC weapons, as opposed to nonproliferation efforts, which have a stronger political, diplomatic, and economic emphasis that is not limited to the DOD.

Counterproliferation involves defusing situations in which nations may be tempted into using NBC weapons against their neighbors; deterring adversarial use through military, political, or economic threats of retaliation; destroying enemy production sites and weapon systems during times of conflict; and defending military forces against the delivery and dissemination of NBC weapons. This policy has, over the years, been crafted into a strategy that has four pillars: counterforce, active defense, passive defense, and consequence management.

Counterforce includes the ability to stop an adversary at any step in the production, storage, transportation, or readying of a CB warfare agent before it is employed. This generally includes (but is not limited to) attacking production facilities, storage complexes, and deployed weapons delivery systems. During the Persian Gulf conflict, special operations forces and dedicated Air Force assets were searching for and destroying these targets to stop their potential employment against U.S. forces. Today, the U.S. Air Force is developing weapons under its Agent Defeat program to destroy, neutralize, or immobilize adversaries' weapons or to deny adversaries access to their own weapons with little or no collateral damage. Other programs include the Hard Target Defeat effort, designed to develop tools to penetrate and destroy hardened and deeply buried targets that may be manufacturing or storing CB weapons.

Active defense measures are those taken to detect, divert, or destroy enemy NBC weapons and delivery means while they are en route to their targets, for instance, destroying theater ballistic missiles in flight, either from airborne platforms or by missile intercepts. These actions reduce the benefit that an adversary might expect to gain by the use of NBC weapons. One of the most visible efforts in this area is the Missile Defense Agency (MDA), formerly known as the Ballistic Missile Defense Organization (BMDO). In addition to its efforts to develop a national missile defense system, the MDA has been researching and developing a capability to provide theater missile defense designed to protect deployed troops, allies, and civilians at risk from theater ballistic missiles. Another effort is the design of the Airborne Laser, a high-energy laser weapon system carried in a modified Boeing 747 airplane. If successful, this laser could destroy or disable a ballistic missile hundreds of kilometers away. If the missile is caught in its boost stage, any debris or potential contamination could fall back on the nation that launched it.

Passive defense refers to defensive measures (rather than the offensive measures in counterforce and active defense) that enable friendly forces to survive, fight, and win military operations despite an enemy's employment of NBC weapons or agents. If counterforce and active defense efforts were 100 percent accurate, there would be little need for passive defense. But since this is not the case, military forces need to be prepared for what will get through counterforce and active defense measures. In the days before the creation of the term "counterproliferation," this area was what one really referred to as NBC defense. These measures largely involve the use of materiel to protect forces against CB warfare agents, such as CB agent detectors, hazard prediction software, protective clothing and masks, medical CB defense countermeasures, collective protection systems in vehicles and in shelters, and decontaminants. Most combat forces do not like to use these measures, because wearing protective clothing and masks, although protecting individuals against CB warfare agents, slows down the tempo of a military force and makes it more vulnerable to conventional weapon systems. The better-trained the force is in using this gear, however, the less degraded their operations are when they are forced to use passive defense equipment under combat conditions.

Consequence management refers to the essential services and activities required to manage or reduce damages or other consequences or problems resulting from the employment of NBC weapons. In general, this means cleaning up after the incident so one can return to an unprotected status. These measures include the long-term actions required to mitigate the effects of NBC weapons resulting from combat operations. Such measures are usually conducted after hostilities die down and dedicated specialists can be brought in to work. During a military conflict, consequence management can also mean the measures the DOD employs to aid a host nation that may have suffered a CB weapons attack from an adversary, whether a nation-state or terrorist group. This is referred to as foreign consequence management.

As one can see, the four measures of counterproliferation are sequential. Ideally, one would like to destroy the adversary's ability to produce and store CB weapons before any weapons are readied for use. If the weapon systems have already been deployed, one would want to intercept them while they are being moved to the front or when the aircraft or missiles are in the air, before they come into range of friendly forces. Failing that, the friendly forces should have measures to find out where the CB warfare agents are and to tell them how to protect themselves and how to reduce the contamination effects so they can carry out their mission. Finally, long-term restoration efforts will return the contaminated area to its former pristine state.

Protecting Military Installations

Since 1983 (the year the Marine Corps barracks was bombed in Beirut, Lebanon), there has been a concern that hostile military forces will try to attack U.S. military bases prior to the formal announcement of hostilities. Since the United States relies on a relatively small number of military bases to project its force overseas, the potential results of CB weapons contamination on these bases could, at best, delay the projection of these forces, giving a critical advantage to the enemy. At worst, such an attack could injure or kill DOD civilians or military dependents. The effects of such an attack against a U.S. military base overseas could similarly create a fatal delay, degrading military operations at the onset of a conflict, the most critical time, when reinforcements are meant to arrive. In a similar fashion, terrorists could attack military bases with CB agents, which might only cause a small number of casualties but would cause mass panic across the nation. Although terrorists would employ much smaller amounts of CB agent than a foreign military power could, the attack could still cause a critical delay in getting forces into action, or at the least, score an international coup against the U.S. government.

All installation commanders have the responsibility to assess their bases' vulnerabilities and to prepare against the potential consequences of a terrorist incident, including preparing for the possibility of a CB terrorist incident. The DOD calls for a force protection plan to be developed at all U.S. military installations.[6] Force protection plans are designed to protect military service members, civilian employees, family members, facilities, and equipment in all locations and situations. They are accomplished through the planned and integrated application of services to combat terrorism, to provide physical security and operations security, and to provide personal protection. These efforts are supported by intelligence, counterintelligence, and other security programs.[7]

There are several components to force protection: antiterrorism, physical security, and consequence management are three major ones. There is a great deal of focus on maintaining perimeter security and on responding to incidents; thus, there is a heavy emphasis on police forces, explosives ordnance disposal (EOD), firefighters, and emergency medical technicians, just as there would be for any city. All military bases do not have the same level of preparedness. Large bases with critical functions will be more heavily protected than most small bases that do not have significant resources. The threat of CB terrorist incidents is a somewhat recent concern, however. The bulk of the DOD's efforts have been applied toward overseas combat operations and not toward the relatively low probability of a terrorist strike within the United States. As one can imagine, this viewpoint has changed since September 11, 2001.

The threat of CB warfare agents is a particular challenge to those who once thought they could stop all threats at an installation's gates. CB warfare agents, particularly those designed to be aerosolized, could be released a mile from a military base and, weather permitting, cross the installation's walls and affect personnel on the base. It might take a considerable amount of agent to actually cause a significant impact, which leads to the second scenario: a terrorist who smuggles in a small canister of CB warfare agent, in a fire extinguisher, for instance. The target might be a particular headquarters building rather than the entire base. There are many challenges to developing enough agent to affect a large base; some theorists postulate that terrorists could just hijack a tanker of industrial phosgene and crash that into the front gates. But, although that would cause an impact, the liquid would evaporate quickly, and at least firefighters know how to deal with a hazardous industrial chemical; they may not be as familiar with handling CW agents.

The focus of force protection is on saving lives prior to and during a terrorist incident, not on maintaining operations. Consequence management reacts to a terrorist incident in order to limit additional casualties and to restore critical services. Similar to the situation discussed for counterproliferation, the DOD can train emergency responders on a base and military CB defense specialists to respond to a CB terrorist incident. By the time the off-post specialists show up, the main damage is done, much as is true in cases where a conventional bomb has been used. All that consequence management specialists can do is to prevent the spread of contamination that might cause additional casualties in the near term and to initiate the steps required to restore the base to its previous state.

The real challenge is that, although the U.S. military understands how to protect its forces from CB warfare agents on the battlefield, protecting civilians at military installations and facilities is an entirely different situation. First, it is very costly. There are more than 600 DOD bases that could require sophisticated detectors and hazard prediction software, there are thousands of buildings that could require collective protection shelters, and the response forces on the bases need their own special detectors, protective gear, and decontaminants to go into hazardous conditions. There are more than 2 million DOD civilians who could require some kind of protective masks and clothing or protective shelter material for their offices, much like the Israeli citizens had during the Persian Gulf conflict, when they feared Iraqi Scuds might carry CB warfare agents.

Second, how does one train all these civilians and keep them prepared for such an incident without overdoing the paranoia? People argue that preparedness for a CB terrorism incident must be maintained at all times, whereas a terrorist only has to be lucky once. Although the actual number of casualties from a terrorist-employed CB weapon might be small, the psychological impact would be significant. Take the Pentagon's issuing of escape masks in March 2003 to all of its workers and its establishment of cabinets with escape masks for visitors, for instance. These masks will probably (hopefully) never be used, yet the Pentagon leadership felt motivated to provide some level of assurance to its workers that there is a plan. Whether this model will be translated to all DOD installations and facilities remains to be seen. It is costly to train and maintain this capability, and the real focus and energy (to be honest) should be on stopping terrorists armed with explosives and handguns.

Third, if such an effort were to be implemented on all military bases, it could divert specialists and equipment from military operations overseas. Although one can make the argument that unprotected military bases are more vulnerable, they are not likely targets for terrorist CB hazard attacks. Military units, on the other hand, recognize that they *are* likely targets of CB weapons when they enter combat operations against nations and terrorists armed with these weapons. The question is one of balance: How much effort should be put toward preparing military forces for CB warfare and how much effort should be put toward preparing installations to respond to CB terrorist incidents? The equipment and expertise for both come from largely the same pool of resources, and this pool is not very big. Rough estimates of the cost of providing such protection to 530 DOD installations exceed $3 billion dollars to establish a minimal capability (let alone a robust capability), and those estimates did not consider manpower costs or the costs of sustaining the capability from year to year. The

DOD plans to spend about $1 billion a year on warfighting CB defense efforts between 2002 and 2007, in comparison.

Homeland Security

Having said that, let us take a hard look at the proposed homeland security effort. The U.S. government and various think tanks have been considering the issue of protecting the U.S. people and the nation's facilities from terrorist attacks since before September 11, 2001. The attack on the World Trade Center and the Pentagon merely hastened the planning process into action a bit sooner than anticipated. The four anthrax-laced letters sent in October 2001 spurred an extreme focus on the potential effects of biological terrorism; although chemical terrorism is still a concern, many analysts feel that an unannounced BW attack against a major metropolitan city would be devastating. By the time the first cases of a contagious disease are identified, its spread could have already impacted thousands, and it could be spreading to other cities. There have been a number of studies on the possibility of a terrorist attack using smallpox, studies that are driving the recent preparations to build a national vaccine stockpile.

The question is, does the nation need a national stockpile? The smallpox virus is relatively hard to get; it is no longer found naturally, and samples are known to exist in only two nations: Russia and the United States. The side effects of this vaccine are worse than those of the anthrax vaccine, which has received much undeserved notoriety. For every million people receiving the smallpox vaccine, fifteen will suffer major complications and one or two will die. A larger group will suffer side effects that are serious but not life threatening, such as blindness or skin ailments. Many will suffer from fevers or malaise.[8] Multiply these numbers by 200, and you get the impact on the total U.S. population. Although these side effects are in part because some of the population are people who would have an increased sensitivity to any vaccines (the old, sick, and very young), there is the possibility that these victims and their families would blame the government.

The U.S. military, in particular, is struggling to determine exactly what its role is in homeland security. Of course, a great deal of attention is focused on how to defend against any repeated use of civilian aircraft as massive explosive devices against cities.

Also of concern is the protection of the sea border, a role shared by the Coast Guard and Navy, and the extensive land boundaries. Although there are limited U.S. military forces working with the Border Patrol, the question has arisen as to the need for an increased military role in guarding the land border. Amid all this discussion is the question of what the DOD's role should be in responding to domestic CB terrorism.

When it comes to biological terrorism, there are many who suggest that the lead federal agency should be the HHS, with its subordinate agencies, the U.S. Public Health Service and the CDC. These agencies have been working with the DOD on related CB warfare issues, but in the past they have not been prepared to respond to the task of preparing the United States to respond to a BW terrorist attack. Given the DOD's large force of specialists and expertise in the subject, we may see a close binding of the two departments in addressing this area.

In the meantime, what is homeland security? President George W. Bush defines homeland security in his national strategy as "a concerted effort to prevent terrorist attacks within the United States, reduce America's vulnerability to terrorism, and minimize the damage and recover from attacks that do occur."[9] One military definition is "the preparation for, prevention of, deterrence of, preemption of, defense against, and response to threats and aggression directed toward U.S. territory, sovereignty, domestic population, and infrastructure; as well as crisis management, consequence management, and other domestic civil support."[10] This proposed military definition breaks homeland security into at least two major areas: homeland defense and civil support.

Not surprisingly, homeland defense includes the protection of U.S. territory, sovereignty, domestic population, and critical infrastructures against external threats and aggression. The extent of these efforts above and beyond force protection (discussed above) is still being developed. For instance, there is an initiative going on to develop urban biological detection sensors for major cities. These sensors might provide an early indication of a terrorist BW attack—if the agent is aerosolized and if the weather cooperates to blow the agent into the detector's sensing apparatus. There may be a great benefit in tying military medical labs and hospitals to the civilian health infrastructure, a move that might improve the early diagnosis and treatment of any contagious diseases outbreaks that may have been caused by BW agents.

Civil support includes military support to U.S. civil authorities for domestic emergencies and for designated law enforcement and other activities. In a broad sense, this means domestic consequence management and responding to state and local agencies' requests for assistance to a CB terrorism incident. The military has already been active in this area: Both the U.S. Army Technical Escort Unit (TEU), stationed at Aberdeen Proving Ground, Maryland, and the U.S. Marine Corps Chemical-Biological Incident Response Force (CBIRF), stationed at Indian Head, Maryland, are practiced in responding to civil requests for assistance in CB terrorism incidents. These definitions and their scope will probably change as the DOD grows into its new role in federal homeland defense issues and as the new command, U.S. Northern Command, assumes responsibility for this function.

There is considerable overlap in the areas of force protection and homeland security; the main difference is in what specific population is being protected. In force protection, installation commanders are protecting their own personnel and dependents on a base. There are limited funds for this task, but there are clear guidelines, and the installation commanders can craft their responses in light of their scope of authority and limited resources. In homeland security, the DOD is supporting other federal agencies to protect U.S. citizens and civil infrastructure. The military is not in charge of funding or leading the response; instead, it defers to federal, state, and local civilian authorities. The funding strategies, degrees of risk, and political actors are different from those of the military. There are, however, similar responses, parallel to what is now used for warfighting, that can be adopted in any examination of the CB warfare threat in force protection or homeland security missions.

Focusing on the Response

The U.S. Army Chemical School, as the DOD's executive agent for CB defense, leads the development of doctrine, training, leader-development materials, and materiel solutions for CB defense challenges. The U.S. Army is also the only branch that dedicates full-time specialists to addressing CB warfare. The U.S. Air Force and Navy include CB defense training through disaster preparedness and counterproliferation officers. The Marine Corps does have CB specialists but not CB defense units (outside of the

CBIRF). As a result, the Army often leads the DOD in developing a joint service response to CB warfare agents.

In 1999, the Chemical School developed a CB defense concept known as sense, shape, shield, and sustain, which emphasizes the need to *sense* CB hazards through reconnaissance, detection, identification, diagnosis, and surveillance; to *shape* the commanders' picture of the battle with timely information on the presence or absence of CB hazards; to *shield* the force from CB hazards through individual protection and mobile collective protection measures; and to *sustain* the force through fixed collective protection, decontamination, and medical restoration efforts. These principles can be executed simultaneously, with some of the force sensing the hazard while others sustain the force in collective protection shelters. Others in "clean" areas (determined from information gathered from networked sensors) do not have to shield themselves with hot and bulky protective suits and masks. These principles can apply equally in the discussion of military, force protection, and homeland security operations. Although the discussion in this book focuses on the U.S. military's approach to CB defense, nearly all countries with a CB defense program address this threat in a very similar fashion.

The capability to *sense* CB hazards generally requires specialized personnel and equipment to provide information to warfighters, commanders, civilians, and other federal agencies (depending on the mission). There are three general areas within this broad area: the ability to provide early warning with sensors prior to the arrival of the hazard; the ability to employ automatic point sensors in the immediate area to warn personnel of the presence of CB warfare agents; and medical surveillance that supports the diagnosing of early stages of exposure. There are distinct differences between sensing for chemical rather than biological warfare agents, in a large part because whereas CW agents stand out as unnatural elements, BW agents are hard to distinguish in an outdoor environment.

With early warning, one can detect and in some cases identify CB warfare agents through stand-off detectors that use infrared or ultraviolet lasers to detect agents kilometers away, through remote point detectors set at a distance from personnel and networked into a command post, or through reconnaissance, provided by mobile specialists actively searching for areas of CB contamination. This capability provides what is termed "detect to warn": Forces can physically avoid the contamination, take shelter, or mask prior to the arrival of the hazard. Early warning capabilities come at a steep price. They require specialized and often very expensive equipment and qualified operators trained to employ and maintain this equipment. Reconnaissance vehicles cost from $1 million to $2 million each, for instance. The U.S. Army and Marine Corps have a specialized NBC reconnaissance vehicle with dedicated operators: the M93A1 NBC Recon System, or "Fox" vehicle. This is a German Fuchs light-armored vehicle that holds three to four soldiers who operate chemical point and stand-off systems from within a collectively protected environment.

As of 2003, there is only one true chemical agent stand-off system, the M-21 Remote Sensing Chemical Agent Alarm, or RSCAAL. This uses a passive infrared sensor to detect aerosol clouds at a distance of up to five kilometers. It has been very difficult to develop BW agent stand-off detectors, because at a distance, it is hard to discriminate man-made BW agents from common biological organisms in the environment. The U.S. military has no early-warning biological detectors, although research continues on developing such a system. Generally, military forces have comparatively few early-warning devices and reconnaissance vehicles (due to their cost and the need for specialists to operate them), but they can cover large tracts of the battlefield very quickly.

Automatic point detectors are usually built to be fielded in large numbers. They cost much less than the sophisticated early-warning devices and can be operated by nonspecialists with minimal training. At least, this is the ultimate goal. Some CW agent point detectors have been built that are small enough to carry in one hand and sensitive enough to give the alarm at less-than-lethal levels. It is more difficult to develop BW agent detectors. Current BW agent detectors are large and expensive, and they do not detect BW agents quickly because they have to sift volumes of air and be triggered by potential BW agents prior to detecting and giving the alarm for an actual threat. The time to alarm can be anywhere from fifteen to forty-five minutes after an attack. This time delay has given rise to the description "detect to treat" devices: All the device tells you is that you have been exposed and must now seek medical attention.

Since BW agents take much more time to affect personnel (from two to ten days), this time lapse is not critical as it would be with CW agents, which can kill exposed personnel in minutes or seconds. Of more concern is the potential for false positives, that is, cases where the detectors give an alarm although nothing is present. False positives can occur because the devices are set to be so sensitive that interferents (such as pesticides or diesel products) can set off the alarms. If the device were not so sensitive, there might be no false positives, but the current trend has been to focus on achieving more sensitivity instead of decreasing the number of false alarms. What one does not want at all are false negatives, that is, cases when the detectors do not give an alarm even though a CB warfare agent is present. Some false positives are acceptable, given the ability to double check with other detectors, but no false negatives can be tolerated, for false negatives mean that people are being exposed without being warned.

There are a number of different chemical point detectors, largely due to the desire to develop tools for different purposes and different missions. For continuous and automatic detection and warning, there are the M8A1 chemical detectors (which detect nerve agent only) and the newer M22 chemical detectors (which detect nerve and mustard agents). These devices are intended to sound an alarm at levels that will permit people to mask before being exposed to lethal levels of agent. There is a strong desire to make these twenty-five-pound detectors more lightweight and portable; detectors have been developed that are as small as forty-two cubic inches and weigh as little as two pounds, but the cost of achieving that has been high. Finally, there is the M1 Chemical Agent Monitor, or CAM, which is used to verify manually the presence or absence of agent on equipment after decontamination operations are completed.

On the biological side, the detectors are often very large and expensive, given the desire to be absolutely sure of finding any BW agent present and to minimize the time from trigger to taking action. Currently, these alarms cannot warn personnel quickly enough for them to take protective action, such as masking or seeking shelter, so this capability is often referred to as "detect to treat," as opposed to "detect to warn." The Army has a few companies of Biological Integrated Detection Systems (BIDS), which allow for the mobile surveillance for BW agents. There are fixed-site biological detection systems called Joint Portal Shields at U.S. military installations in southwest Asia and northeast Asia, built on similar technology. The Joint Biological Point Detection System (JBPDS) is nearly ready for fielding at the time of this printing. These systems all operate on similar technologies: They constantly sample the air until a large biological presence is detected, triggering the system to take a sample. This sample is tested on antibody-antigen-detector assays. If there is a positive identification, the operator alerts the command. This process can take twenty-five to thirty minutes from the initial trigger. Although people will be exposed to the agent, because BW agents take so long to affect their host, there is ample time for medical countermeasures.

Medical surveillance relies on the fact that humans are ultimately the detection device for any CB warfare agents that are not detected by early warning or point detectors. Because medical personnel monitor the health of any deploying force or civilians on a base, they will note any outbreaks of disease or patterns of exposure that match the signs and symptoms of exposure to CB warfare agents. They also monitor what are known as disease nonbattle injuries, which can be an indication of an undetected biological agent attack. One difficulty in this process is that medically trained personnel can be hard to retain in the military; there are never enough medical personnel to watch over everyone. Medical personnel also require field laboratories or backup capabilities if they are to be able to analyze clinical and environmental samples to diagnose and treat CB warfare casualties.

The capability to *shape* CB hazard information requires the integration of CB warfare sensors across the operating environment to provide near-real-time data to warfighters, commanders, civilians, and other federal agencies. This capability does not focus merely on CB hazard information; it must also include medical data, logistics data, and meteorological and terrain data if it is to be successful. In addition to networking the CB warfare sensors, one must have some kind of hazard prediction software to analyze potential scenarios and to predict where the hazard could be, in addition to mapping where the sensors have reported contamination.

The two hazard prediction software packages adopted by the U.S. military include Hazard Prediction and Assessment Capability (HPAC) and Vapor, Liquid, and Solid Tracking Model (VLSTRACK). The Defense Threat Reduction Agency developed and maintains HPAC, giving it to military and defense agencies that desire an ability to model CB warfare. Through HPAC, a skilled operator can predict the effects of hazardous-material releases into the atmosphere and their impacts on civilian and military populations. It models CB warfare releases resulting from strikes by conventional weapons against enemy CB warfare production and storage facilities or from accidental releases, and it models the downwind hazard areas of such releases. VLSTRACK was developed by the Navy as an operational model and simulation tool, providing downwind hazard predictions for a wide range of CB agents and munitions. It can take into account weather and terrain effects, high-altitude releases, and other variables. These models do not run quickly; the amount of data required can be staggering, including the exact type and number of munitions, agent purity, height of burst, wind speed and direction at different altitudes, 3-D terrain reliefs, temperature data, and so on. It takes even experienced operators hours to run some iterations, and even then there are disagreements.

Consider the Khamisiyah depot demolition in 1991. When the DOD and the CIA asked their modelers to estimate the downwind hazard area using a very low level of nerve agent, the resulting pattern looked like two rabbit ears splitting away from a central source.[11] Neither model was "wrong"; they just ran differently based on their exact methodology. There are a number of other CB warfare agent models: CALPUFF, D2PC, D2-PUFF, MIDAS, NUSSE4, PEGEM, SCIPUFF, and many others, if one includes the hazardous-material models. The challenge is validating and verifying that the models will accurately tell the operator how the CB warfare cloud will actually move in real situations. Because the U.S. government does not permit open-air CB warfare testing anymore, it is nearly impossible to verify that these models actually perform as advertised. We think the models are accurate, based on particle physics, but there is nothing like observing the real thing to prove that the model works.

Many military forces, emergency centers, and hazardous-materiel units have predictive software that can assist in estimating where the contamination is. The problem has been how to connect all the sensors to the command, communications, control, computers, and information (C4I) system. Each branch in the U.S. military has a distinct C4I system, and they do not always talk to each other. A similar lack of interdepartmental communications is often seen between firefighters and police in the same city, for instance. However, steps are being made to standardize the C4I systems. The potential benefits of networked sensors providing instantaneous data to the commanders is an intoxicating idea, since this capability could literally allow many individuals to take actions preventing or limiting their exposure to CB warfare agents. On the other hand, one has to be concerned about the possibility of false alarms, which may spook the force instead of protecting it.

In the meantime, there is always the manual method of data collection and analysis: Military personnel have a standard NBC warning and reporting format to report CB warfare alarms and indications. These data are relayed to higher commands, analyzed, and disseminated to whomever needs the information. This system worked well in the Persian Gulf conflict to follow up and investigate potential CB warfare attacks that later were discovered to be false alarms.

The capability to *shield* personnel from CB hazards requires an integration of manual detectors and monitors, protective suits and masks, individual decontamination kits, and medical pretreatments and vaccines. The capability to shield major weapon systems such as tanks, aircraft, and ships from contamination requires the addition of collective protection equipment to mobile platforms and the use of barrier materiel (plastic sheets) for critical equipment. In general, the military has invested considerable time and money into shielding its personnel and equipment from CB hazards.

The most obvious example of this is the protective suits and masks. The older protective suit for the U.S. Army was the Battledress Overgarment, or BDO. This suit is being replaced by the Joint Service Lightweight Integrated Suit Technology, or JSLIST, ensemble. This semipermeable protective suit can be worn for up to forty-five days without loss of ability to protect an individual from vapor or liquid contact with the skin. It is designed and tested to protect the wearer from up to ten grams of liquid agent per square meter of cloth for up to twenty-four hours. This level of contaminant is roughly equivalent to what one would get standing directly under a plane or artillery shell that is dispensing liquid CW agents. This ensemble is not approved to the level of the garments worn by those who handle hazardous materiels, however; emergency responders reacting to a CB terrorist incident must obey more stringent occupational safety regulations. This is not to say that military personnel are not safe: They are safe for short-duration attacks, and the protective suits and masks do not overly interfere with their ability to execute a mission.

The new protective masks have improved vision and breathing resistance over their Cold War precedents, and they can filter out all chemical vapors, biological particles, or radiological particles. The M40-series and M42-series protective masks are worn by the Army and Marine Corps; the Air Force and Navy use the older MCU-2A/P mask for their ground forces. Aviators have special requirements for their masks, given the interfaces they have with their aircraft (both for electronics or for oxygen) and the need to keep their vision completely unobstructed. Apache pilots need the M45 mask, which interfaces with their unique targeting systems, and fixed-wing pilots are integrating their CB Respiratory Mask (Navy) or Aircrew Eye/Respiratory Protection Mask (Air Force) into their flight ensembles and specific airframes. By the year 2010, the DOD plans to modernize the protective masks by moving to one general mask for all military personnel on the ground and one aviator mask for all rotary-wing and fixed-wing pilots.

Military personnel can carry a number of inexpensive, manual monitors to identify the hazards in their immediate area, allowing them to confirm whether it is safe to unmask and take off their protective clothing. They carry detector paper for liquid and aerosol CW agents, manual kits and monitors for sampling for low levels of CW vapors, and hand-held bioassays to sample for the presence of BW agents. Radiation monitors called dosimeters have been around for decades and continue to be part of the individual service member's protection package. The basic military individual protection package has a few inexpensive manual tools for determining if there is a chemical hazard, including M8 paper (very much like litmus paper), M9 paper (which has a sticky back so it can adhere to surfaces), and an M256A1 chemical detector kit, which is more sensitive than the automated detectors. Service members also carry individual decontamination kits, which are hand-sized pads of a dry resin that can absorb any liquid agent that may have been deposited on their body or personal equipment. The U.S. military version is called the M291 skin decontamination kit, and there is also a larger M295 hand-sized individual equipment decontamination kit.

Medical pretreatments provide additional protection, and medical countermeasures support those individuals who do not get their suits or masks on in time. Pretreatments include biological pretreatments (anthrax and smallpox vaccines, for instance) and chemical pretreatments such as pyridostigmine bromide, which assists in blocking nerve agents. Medical chemical defense countermeasures include atropine and 2-PAM chloride for countering exposure to nerve agents, and the antibiotics ciprofloxacin and doxycycline to counteract bacterial BW agents. There are no treatments for viral agents; about the best one can do is get medical treatment for the symptoms and ride the virus out. The challenge with medical countermeasures is to get these drugs approved by the FDA, which demands that both efficacy and safety be proven for all military items. As a result, several biological vaccines are at least a decade away from being ready for use.

For vehicles, including vans and ships, there are two main forms of shielding. One is the use of collective protection systems. Tanks, armored personnel carriers, ships, and some trucks have filtered ventilation systems to which personnel can hook their masks, relieving some breathing resistance and cooling the person down. In addition, the interior of some armored vehicles can be kept at above-atmospheric pressures to keep aerosols and vapors out. These filters are much larger than the ones found on masks, for they have to channel up to hundreds of liters of air per minute. There are also equipment design features that can reduce the possibility that CB warfare agents might get into areas that cannot be decontaminated (cracks, crevices), and there are materials that survive the corrosive effects of CB contamination and the decontaminants used to clean the equipment.

Last, there is the capability to *sustain* operating forces and installations during CB warfare attacks or terrorist CB incidents, allowing them to operate for extended periods despite the hazards of contamination by CB agents. These measures include fixed-site and temporary collective protection, operational and thorough decontamination operations, medical diagnosis and treatments, and logistics. Most military forces have a high "tail-to-tooth" ratio, meaning they rely on a large number of combat-support forces at air bases, seaports, medical facilities, command-and-control nodes, and logistics sites to keep the combat forces supplied and engaged. If the rear area goes down, so does the warfight.

The first measures to protect these rear-area fixed sites include the use of temporary collective protection shelters and collective protection systems installed in buildings. If the personnel at a fixed site can operate freely within these shelters despite the presence of contamination outside, then military operations can continue. These shelters use plastic liners, airlocks, large filters, and powered generators to maintain a clean environment. One drawback is that they can be difficult to set up quickly and thus must be installed prior to any attacks. The other drawback is that there really are not that many shelters beyond those used by medical field hospitals. Because of the size and power requirements of these shelters, and perhaps because of the difficulty of integrating this protection into current military shelters, most military forces choose to rely on individual protective suits rather than on shelters.

As forces become contaminated, they lose momentum due to the need to wear protective suits and masks. Operational decontamination amounts to spraying high-pressure hot water on vehicles to remove most of the contamination, reducing the hazard to the crew. Thorough decontamination requires specialists with decontaminants developed to completely eliminate the CB warfare agents in order to allow the crew to resume unprotected operations. Ideally, one would want a decontaminant to be easily applied, to act quickly to neutralize or remove the contamination completely, and not to have harmful effects on people, equipment, or the environment. Decontaminants should also be inexpensive (since tens of thousands of gallons may be needed in decontamination operations), produce no toxic end products, and be stable for long storage periods. The old decontaminants, STB and DS-2, are very corrosive and are not great for the environment, but they work very well in destroying CB warfare agents. Commercial decontaminants include high-test hypochlorite bleach, soap and water, and fuller's earth (a clay-like substance), which work well, but not as well as DS-2 in some cases.

In general, military forces also have smaller operational decontamination applicators that they can carry with their maneuver forces. The U.S. military standard is the M17A1 Lightweight Decontamination System, which was modified from a Norwegian system called the Sanator. The thorough-decontamination system for the Army is the M12A1 Power-Driven Decontamination Apparatus, a veteran from the days of the Korean conflict that is expected to be replaced in the next few years. These systems are only found in Army decontamination companies, and they are usually set up at thorough-decontamination sites, to which operators drive their contaminated vehicles. The vehicles are decontaminated to a level where they can be operated without requiring their crews to wear protective ensembles.

Medical diagnosis and treatments allow military forces to rapidly assess their exposed personnel and to continue long-term treatments that increase the odds of survival and of restoring the force to its full potency. Medical specialists train to recognize the signs and symptoms of exposure to CB warfare agents. Since not all CB warfare agents have vaccines or pretreatments, patients may require long-term care to return to full health.

Last, but perhaps most important, CB defense is very logistically demanding. The capability to resupply the force with protective suits, filters for the masks and collective protection systems, parts for the detectors, and decontaminants in bulk quantities is critical to success in responding to the threat of CB warfare agents.

Summary

The preceding section on response focused on the warfighting aspects, but the responses undertaken by forces responding under consequence management, force protection, and even homeland security missions are very similar. The basic differences are the populations being protected (military, DOD civilians, or the general public), the level of risk assumed (high for warfighters, low for civilians), the exact equipment design (for short durations or for long durations), and the funding available to execute a strategy (a big factor). For homeland security, for instance, it has been suggested that urban biological detectors should be developed for cities (sense), that all the nation's medical centers should be networked into a disease surveillance system (shape), that all local emergency responders should be given suits and masks tested for CB warfare agents (shield), and that the EPA and DOD forces should be called on to help clean up contamination after an incident (sustain). Consequence management forces need very sensitive and expensive detectors to ensure that contamination is gone and that it is safe for civilians to return (sense). They must wear hazardous-materiel suits (shield) and use hazard prediction software to make decisions about where contamination hazards may remain (shape). And of course, they direct the level of cleanliness, such as the efforts to decontaminate the Hart building (sustain).

This chapter has intended to emphasize that it is not the end of the world merely because nations invest in offensive CB warfare capabilities. There are strategies intended to address these hazards and to allow military forces to continue their missions despite the presence of CB contamination. Although military personnel may wish this hazard did not exist, the fact is that CB warfare agents do exist and can kill unprepared people, potentially in large numbers. As a result, military forces across the world dedicate time and resources to understanding the threat and to developing a capability to defeat adversaries despite the employment of CB warfare agents.

This combat edge is fragile, however. Military forces that do not train for the possibility of CB warfare and that neglect to stockpile the materials necessary to conduct operations in a CB warfare environment will suffer the consequences. The defensive equipment and procedures exist, but it is up to the military leaders to ensure that their troops maintain their equipment and train to operate under CB-contaminated conditions. Because CB warfare agents are not always seen as a credible or likely threat to deployed forces, troops sometimes stop training. The equipment does not work if it is not maintained, and then the problems return. That lack of preparedness nearly cost the U.S. forces that were preparing to oust Iraqi forces from Kuwait in 1991.

Notes

1. Charles E. Heller, *Chemical Warfare in World War I: The American Experience, 1917–1918* (Washington, DC: Government Printing Office, 1984), 91.

2. The concept of force protection actually started before 1996. One can cite the bombing of the Marine Barracks in Beirut, Lebanon, in October 1983 as the event that really woke people up to the fact that military forces were being targeted off the battlefield. Other such incidents include the April 1986 bombing of a Berlin disco targeting U.S. service members, the August 1998 bombing of U.S. embassies in Kenya and Tanzania, the USS *Cole* incident in Yemen in September 2000, and of course, the September 11, 2001, attack against the Pentagon.

3. National Security Council memorandum, February 18, 1994.

4. Barry R. Schneider, *Future War and Counterproliferation: U.S. Military Responses to NBC Proliferation Threats* (Westport, CT: Praeger, 1999), 47.

5. Chairman of the Joint Chiefs of Staff Counterproliferation Charter, September 1996.

6. DOD Directive 2000.12, *DoD Antiterrorism/Force Protection (AT/FP) Program,* April 13, 1999 (on-line; available: http://www.dtic.mil/whs/directives/corres/html/200012.htm; accessed March 2003).

7. Joint Publication 1-02, *DoD Dictionary of Military and Associated Terms,* April 12, 2001 (on-line; available: http://www.dtic.mil/doctrine/jel/doddict/; accessed November 2002).

8. "New Set of Potential Risks: Experts Say Vaccine Would Kill Some, Injure Others," *Washington Post,* October 5, 2002, A-9.

9. Office for Homeland Security, "National Strategy for Homeland Security," July 2, 2002 (on-line; available: http://www.whitehouse.gov/homeland/book/nat_strat_his.pdf; accessed March 2003).

10. Chairman's Memo 213-02, "Terms of Reference for Establishing U.S. Northern Command," March 7, 2002.

11. For this case study, see Office of the Special Assistant for Gulf War Illnesses, "Case Narrative: US Demolition Operations at Khamisiyah" (on-line; available: http://www.gulflink.osd.mil/ khamisiyah_ii/; accessed February 14, 2003).

7

Case Studies

One of the challenges resulting from talking about CB warfare in the abstract is that it can lead to further misunderstanding. People often cannot accurately visualize what a battle would be like if one or both sides used chemical or biological weapons, or if one or both combatants had the potential to use CB weapons but deliberately chose not to. What decisions are made? What assumptions are driving the decisions? On one side are arms control proponents and medical specialists who see CB warfare as an abomination to humanity and science and refuse to conceptualize how the weapons work; they would rather see all these weapons simply eliminated. On the other side are the conventional military experts who, far from understanding the effects of CB warfare, "wish" the weapons away because they complicate what would otherwise be a clean and predictable battle. This lack of perception of the true limitations of CB warfare feeds the mythology that surrounds this subject.

We can take a look at several case studies that exemplify the nature of CB weapons throughout history. The first will be the use of gas at Caporetto, Italy, which resulted in one of the worst routs of Italian forces during World War I. The second will be an evaluation of the use of chemical weapons by Egypt against the

Yemeni royalists in 1968. Third will be the use of chemical weapons during the Iran-Iraq War. Fourth will be the preparations and actions taken by the United States during its military operations against Iraq in 1990–1991. The first two cases will be relatively short snapshots of the tactical use of chemical weapons in specific battles, and the latter two will be longer discussions on the operational employment of chemical weapons through an entire conflict. Finally, we will review the anthrax letter incidents of October 2001 as a terrorism case.

Gas at Caporetto

Most military analysts believe the use of chemical weapons was inconclusive in causing any changes in the outcome of World War I. The German military's superior execution of gas warfare did not shift the tide of the war in their favor, though not for lack of effort. In most cases, British and German use of gas weapons was not significant enough to give the side using the weapons the edge required to overcome the significant defenses and depths of trench works. On the western front at least, the two sides were simply too well-matched for chemical weapons in and of themselves to tip the balance of combat. The use of chemical weapons on the eastern and Italian fronts, however, proved to be much different, in large part because the military commanders used chemical weapons as a combat multiplier in addition to sound military tactics instead of relying on chemical weapons alone to win the battle. The best example of this in World War I was the use of gas against the Italian army at Caporetto in the fall of 1917.

Italy was a late joiner to the Great War, declaring war against Austria-Hungary in May 1915 and against Germany in August 1916. The Italian offensives against Austria were called the Battles of the Isonzo, of which there were twelve defined campaigns between July 1915 and December 1917. The eleventh battle had ended in September 1917 with the Italian army in full command of the mountain passes between the two countries and inside Austrian territory. The Italian fortifications, combined with the rough terrain, made it nearly impossible for the Austrian army to attack effectively.

Upon the Austrian government's request to the German government, six German divisions joined nine Austrian divisions to attack a twenty-five-kilometer stretch of lightly defended Italian positions in front of Caporetto on October 24, 1917. The Germans planned an initial barrage of gas and would use newly developed infiltration and shock tactics to overcome the fortifications and their defenders. (As an anecdotal note, one of the German officers that would be decorated for his actions during this offensive was Lieutenant Erwin Rommel.) Although the Italian army was aware that the Austrian and German forces were preparing an offensive, they either did not expect a gas attack or were confident that their positions were defensible enough, given the rugged mountains and their past successes against the Austrians, to stop any offensive. In fact, the local Italian commander near Caporetto had aggressively organized an offensive operation to attack the Germans' southern flanks.

The German divisions attacked at two in the morning using a mixture of phosgene and chlorine, employing more than 800 projectors and six tons of gas during an initial artillery barrage that lasted four hours. The Italian forces had no intelligence suggesting that a gas attack would occur, and they had little protection. Although this was not a heavy barrage compared to gas attacks against the British and French, the Italian gas mask, a copy of a French respirator, was of practically no use against phosgene. The chemical barrage had an instantaneous effect, and the Italians began to panic and retreat almost immediately. Their artillery could not counterattack with their crews helpless or deserting their posts. Because this mixture was not a persistent chemical agent, Austrian and German troops could attack the fortifications with limited protection and little danger to their own forces.[1]

By that afternoon, Austrian-German forces had taken Caporetto and penetrated about twenty-three kilometers into Italian territory. They continued to push into Italy until, running out of supplies and beginning to face stiffer resistance, they stopped on November 12 at the Piave River, about thirty kilometers north of Venice. Between 275,000 and 300,000 Italian soldiers were captured or became casualties (90 percent had surrendered), and the Italian forces lost all their trench artillery. The British and French forces, alarmed at the near-collapse of the Italian army, rushed several divisions down to the Alps in November to stanch the impact of the offensive.

As suggested at the beginning of this section, the battles where the use of chemical weapons resulted in a success for the attacker were few and were definitely not the norm. Caporetto does demonstrate, however, two important factors. First, the use of chemical weapons combined with conventional forces against an unprepared force resulted in a successful offensive operation. The use of chemical weapons was instrumental in providing Austrian-German forces with the key to overcoming mountain fortifications that conventional weapons and forces were unable to defeat. Second, this use of chemical weapons was a tactical success; although the Austrian-German force penetrated deep into Italian territory, the operation itself did not lead to their winning the war or forcing Italy to withdraw from the war. Chemical weapons were not seen as an operational or strategic weapon, and they were certainly not seen as a weapon of mass destruction. The chemical weapons had not killed thousands of soldiers; they had merely disrupted the effectiveness of the Italian units to the point where they collapsed under pressure.

Egyptian Use of Chemical Weapons

The Yemeni civil war (1962–1970) pitted the Yemeni royalists of the deposed imam against the Yemen republican forces in North Yemen, with Saudi Arabia and Jordan supporting the royalists and Egypt supporting the republican forces. This war was fought for five years until the two forces reached a stalemate in 1967. Although there had been occasional mentions of Egyptian military employment of mustard agent–filled bombs between 1963 and 1966, in 1967 these attacks became more frequent. International journalists began reporting that Ilyushin heavy bombers were dropping mustard-filled and phosgene-filled bombs on cities and rebel bases.

In January 1967, a gas attack near Sada killed more than 125 people. In May, two villages suffered 75 casualties from phosgene-filled bombs. Between 1967 and 1968, it is estimated that more than 1,000 Yemeni were killed as a result of exposure to chemical warfare. An International Red Cross mission sent doctors to assist the wounded, and the doctors testified to what they saw. Although they were careful to clarify that they did not see any evidence of actual attacks taking place, the signs and symptoms of the victims included burning eyes and trachea, pulmonary edema, internal thorax pain, extreme fatigue, and anorexia. Their findings were that in all probability these victims had inhaled toxic gases.[2]

The doctors were reluctant to identify the specific chemical warfare agents used. Although it appeared conclusive that mustard and phosgene had been used, there were a few cases that suggested the use of nerve agent–filled bombs as well. The problem was how to prove the use of chemical warfare agents and who was responsible for using them. Because there were no arms control experts assigned to monitor or investigate these attacks, there was very little evidence other than eyewitness accounts from civilians and what could have been propaganda from the royalists. Although bodies and samples were sent to Saudi Arabia for more study, again, it was difficult to accuse any specific nation. Egypt claimed it had not used chemical weapons in Yemen, and according to some sources, this may have been true if Soviet bomb crews were manning the Egyptian-marked bombers that attacked those cities.

When Saudi Arabia and the royalists tried to get the United Nations to investigate, the UN's secretary-general, U Thant, declined. On March 1, 1967, he stated that he was "powerless" to investigate the issue and that the facts were in sharp dispute. Although he almost certainly knew exactly what was going on in Yemen, he had made a political decision to stay out of the affair. The U.S. government, occupied with answering criticisms about the use of Agent Orange and riot-control agents in Vietnam, also chose not to get involved. The U.S. military decided that the chemical warfare attacks were an aberration and did not give rise to any need to worry about future chemical warfare attacks (and, in 1972, chose to disestablish the Chemical Corps). The United Kingdom was attempting to reestablish relations with Egypt at that time, so it chose not to say anything publicly against Egypt or Soviet affairs in the Middle East.[3] The incident became a political nonevent, fodder for the arms control community but not much else.

This incident teaches several interesting lessons. The first is the failure of the world's nations to react against the use of chemical weapons against civilians and military forces that were not similarly armed. This was not a clear violation of the Geneva Protocol of 1925, since Egypt was not then (and still is not) a signatory of the Geneva Protocol, unless it could be proved that Soviet crews were in the bombers that spread the chemical weapons. The reason why some military analysts believe there were Soviet crews in the bombers is twofold: First, they do not believe that the Soviet Union would have allowed Egypt to own or employ chemical weapons in 1967, Egypt having just started its interest in an offensive CW program. Second, the bombers dropped their munitions upwind of their targets for maximum effect, and in some cases, MiG fighter planes came back to drop high explosives or napalm on and near the targets to reduce or eliminate the evidence. These same tactics were seen years later when the Soviet Air Force attacked Afghani villages with chemical weapons. Because the attacks occurred in such remote locations and because postmortem examinations took place days or weeks later, it was very difficult to directly attribute the cause of death to the bombing attacks.

This was the first instance of Arabs attacking Arabs with chemical weapons, but what is important is not to note whom they attacked but to understand why they did it. And again, the reason is that the two forces were at a stalemate using conventional arms, and one side decided to break the stalemate by adding the use of an unconventional munition. These unconventional arms succeeded in hastening the collapse of the royalist forces, and, as in the Caporetto case, the attacks cannot be described as the use of "weapons of mass destruction." Although in some cases more than 100 civilians died, this level of casualties could just as easily have been caused by a few extra bombing runs using high explosives. Using chemical weapons was more efficient than conventional munitions, and the attacks were limited to tactical applications.

The Iran-Iraq War

In most accounts, Iraq's initiation of a war against Iran is seen as a mistake of bad timing and poor judgment. Saddam Hussein had been president of Iraq for about a year. Iran was in the throes of a civil war and its leader, Ayatollah Ruholla Khomeini was calling for an overthrow of the Iraqi Ba'ath Party. Iran had alienated its former supplier of military equipment and training, the United States, through the Iran hostage crisis of the previous year. It looked like an easy win to Iraq. Two years later, Iraq was on the ropes fighting for its life against heavy Iranian offenses driving into its oil-rich southern regions.

In mid-July 1982, Iraqi artillery fired artillery shells filled with riot-control agents into the advancing infantry to break up the unprotected troops. This attack, combined with heavy air and mechanized infantry attacks, stopped the Iranian infantry, who thought they were being attacked with chemical weapons. Iraq began firing Scud rockets against Iranian cities near the Iraqi border. Rather than capitulating, the Iranian army came back harder in human-wave attacks and night attacks.[4]

In the summer and fall of 1983, Iraqi forces began to use mustard agent delivered by aerial bombs, helicopter sprayers, and artillery shells against the human-wave attacks. The unprotected forces suffered thousands of casualties and were effectively driven back to the defense. When Iran reported these attacks to the United Nations, Belgian firms that had delivered thiodigycol, a key chemical precursor for mustard agent, to Iraq stopped their shipments. By this time, Iraq was well on its way to developing an indigenous capability for producing mustard agent at its al-Fallujah complex.

In March 1984, Iranian forces attempted to force their way into central Iraq. They pushed through the wetlands, where they thought that Iraqi armor and artillery would be slow to react. In some of the most ferocious fighting of the war to date, the Iraqi military threw the Iranian forces back, using conventional forces and chemical artillery. These failures effectively stopped the Iranian military from assuming the offense through spring 1985. Iraq, however, was not sitting passively. It had been building more chemical munitions factories with the intention of developing nerve agents. Some analysts feel that Iraq used tabun and mustard agent to counterattack against Iranian pushes in that spring. Although Iranian forces were somewhat better prepared, having bought chemical defense equipment on the global market, they were still sufficiently damaged by the attacks to fail to make any significant gains.

In 1986, Iraqi scientists began their biological weapons program at Muthanna State Enterprise. These studies would yield the needed experience to develop pilot plants and to initiate batch production of such BW agents as anthrax and botulinum toxin. Although Iraq did not have a sufficiently mature program to weaponize and employ these agents against Iran prior to the end of the conflict, this move to develop biological weapons was a clear and natural progression of developing the tools they felt they needed to combat Iran's forces.

In 1987, Iraqi military forces finally had enough hands-on training in using chemical munitions and incorporating them into military operational plans to become truly effective. The preceding years had seen the occasional mishaps when Iraqi forces were mistakenly gassed by their own forces, but practice made perfect, as the Iraqi forces increasingly used chemical weapons to beat back the Iranian offensives. At least four times in 1987, Iraq used mustard and nerve agents to disrupt Iranian troop buildups around Basra. Iran's enlistment of Kurds in the north to attack Iraqi forces resulted in Iraq's use of chemicals against the towns from which the suspected fighters originated. Although there were no major offensives in 1987, both sides rearmed to prepare for further conflicts.

When Iranian attacks into Iraq began to make headway in the north, Iraq responded by reinitiating attacks on Iranian cities with redesigned Scud missiles, which had a range that brought Tehran under fire. Iran responded as best it could with its ballistic missiles. During this "war against the cities," Iraq fired more than 200 Scud missiles at Iranian cities; although none had chemical or biological warheads, many Iranian citizens fled the large cities in the fear that the next Scud would. Two major offensives in 1988, both of which featured chemical attacks, would cause Iran to eventually sue for a cease-fire.

The first offensive was Iraq's attempt to win back the Al Faw peninsula, which had fallen to Iranian forces years prior. On the first day of Ramadan, Iraqi forces massed and attacked a weakened and much smaller Iranian presence. The Iraqi army used artillery-delivered nonpersistent nerve and blood agents on the front lines, while its air force bombed the rear-area troops, command centers, and reinforcements with mustard and nerve agent bombs. The combination of the six-to-one odds in troop numbers, two amphibious assaults, and good close air support resulted in a decisive defeat for the Iranian forces. Not more than a month later, Iran attacked to push Iraqi forces away from their defensive positions around Basra. In June, Iraqi use of chemical weapons continued to drive Iranian forces back. Continued attacks in the central and north sectors had similar results, allowing Iraq to regain all the territory that it had lost in the earlier years, including the Majnoon Islands and Hawizeh marshes. This series of successes led Iran to formally ask the United Nations to implement a cease-fire in August.

This is a very small snapshot of a long and dirty war, but there are several key points that one can take from this conflict. One is the relatively low loss of life from modern chemical weapons. About 45,000 Iranian casualties resulted from the direct employment of chemical weapons in a conflict that caused more than a million military and civilian casualties. The prediction that chemical warfare would result in hundreds of thousands of deaths was shown to be an overstatement. What military analysts observed was that CW agents did not have to kill all the troops to be effective; demoralizing the enemy force and degrading its units' capabilities to function was enough to tip the battle to the attacker's favor. Prompt attacks by conventional combat arms units against an unprepared adversary who was reeling from a chemical attack often, if not always, resulted in a successful operation. Iraq did not fully master this operational strategy until 1987, when its forces had the requisite training and experience in chemical target analysis to mount effective attacks and to follow up on them. The end result of the offensive use of chemical weapons was that Iraq was able to stave off defeat from a numerically superior foe until that foe had become exhausted and worn down by these attacks.

This narrative focuses on the battlefield applications of chemical warfare, but how Iraq developed its chemical and biological weapons is also of interest. Like many other countries, Iraq started with a basic knowledge of CB warfare, supported by the Soviet Union, and developed its chemical weapons production capability by purchasing equipment and materials from U.S. and European industrial firms. When these firms stopped their shipments, Iraq developed an indigenous capability to continue production. It was not until Iraqi scientists and military became comfortable with chemical warfare agents and munitions that Iraq moved on to the development of an offensive BW capability. Iraq is not believed to have employed BW agents against Iran, but had the conflict not ended when it did, it may have been only a matter of time before Iraq did use BW agents.

Another point to observe is the relatively muted (again) tones of outrage from the rest of the world on the large-scale use of chemical weapons. Although European and U.S. government agencies moved to enact controls on the export of the specific precursors needed for chemical weapons, Iraq was already deeply involved in its chemical weapons program. Through dummy corporations and transactions through other countries, Iraq used the global economy to its benefit, creating a virtual model for developing countries that wanted a similar offensive CB warfare capability. There was very little response from the international community outside of public scoldings; in fact, a U.S. congressional delegation visited Saddam Hussein shortly after the Iran-Iraq War ended to resume trade talks on agricultural products. There were no calls for bringing Saddam Hussein to justice for using chemical weapons against Iranian military forces or even for using them against his own people (until President George W. Bush noted these issues nearly fifteen years after the fact).

This conflict did have the result of increasing discussions on the issue of nonproliferation options. In 1984, while the Geneva talks on the Chemical Weapons Convention languished, a small group of fifteen nations (led by Australia) started the Australia Group to discuss nonbinding resolutions to reduce the chance of nations' developing offensive CB warfare programs by cooperatively developing measures aimed at controlling exports of dual-use chemicals and equipment. They recognized that the Geneva Protocol had done nothing to stop the use of chemical weapons in this conflict and that Iraq had clearly benefited from the international chemical industries in other nations. This group has doubled in size, to thirty-three plus the European Commission, and it continues to meet annually in Paris.

The irony of this conflict is, of course, that the United States would soon face the same threat they had casually observed going on for years. The fears that U.S. military forces would face an actual CB warfare threat other than from the Soviet Union's past capabilities led to a great deal of soul-searching and scrambling to discover what the Iraqi threat really meant to the U.S. military, what steps they would have to take to protect their forces against CB warfare agents, and how they should attempt to respond to the threatened use or actual employment of these agents against U.S. forces.

Operations Desert Shield and Desert Storm

The question of how U.S. military forces faced the Iraqi chemical warfare threat in 1990 is controversial for several reasons. First, a General Accounting Office review of military forces in 1990 found there to be a general state of unreadiness. This report was initially classified and was not released to the public until after the conflict, in May 1991. To this day, some military personnel, veterans' groups, and other critics feel that a large number of U.S. military forces were exposed to chemical or biological agents, despite overwhelming medical evidence to the contrary. The lack of any

CB warfare attacks by Iraq made it difficult to really tell whether U.S. military forces were adequately protected and prepared during Desert Storm. The constant fear of an incoming Scud missile carrying CB agents, the many false alarms, and the unanswered questions about Gulf War illnesses seemed to contradict the DOD's assertion that there were no Iraqi CB warfare attacks and that the troops were not exposed to CB warfare agents.

Initially, U.S. military forces were not well prepared to fight on a CB-contaminated battlefield, similar to their readiness at the onsets of the two world wars. They had modern CB defense equipment and enough specialists, but their training was not as good as it should have been. As in those previous conflicts, the military developed a capability to survive and sustain operations in this environment through hard training and by fielding specialized CB defense equipment, assisted by the efforts of more than 4,000 Army chemical specialists deployed throughout the force. Without the six months of preparations between August and February, however, this capability would not have been present.[5]

Although the Army's CB defense program had its renaissance period in the 1980s following its near demise in the 1970s, by the end of the 1980s the U.S. Army had become complacent. With the fall of the Berlin Wall and the apparent end of the Cold War, it appeared there was no longer any peer adversary against which the United States would have to fight a sustained military conflict. Many military analysts had seen the Soviet Union as the only adversary against which U.S. armed forces needed to develop CB defense programs. Without the European conflict scenario of NATO versus the Warsaw Pact, many began questioning the need for a continued CB defense program. Even as the Iran-Iraq conflict dragged on for years and included chemical warfare, there were no concerns within the Pentagon until August 1990, when Saddam Hussein's forces invaded Kuwait.

To say that the U.S. military and civilian leadership were concerned would be an understatement. The Defense Intelligence Agency and the CIA dug up their assessments of Iraq's military operations during the Iran-Iraq conflict and identified the major CB weapon systems. They assessed Iraq as having mustard agent and the nerve agents tabun, sarin, soman, VX, and possibly BZ. Iraqi chemical weapon systems included the Soviet-built 122 mm rocket launchers, helicopter-launched 90 mm rockets, 250- and 500-kilogram aerial bombs, 120 mm mortar shells, and 155 mm artillery projectiles. Israeli intelligence stated the existence of

Scud chemical warheads, but the main threat was seen to be the 155 mm artillery systems, since they had a greater range than the U.S. Army's 155 mm artillery and most of the chemical munitions were thought to be delivered via artillery projectiles. It was estimated that Iraq had up to 4,000 tons of chemical agents.

As for biological agents, all the intelligence community had were guesses. Because Iraq had not used BW agents in its previous conflict, there were no hard data to go on. Analysts predicted that Iraq had anthrax and botulinum toxin in weaponized form and was probably working on *Clostridium perfringens* (which causes gas gangrene in wounds), SEB, and cholera. The intelligence community listed the same weapon systems as the ones used for CW agents, with the addition of ground and air spray generators. Between the Air Force and the intelligence community, the targeting list of CB weapons production and storage sites grew quickly.

The official estimate was that Iraq was likely to use chemical weapons as a part of tactical operations to protect against any offensive actions taken by the coalition forces. Chemical weapons would cause high casualties, and that was bad news, but not the worst. The military and political leadership knew that the coalition military forces would be very vulnerable to any biological attack: There was no vaccination program, there were no detectors, there was very little training on recognizing that a BW attack was taking place other than medical epidemiology after the fact. No one had any estimates on what the overall casualty rates would be from a BW attack, whether the agent were to be delivered by a Scud missile or released by a covert operation behind friendly lines.

When the Army's Eighty-Second Airborne Division deployed to go into Saudi Arabia along with the early-deploying Marine Corps and elements of the Air Force, the forces realized that they would, for the first time in decades, face off against a credible foe with CB weapons. The Eighty-Second discovered that the soldiers' masks did not fit well, since many soldiers had selected larger masks than necessary, allowing for easier breathing with a loose seal. That would not do now that there was a real threat, but there was little time to replace them. The Marine Corps' pre-positioned stocks included dry-rotted protective masks and only one-tenth as many protective suits as it thought were stored in war reserves. The Air Force and Navy had similar problems, lacking the protective suits and decontaminants they needed but had not purchased in years. There were a number of new detectors and a new protective mask ready to come out of research and development, but there were not nearly as many as were required. The Saudi armed forces were in even worse shape, lacking any basic CB defense equipment and looking to the United States for assistance. On top of all these logistical issues, all the military forces knew that their soldiers, sailors, airmen, and marines were trained only on individual survival skills; very few military units had practiced CB defense in the field to gain the proficiency required to sustain operations in a CB-contaminated environment.

Because the Army was the only service that had a dedicated force structure for chemical defense, it moved to deploy these assets as quickly as possible. Most of the decontamination companies in the Army are in the reserves, which means that more time was required to activate and prepare the soldiers for deployment. Although each Army division had a chemical company within its force structure, these were not enough to fully cover all the decontamination requirements in the theater. The first chemical decontamination companies deploying from the United States would come under the Second Chemical Battalion, but they would not arrive until late September. Given the lack of supplies, the poor level of training, and the lack of dedicated CB specialists in theater, the forward forces would be very vulnerable for several months to any Iraqi combat action that included CB warfare.

What this meant to the political leadership was that they needed to bluff and gain some time. A massive media coverage of the troops showed every soldier and marine practicing his or her mission in a chemical suit, or at the least, walking with a protective mask at his or her side. All military service members in theater, no matter where they were or what they were doing, kept their masks nearby. The Bush administration sent Patriot missiles to Israel and Saudi Arabia, touting their protective features, which would knock any Scuds out of the sky. It certainly appeared that the use of CB weapons would have little effect other than to make the United States mad.

The Air Force Component (CENTAF) of the Central Command (CENTCOM) continued work on their targeting strategy, in which Iraq's NBC weapons sites would be one of the top priorities of offensive air operations. They also developed a Punishment Air Tasking Order that outlined the retaliation options if Iraq did release the use of chemical weapons. Secretary of State

James Baker would meet with Iraqi Foreign Minister Tariq Aziz in Geneva to deliver a letter from President Bush warning the Iraqi government of the consequences of engaging in unconventional warfare. Along with other veiled (and not so veiled) warnings from administration figures and military analysts, the tone was set to inform Saddam Hussein that there would be a heavy price if he were to use these weapons. Nonetheless, the military service members worried and trained harder.

For the first five months, the coalition forces brought in additional CB defense specialists and equipment while staying on the defense. Two chemical battalion headquarters deployed to support the Army corps, along with seven decontamination companies, seven dual-purpose (decontamination and smoke-generator) companies, four NBC reconnaissance platoons (outfitted with donated German Fuchs vehicles), and several staff-augmentation cells. In addition to the 4,000 chemical specialists attached to Army units, these 2,000 chemical specialists would give the coalition forces a robust support base. More than 1,500 physicians, nurses, and medical assistants would receive special training in the medical management of chemical and biological casualties.

Protective suits were initially in short supply, and none featured a desert camouflage pattern (the Army's focus being on the woodlands of Europe). More than 1.1 million protective suits were transferred from the United States and South Korea, while the Defense Logistics Agency awarded several contracts for accelerated production of more suits. Most of these would not arrive until March and April 1991, and as a result, most troops had only two protective suits each. Pine Bluff Arsenal sent a mask repair team into theater to inspect and repair as many masks as they could.

The time between August and December allowed the United States to borrow more than 1,000 Chemical Agent Monitors (CAMs) from Canada and the United Kingdom. Although nearly every unit had an M8A1 Automatic Chemical Agent Alarm, the CAM, being a more sensitive manual detector, allowed for postattack monitoring and verification that personnel and equipment were "clean." The M8A1 alarms came under suspicion due to a number of false alarms; however, the false alarms could be attributed to one of three major causes: poor training (hitting the wrong switch), low batteries (which would cause the alarm to sound), and interferents such as pesticides or diesel products. In all cases of alarms, soldiers were trained to use the more sensitive M256A1 chemical detector kit to verify the presence or absence of agent.

The lack of means for biological detection was a serious shortcoming. Because biological detectors had been assigned a lower research priority during the Cold War[6] and because biological detection is very difficult in the first place, there were no devices available from any country. The U.S. military pulled a former BW detection system out of mothballs, stripping it down and basically taking to the field an air sampler made sturdier to withstand field conditions. Along with several commercial air samplers and BW assay tickets, twelve teams of specialists spread out across the theater to provide an initial detection and verification of BW use if it were to occur. The problem was the time involved: The air sampler took an air sample every forty-five minutes, then an operator needed to check the samples, which then needed to be verified at an in-theater laboratory; during this time, the forces would be exposed to the BW agent, whatever it was. Although this was not optimal, at least U.S. forces would be able to verify whether they had been attacked with a weaponized agent and could begin to take the appropriate medical countermeasures.

The military's solution to this shortfall was to rely on vaccines. There was the good news, that the United States had an FDA-approved anthrax vaccine, and bad news, that the military didn't have enough to vaccinate the entire force. Every soldier required six shots for the full vaccination therapy; after the first shot, a service member would receive a second shot two weeks later, a third at the four-week mark, then one shot at the six-, twelve-, and eighteen-month marks. The doctors theorized that at least two shots would give a person more than an 85 percent chance of resisting anthrax infection. Even with a reduced shot schedule, only 150,000 of the half-million troops in theater could get the required shots.

The botulinum toxoid was not available for general release, so personnel receiving a shot had to volunteer to take the vaccination after being advised of its safety risks. Only 8,000 doses of botulinum toxoid were available. If there was a way to delay the start of operations to May, the entire force could have been vaccinated, but there was no time. Britain and the United States announced their plans to vaccinate the troops at the end of December. The challenge was to determine who was at the greatest risk from BW attacks and who should receive the shots. Some thought the rear area was the more logical target; others felt the front-line troops should receive the medications. The division and corps commanders were very upset about being forced to choose who would receive the shots and who would not, stating that there should have been vaccine shots for everyone or for no one.

The coalition forces initiated their air offensive in mid-January, attacking Iraqi CB production and storage sites along with key leadership and communication centers, air bases, and key military infrastructure and military forces in Kuwait. Although the NBC sites were pounded, only about half of the Iraqi CB warfare program was destroyed. More than 75 percent of production sites were out of business, but as the postwar investigations would reveal, most of the munitions were still in play.

On the second day of the air offensive, Iraq countered with Scud missiles fired from mobile launchers moving around the desert. In the first week, twenty-five Scuds hit Israel and twenty-four Scuds hit Saudi Arabia. As the first missiles hit Tel Aviv, reconnaissance teams raced out to inspect the sites for the presence of chemical agents. Initial police reports indicated the presence of nerve agents, but the reports were later corrected as false alarms triggered by the nitric acid that fueled the Scuds. All the Scuds were armed with high explosives. The Patriot missiles made for a great light show, but their overall effectiveness was later proven to be less than optimal. The Scud attacks caused a political outcry for CENTCOM to hunt down and eliminate this threat. Searches from fighter plane sorties and special operations forces caused a decrease in the number of Scuds being launched, not due to any successful attacks but merely because of the increased urgency felt by the mobile launchers to "shoot and scoot" to cover.

In February, as the ground forces maneuvered to their starting positions, the fear continued that Iraq would attack any forces entering Kuwait or Iraq with chemical weapons. When the ground offensive kicked off on February 24, all forces crossing into the badlands were outfitted in protective clothing. A massive artillery and air attack on Iraqi forces was intended to keep any artillery from being able to target coalition forces with chemical weapons (the Iraqi Air Force had been absent from the fight for several weeks). As the forces moved swiftly through the Iraqi front lines, it appeared that there would be no chemical attacks. There was one incident in the Marine Corps' First Marine Division sector: A mine had exploded with what some engineers thought was suspiciously low sound, a possible indication of a chemical-filled mine. The force stopped and assumed full protective posture. One NBC reconnaissance vehicle moved in to take a preliminary sample, which seemed to confirm a mustard agent, but subsequent tests with M8A1 alarms and M256A1 kits did not detect any agent. The marines unmasked and drove on.

There were similar false alarms going on within the four days of military operations, but they had all been confirmed as negative. Either the speed of the military forces, the devastating air and artillery attacks, or the veiled threats of "massive retaliation" from the coalition allies had prevented Iraq's military commanders from employing chemical warfare agents. The only case of exposure to a chemical agent occurred after military operations had ceased, when Private First Class David Fisher, a cavalry scout from the Third Armored Division, was inspecting an empty bunker in northern Kuwait for intelligence material. He brushed up against the wall of the bunkers and, several hours later, experienced blistering and pain along his arms. The medics evaluated him as a mustard agent casualty; Iraq had probably stored chemical munitions in this bunker during the Iran-Iraq conflict and later removed them. Outside of four blisters about an inch in diameter, the soldier was fine.

Concerns about potential Gulf War illnesses emerged years later, as controversies emerged regarding whether the coalition bombings of Iraqi production plants had exposed forces to low levels of chemical agents, whether Iraq had attacked coalition forces with CB warfare agents and the U.S. government had concealed these actions, and whether the postconflict demolition operations at Khamasiyah were a source of low-level chemical agent exposure. All these cases are interesting discussion points, but they have nothing to do with the discussion of military operations against Iraq (and it would take another book to give these topics the proper details for that discussion).

Part of the reason this debate is so fierce is that everyone was so convinced that Iraq would use CB warfare agents against the coalition that it was almost a self-fulfilling prophecy. The United States knew that Iraq had CB weapons—many of them were found after the war—and that the Iraqi military had the weapon systems and knowledge to effectively use CB warfare agents. We knew that U.S. forces were not well prepared or trained, and some of the chemical detectors had kept alarming. Why would Iraq not have used these weapons? Weren't the 70,000 plus cases of Gulf War illnesses a sign that something had occurred?

Barry McCaffrey, then a major general commanding the Twenty-Fourth Infantry Division, offered two insights as to why there had been no chemical warfare incidents: The forces had been equipped and trained well prior to the onset of offensive operations, and they had demonstrated this capability to the news media at every opportunity. In August 1990, they had not been ready, but in February 1991, they were, in part due to the chemical specialists in their units and in part due to the massive influx of CB defense material. They were prepared; they would have been miserable if attacked by chemical weapons, but the overwhelming majority knew they would survive.

These defense preparations may not by themselves have convinced Iraq that it would not benefit from the use of chemical weapons, but other factors may have. U.S. policy asserted the right to retaliate, and the Iraqi military did not know whether such retaliation would have been with chemical weapons (as the national policy would have allowed at that time), massive conventional strikes, or nuclear weapons. Steady diplomatic pressure from an international front, backed by promised retaliatory measures and a strong psychological warfare operation against Iraqi commanders warning them against using CB weapons, could have been a strong factor.

Other analysts postulate that Saddam Hussein was merely using the threat of CB weapons as a strategic bluff to keep the coalition forces out of Kuwait and Iraq. Certainly the threat had held up the coalition forces for several months as they developed their options and gathered more materials. Or maybe Iraq refrained from using chemical weapons because coalition forces stopped prior to reaching Basra; had they started taking cities in Iraq, maybe the order to use chemical weapons would have been given, as had happened when Iranian forces threatened Basra in the 1980s.

Nevertheless, it can be said, without going into a great deal of detail, that there was essentially no medical or forensic evidence of any chemical or biological weapons use, and the thousands of medical and chemical defense specialists were looking very hard. Chemical weapons have very distinct signs and symptoms, and if anyone had been exposed to a CW agent (as Private Fisher was), he or she would have known about it immediately, not three or four years later. Many medical studies have pointed to other possible factors causing Gulf War illnesses, but all the experts have declared CB weapons as one of the least likely causes of Gulf War illnesses, if not flatly ruling them out altogether.

The lack of CB warfare has actually caused more questions as to the proper defense against CB weapons than answers. Many combat leaders feel that the Gulf War illustrated that one does not need CB defense equipment as much as one needs a heavy conventional attacking force and threats of massive retaliation. Although the debate over the continued need for CB defense equipment continues to this day, the U.S. military was convinced that they needed a strategy to counter nonnuclear countries' potential use of CB weapons. This led to the development of the counterproliferation strategy, which was detailed earlier in the book.

Mr. Anthrax Goes to Washington

Because of the recent concerns about the threat of CB terrorism, it may be instructive to discuss the anthrax-filled letters received in October and November 2001. Although these letters were received shortly after the September 11, 2001, terrorist incident, there has only been speculation as to whether there is a connection or if this connection is merely coincidental. Four letters containing a high-grade "weaponized" form of anthrax were sent from a post office in Trenton, New Jersey. Two of these went to media outlets in New York City, and two were sent to the Washington offices of Democratic senators.[7] Prior to the discovery of these letters, however, a citizen in Boca Raton, Florida, died as a result of pulmonary anthrax exposure.

Robert Stevens, a photo editor working for the tabloid *The Sun*, published by American Media, Inc., had fallen ill on September 30 and was brought to a hospital on October 2. When the hospital treating Stevens suspected he had pulmonary anthrax and alerted the CDC, the Federal Bureau of Investigation (FBI) came in to investigate. It was too late for Stevens, who died on October 5, 2001. At first, it was suspected that perhaps Stevens had contracted anthrax naturally, since this incident represented the first appearance of inhalation anthrax in the United States in several decades. When another employee at the facility, a mail supervisor, contracted anthrax a few days later, it quickly became clear that this was not an accident. The second employee recovered after treatment with antibiotics. Although the FBI did not discover a letter, it was suspected that Stevens had opened a letter at his desk prior to leaving on vacation on September 26 and had inhaled a lethal dose of the spores.

About the same time as Stevens had received his letter, a staff member working for NBC News in New York City opened a letter addressed to Tom Brokaw. She saw a doctor on October 1, who suspected she had contracted cutaneous anthrax. The letter was postmarked September 18 from Trenton and had no return address. Both she and another employee were treated for anthrax and recovered. Two weeks later, reports surfaced in New York City that the young child of an ABC employee and a staff member from CBS had tested positive for cutaneous anthrax. Although no letters were discovered, it was suspected that letters had been sent to these studios. These events, combined with the Florida incident, made it clear that these were not accidents but a deliberate terrorist incident.

On October 15, a staffer for Senate Majority Leader Tom Daschle (D–SD) opened a letter also postmarked from Trenton, dated October 9. It contained a brief message and a white powder, which was later identified as anthrax. Nearly thirty people in the building had been exposed, and treatments of ciprofloxacin were initiated almost immediately. Only a few people were thought to have actually contracted inhalation anthrax. The House of Representatives recessed in a panic, and investigators fanned out to identify where anthrax contamination may have spread and what other letters may have been sent. What they had overlooked was the main postal facility through which the letter had probably been sent. Postal workers in Trenton developed symptoms of cutaneous and inhalation anthrax. Two postal workers from Washington's Brentwood postal facility died of inhalation anthrax on October 22. Two additional workers were confirmed as having inhalation anthrax the next day, with nine others showing symptoms. They have all recovered, following intense antibiotic treatments.

Federal agencies all over Washington implemented security measures to screen all incoming mail, with some deciding to irradiate all mail prior to allowing it forward. Although they set everyone's mail back for up to three months, these measures were successful in stopping a fourth letter, addressed to Senator Patrick Leahy (D–VT). Like the Daschle letter, it had a return address from a Greendale School in Franklin Park, New Jersey (although there is no such school in that town). This letter, being unopened, was chock-full of anthrax spores and represented an important find for the investigators, who took this (and all other letters) to the laboratories at Fort Detrick for analysis.

The anthrax powder was finely milled and coated with a surfactant that allowed the particles to literally "float" like a vapor.

It was in a form that would have made it an ideal weapon, thus the term "weaponized" anthrax.[8] This peculiarity made some believe that the anthrax had to have come from a nation that had invested in an offensive biological weapons program. Others suspected that the person who sent the letters could be someone inside the U.S. Army's CB defense community, perhaps a scientist from Dugway Proving Ground or Fort Detrick. Yet FBI profilers do not believe this is necessarily the case; the pattern of sending these letters to media outlets and Democratic senators seems to be the pattern of a male loner or militant with a scientific background. Despite a national investigation, the perpetrator has remained at large. Whether he or she will strike again is unknown; did the perpetrator use up all the available stocks, or is this individual just afraid of being caught? In all, it is believed that at least twenty-two people contracted anthrax, of whom eleven contracted cutaneous anthrax and eleven contracted inhalation anthrax. Five people died, including an elderly woman in Connecticut (demonstrating the frightening aspects of the perhaps unintentional cross-contamination of letters in the postal delivery service).

Without going too much into depth here, there are a number of interesting follow-on issues arising from this incident. One might comment on the vulnerability of the public within the United States to acts of terrorism, when this case of deliberate and repeated attacks cannot be tracked down and closed. One might also observe the thousands of hoax incidents that arose from these events, some of them meant to be in jest and many others merely capitalizing on people's fears. This incident has driven a strong response from the U.S. government to prepare and issue guidance to federal, state, and local agencies on how to address future CB terrorism incidents. However, in the opinion of this author, the U.S. government guidance that citizens should prepare "safe rooms" in their homes, using plastic sheeting and duct tape, is very misguided. No amount of plastic sheeting would have saved the five individuals who died from inhalation anthrax in 2001, and certainly no safe rooms would have protected the hundreds of people who were exposed to anthrax while they were at work. It will take a more serious analysis and understanding of the threat of CB terrorism and effective measures to counter these incidents before the American public can take rational steps to be prepared against future attacks.

Summary

Whenever one force has used CB weapons in conjunction with conventional weapons against an unprepared force, the offensive force wins, and wins quickly. That is the value of CB weapons. If the defending force fails to persuade the attackers not to use CB weapons, whether through diplomacy or threats of retaliation, or fails to intercept the weapons prior to their dispersing their payloads, it will require the appropriate protection to maintain its continuity. This lesson has been repeated throughout history, and the military force that does not understand this lesson will ultimately be defeated.

The first four case studies have nothing in common with the more recent issue of CB terrorism, for the terrorist incidents target civilians completely unprepared and unschooled in the area of CB warfare, but one parallel can be offered: The key to responding to CB warfare, whether on the battlefield or in a city, lies in knowledge, training, and equipment. If our investments in any of these three areas decline, then the potential impact of a CB warfare attack increases in scope. Consider that the DOD investment in CB defense has amounted to less than one-half of one percent of the total DOD budget for decades. When an actual threat arises, the military and political leadership often think a quick transfusion of funds to buy the necessary equipment right before the troops hit the field will solve the matter. This simplistic attitude continues to be the true source of risk for U.S. forces on the modern battlefield, forcing the troops to "cram" to increase their readiness rather than to maintain an acceptable defensive level before the crises occur. Unfortunately, as long as the military and political leadership view CB warfare as an aberration and not a constant threat throughout history, the failure to adequately invest in a robust CB defense capability will continue to put both military service members and civilians at risk.

Notes

1. L. F. Haber, *The Poisonous Cloud: Chemical Warfare in the First World War* (Oxford: Clarendon Press, 1986), 77, 186. Also see "Battles: The Battle of Caporetto, 1917" (on-line; available: http://www.firstworldwar.com/battles/caporetto.htm; accessed November 2002).

2. John Cookson and Judith Nottingham, *A Survey of Chemical and Biological Warfare* (New York: Monthly Review Press, 1969), 9–10.

3. Sterling Seagrave, *Yellow Rain: A Journey through the Terror of Chemical Warfare* (New York: M. Evans, 1981), 124–125.

4. Albert J. Mauroni, *America's Struggle with Chemical-Biological Warfare* (Westport, CT: Praeger, 2000), 199–214. A more detailed description of the Iran-Iraq War can be found in Anthony H. Cordesman and Abraham R. Wagner, *The Lessons of Modern War*, vol. 2, *The Iran-Iraq War* (Boulder, CO: Westview Press, 1990).

5. Albert J. Mauroni, *Chemical-Biological Defense: U.S. Military Policies and Decisions in the Gulf War* (Westport, CT: Praeger, 1998). This section, discussing the U.S. CB defense preparations for the Gulf War was derived from this book, which goes into much more detail on the specific issues, including the Khamisiyah depot incident.

6. This probably sounds strange today, but the truth of the matter was that U.S. war plans assumed the Soviets would use chemical weapons in heavy concentrations. If the Soviets were to have used biological weapons, things would have gotten ugly very quickly. Because biological organisms do not stand out in the natural environment and because detectors for biological agents have to be much more sensitive than detectors for chemical agents, the decision was made to focus on the easier and more relevant systems: chemical detectors. Of course, since then, things have changed. Military and civilian leadership have put more money into the program, and today biological detection takes priority over chemical detection.

7. For illustrations of the letters, see the web page http://www.fbi.gov/pressrel/pressrel01/102301.htm; accessed March 2003.

8. An excellent discussion on the research conducted on the anthrax samples can be found in Richard Preston, *The Demon in the Freezer* (New York: Random House, 2002), 163–202.

8

Organizations, Associations, and Government and International Agencies

There are a number of organizations, associations, and private and governmental agencies involved in the business of CB defense and CB warfare (CBW), and more are coming into existence every year. A small number are arms control agencies, some are think tanks, others are commercial companies supporting the military, and most are government agencies. In the past, this area has not had much commercial interest. However, there is a growing interest by those who have begun looking into the CB defense aspects of homeland security. This chapter will focus more on the agencies that primarily work in CB defense and what they do rather than on the many industries involved in the business of producing CB defense products. Chapter 9 will include sources of information for companies and other players that are involved in CB defense but not necessarily as primary agents.

As with any reference book, this information may be ephemeral. Internet addresses change; agencies change their names or reorganize. But the majority of these groups should remain active. Some of these agencies are relatively young, whereas others have worked in this area for many years, and, no doubt, new ones are coming. Some agencies will not be open to research questions from the general public, but one can always ask the questions and start a dialogue.

The Australia Group
c/o The Australian Embassy
4 rue Jean Rey
Paris 75724 France
Internet: http://www.australiagroup.net/index_en.htm

The Australia Group is an informal group that aims to allow exporting or transshipping countries to minimize the risk of assisting CB weapons proliferation. The group meets annually to discuss ways in which the national export-licensing measures of its thirty-four participants can collectively be made more effective in ensuring that would-be proliferaters are unable to obtain necessary ingredients for CBW programs, which are banned under international law.

Participants in the Australia Group do not undertake any legally binding obligations: The effectiveness of the cooperation between participants depends solely on their commitment to CB weapons nonproliferation goals and on the effectiveness of the measures they each take on a national basis. All states participating in the Australia Group are parties to the Chemical Weapons Convention and the Biological Weapons Convention and strongly support efforts under those conventions to rid the world of chemical and biological weapons.

Carnegie Endowment for International Peace (CEIP)
Non-Proliferation Project
1779 Massachusetts Avenue, NW
Washington, D.C. 20036
(202) 483-7600
Internet: http://www.ceip.org/files/nonprolif/

The Carnegie Endowment for International Peace is a private, nonprofit organization dedicated to advancing cooperation between nations and promoting active international engagement by the United States. Its focus is on public policy analysis of international politics. Its nonproliferation site offers research, analysis, and comments on the nation's programs, CBW agents, links to on-line resources, and recent news on CBW issues. The Endowment publishes *Foreign Policy*, one of the worlds leading magazines on international politics and economics, reaching a readership in more than 120 countries.

Center for Counterproliferation Research (CCR)
300 Fifth Avenue, SW
Fort Lesley J. McNair
Washington, D.C. 20319-5066
Internet: http://www.ndu.edu/centercounter/

The CCR has a broad mandate for education and research in the areas of nonproliferation and counterproliferation policies and programs, doctrine and training, and NBC operational effects. Their small staff, residing at the National Defense University, conducts its research and hosts collaborative meetings with defense civilians and military leaders to enhance their awareness of the challenges and requirements for operating in an NBC environment and to shape defense policy, programs, and military operations.

Centers for Disease Control and Prevention (CDC)
1600 Clifton Road
Atlanta, Georgia 30333
(404) 639-3311
Internet: http://www.cdc.org/

The CDC falls under the Department of Health and Human Services and is recognized as the lead federal agency for protecting health and safety. It focuses on developing and applying disease prevention and control, environmental health, and health promotion and education activities designed to improve the health of those living in the United States. The CDC has been involved with CB warfare and defense issues since at least 1970. Its activities in this area include reviewing aspects of the chemical demilitarization program, creating acquisition and transfer protocols for selected biological agents within the United States, and working with the Department of Defense on medical surveillance and occupational health safety standards related to CBW agents. It is, of course, deeply involved in national issues involving the preparations for and response to a potential BW terrorist incident in the United States.

Chemical and Biological Arms Control Institute (CBACI)
1747 Pennsylvania Avenue, NW
Washington, D.C. 20006
(202) 296-3550
Internet: http://www.cbaci.org

The mission of the CBACI is to address the challenges to global security and stability with a special focus on CB weapons, arms control, and nonproliferation issues. It exercises this role through the development of programs, training, and outreach to communicate issues of immediate national concerns to national and international leaders. The staff produces a large assortment of publications and reports on CBW issues, training modules for those involved in arms control efforts, and briefings for industry, government, and the media.

Chemical and Biological Defense
Information Analysis Center (CBIAC)
P.O. Box 196
Gunpowder, Maryland 21010-0196
(410) 676-9030
Internet: http://www.cbiac.apgea.army.mil/

The CBIAC is one of a number of information analysis centers overseen by the Defense Technical Information Center (DTIC). Its mission is to generate, acquire, process, analyze, and disseminate CB science and technology information for the government, military agencies, and private agencies under contract to the government. Its information collection contains just about every aspect of technical analysis of CB warfare, from warfighting requirements to domestic preparedness to treaty issues. Its products include handbooks, databases, and a quarterly bulletin, in addition to its data-gathering and dissemination function.

Chemical Corps Regimental Association (CCRA)
P.O. Box 437
Fort Leonard Wood, Missouri 65473
(573) 336-2049
Internet: http://www.nti.net/ccra/

The CCRA is an organization of military (active and retired) and civilian supporters of the Army Chemical Corps. Its purpose includes promoting the heritage, esprit, and professionalism of the

Chemical Corps, including soliciting donations and gifts of funds, materials, services, and artifacts on behalf of the Chemical Corps Museum. Members meet annually at the Worldwide Chemical Conference, held at Fort Leonard Wood, Missouri. The CCRA links the active-duty military members of the Chemical Corps with its history.

Chemical Weapons Working Group (CWWG)
P.O. Box 467
Berea, Kentucky 40403
(859) 986-7565
Internet: http://www.cwwg.org/

The CWWG is a coalition of U.S. citizens formed to oppose the incineration of chemical weapons as an unsafe disposal method and to work with government officials to promote disposal technologies that do not rely on open emissions. The group coordinates with a wide number of grassroots organizations in other states on the issue of chemical demilitarization.

Defence Research Establishment—Suffield (DRES)
Box 4000, Stn Main
Medicine Hat, Alberta T1A 8K6, Canada
(403) 544-4655; (403) 544-4656
Internet: http://www.dres.dnd.ca/ResearchTech/Products/
CB_PRODUCTS/index_e.html

DRES is the Canadian government laboratory equivalent to the Defence Science and Technology Laboratory (Dstl) and Edgewood, researching and developing CB defense equipment to provide Canadian forces with the capabilities required to survive and sustain combat missions in contaminated environments. Its scientists have cooperatively worked on research and development efforts with the United States and the United Kingdom since World War II.

Defence Science and Technology
Laboratory (Dstl)—Porton Down
Dstl Porton, Salisbury
Wiltshire SP4 0JQ, United Kingdom
Internet: http://www.dstl.gov.uk/

The Dstl was formerly known as the Defence Evaluation and Research Agency (DERA), the U.K. Ministry of Defence's military science and technology advisor and developer. Porton Down, in particular, is the main U.K. laboratory that researches chemical and biological defense issues. Porton Down and the U.S. equivalent, Edgewood Arsenal in Maryland, have been cooperatively working together on CB defense topics since 1917. In addition to sharing a past in weaponizing CBW agents, the two sites also share some controversy as to human volunteer testing of CBW agents.

Defense Advanced Research Projects Agency (DARPA)
3701 North Fairfax Drive
Arlington, Virginia 22203-1714
(703) 526-6630
Internet: http://www.darpa.mil/

DARPA is the central research and development organization for the DOD in the area of basic science and technology and applied research and development projects. It specializes in pursuing areas that have both a high risk and potentially high payoff, areas that may be commercially risky for private agencies to explore. In the CB defense area, it tends to specialize in biotechnology, decontamination, and medical biological defense efforts. When these areas become mature and show potential for applications, DARPA transitions the information to the appropriate military laboratories.

Defense Logistics Agency (DLA)
8725 John J. Kingman Road
Suite 2545
Fort Belvoir, Virginia 22060-6221
(703) 767-6200
Internet: http://www.dla.mil

The Defense Logistics Agency supplies the nation's military services and several civilian agencies with equipment, spare parts, and practically all the consumable items the military needs to operate. In regards to CB defense, DLA procures and distributes the protective clothing (jackets, trousers, boots, and gloves), medical defense countermeasures, and decontaminants. Its headquarters is at Fort Belvoir, Virginia, but its Defense Supply Center in Philadelphia is the main hub for distributing CB defense protective clothing.

Defense Threat Reduction Agency (DTRA)
8725 John J. Kingman Road
Suite 6201
Fort Belvoir, Virginia 22060-6201
(703) 767-5870
Internet: http://www.dtra.mil/cb/cb_index.html

DTRA was formed in 1998 from the former Defense Special Weapons Agency (which was the Defense Nuclear Agency and, before that, the Defense Atomic Support Agency, and originally the Armed Forces Special Weapons Project) and other government agencies, created under Defense Secretary William Cohen's Defense Reform Initiative. DTRA has a wide mission as a defense agency to assist the DOD in reducing the threat of NBC weapons and preparing for the future threat. This include arms control research and development, CB defense science and technology, and support to military forces that have systems designed to counter CB weapons proliferation.

Department of Energy (DOE) CB Nonproliferation Program (CBNP)
1000 Independence Avenue, SW
Washington, D.C. 20585
(800)-dial-DOE ([800] 342-5363)
Internet: http://www.energy.gov/aboutus/org/natlabs.html

The DOE has several initiatives in the area of CB defense, most executed through its national laboratories. Sandia National Laboratory is in New Mexico, Lawrence Livermore National Laboratory is in California, and Los Alamos National Laboratory is in New Mexico. These labs, once more prominent in nuclear arms research, execute most of the DOE's CB defense research and development efforts, often with an eye to developing CB defense equipment for emergency responders, while coordinating their technology efforts with the DOD. Oak Ridge National Laboratory has supported several chemical demilitarization analyses. The DOE CBNP has been transferred to the Department of Homeland Security to continue its work there.

Department of Justice Office for Domestic Preparedness (ODP)
810 Seventh Street, NW
Washington, D.C. 20531

(800) 368-6498
Internet: http://www.ojp.usdoj.gov/odp/

The ODP is the program office within the Department of Justice responsible for enhancing the capability of state and local jurisdictions to respond to and mitigate the consequences of incidents of domestic terrorism, with a focus on CB incidents. Attorney General Janet Reno established this office in 1998 to develop and administer training and equipment-assistance programs for state and local response agencies. In October 1999, it assumed the 120-city training program that had been initiated by the DOD in 1997. The agency addresses equipment acquisition and support, training and technical assistance, and exercise development and support. This includes the operation of a helpline for state and local emergency responders and running the Center for Domestic Preparedness in Anniston, Alabama. This office has been transferred to the Department of Homeland Security.

Department of Veterans Affairs
Washington, D.C. 20111
Internet: http://www.va.gov/

The Department of Veterans Affairs has been closely involved with health issues related to exposure or suspected exposure to CBW agents and herbicides. This work includes funding several grants at universities and other academic centers for research into the potential effects resulting from CB warfare exposure. It is currently working with the Defense Department on issues such as Project SHAD, Agent Orange, Gulf War illnesses, and studies on low-level exposure to chemical warfare agents.

Dugway Proving Ground
Commander, U.S. Army Dugway Proving Ground
Attn: Public Affairs Office
Dugway, Utah 84022-5000
(435) 831-3409
Internet: http://www.dugway.army.mil

Dugway Proving Ground is the Army's test and evaluation center for CB defense, smoke and obscurants, illumination, and munitions research and development efforts. It is a designated DOD major range and test facility base. Built during World War II, located nearly ninety miles from Salt Lake City, the center is most famous for its role in the alleged sheep-poisoning incident of 1968. Although there are no more open-air toxic CB agent tests at the site, it does continue to support open-air simulant tests of CB defense equipment as well as toxic-agent tests of equipment within specially designed and protected facilities.

Edgewood Chemical Biological Center (ECBC)
5183 Blackhawk Road
Building E3330
Attn: AMSSB-RAS
Aberdeen Proving Ground, Maryland 21010-5424
(410) 436-4347

ECBC is the Army's principal research and development center for CB defense technology, engineering, and service. Although the organization's name has changed several times since 1917, its mission of providing the military with the majority of its detection, protection, and decontamination equipment has remained constant. It was responsible for the development of CBW munitions before the United States ended its offensive programs, and it continues to support smoke and obscurant programs for the Army in addition to CB defense equipment. An Army reorganization created a higher headquarters, the U.S. Army Soldier and Biological-Chemical Command (SBCCOM), to supervise the center and the Army's soldier system products at Natick, Massachusetts.

Federal Emergency Management Agency (FEMA)
500 C Street, SW
Washington, D.C. 20472
(202) 566-1600
Internet: http://www.fema.gov/

FEMA's mission is to respond to, plan for, recover from, and mitigate against disasters. Its normal practice is to respond to natural disasters, but in this area, it also leads the preparation for potential chemical agent accidents and incidents in communities near the eight chemical weapons stockpiles in the United States. It is the keeper of the Federal Response Plan, which establishes the process and structure for a coordinated delivery of federal assistance to address the consequences of any major disaster or emergency declared under the Stafford Act. This includes preparing for CB terrorism incidents, both reducing the vulnerability of people and property to terrorist acts and preparing for the response and recovery from a terrorist act.

**Federation of American Scientists (FAS) Chemical
and Biological Arms Control Program**
1717 K Street, NW
Suite 209
Washington, D.C. 20036
(202) 546-3300
Internet: http://www.fas.org/bwc/index.html

Founded in 1945 by scientists of the Manhattan Project, FAS is dedicated to the responsible use of science and technology. It is a nonprofit group engaging in analysis and public education on a broad range of science, technology, and public policy issues. Its CB Arms Control Program features current news and analysis on CBW issues as well as a comprehensive section discussing the CWC and BWC treaties.

**Harvard-Sussex Program (HSP) on CBW Armament
and Arms Limitation**
University of Sussex
Brighton, East Sussex, BN1 9RF, United Kingdom
+ 44 (0) 1273 678 172
Internet: http://www.susx.ac.uk/spru/hsp/index.html

HSP is a long-standing collaboration between Harvard University in the United States and the University of Sussex in the United Kingdom. The program undertakes research, publication, and training in support of informed public policy on international CBW issues. Its aim is to promote the global elimination of CB weapons and to strengthen constraints against the hostile use of biomedical technologies. Its quarterly *CBW Conventions Bulletin* is available on-line.

Henry L. Stimson Center's CBW Nonproliferation Project
11 Dupont Circle
Suite 900
Washington, D.C. 20036
(202) 223-5956
Internet: http://www.stimson.org/cbw/

The Stimson Center is a nonprofit, nonpartisan institution devoted to enhancing international peace and security through a combination of analysis and public outreach. Its work covers a range of topics, from the elimination of NBC weapons to the roles and missions of the U.S. armed forces. Its CBW Nonproliferation Project examines a wide range of topics, including arms control, CB terrorism, and general CB weapons issues, not restricted merely to the United States. The project also issues a *CBW Chronicle* discussing recent events in these areas.

Johns Hopkins University Center for Civilian Biodefense Strategies
Hampton House
624 North Broadway
Baltimore, Maryland 21205
(410) 223-1667
Internet: http://www.hopkins-biodefense.org/

The Center for Civilian Biodefense Studies seeks to guide policy and practices that will reduce the likelihood that biological weapons are used and that will, should prevention fail, lessen the suffering and consequences that would result from their use. The Center is a nonprofit organization chartered under Johns Hopkins University. They coordinate events, provide information on BW issues, and frequently write articles and meet with government representatives to discuss BW issues.

Joint Requirements Office for Chemical, Biological, Radiological, and Nuclear Defense (JRO-CBRND)
Joint Chiefs of Staff
Attn: J8/JRO
The Pentagon
Room 1E973
Washington, D.C. 20318-8000

The JRO-CBRND formally began operations on October 1, 2002, as the single office within the Department of Defense under the chairman of the Joint Chiefs of Staff to be responsible for the planning, coordination, and approval of joint chemical, biological, radiological, and nuclear defense operational requirements, medical and nonmedical, and to serve as the focal point for service, combatant command, and Joint Staff requirements generation. This office addresses all requirements generation and program analysis issues within passive defense, consequence management, force protection, and homeland security, and it collaborates with appropriate Joint Staff elements on chemical, biological, radiological, and nuclear defense policy, operational readiness, logistics, and sustainment issues.

Monterey Institute of International Studies (MIIS)
CB Weapons Nonproliferation Program (CBWNP)
460 Pierce Street
Monterey, California 93940
(831) 647-4154
Internet: http://cns.miis.edu/cns/projects/cbwnp/index.htm

The MIIS CBWNP monitors the global proliferation of CB weapons and develops strategies for halting and reversing their spread. The program's research focuses on understanding why states and subnational groups are motivated to acquire CB weapon systems. Its products include reports on current CBW issues, nonproliferation treaties, and country CBW capabilities; a database of terrorist incidents involving CBW materials; and case studies.

Natick Soldier Systems Center (NSSC)
Kansas Street
Natick, Massachusetts 01760
(508) 233-4001
Internet: http://www.natick.army.mil/

Natick Soldier Systems is responsible for researching, developing, fielding, and managing food, clothing, shelters, airdrop systems, and soldier support items. Although they are perhaps better-known for having developed Meals Ready to Eat (MREs), tents, parachutes, soldiers' uniforms, and other clothing items, in the CB defense sector they develop chemical protective suits and transportable collective protection shelters. The labs came under U.S. Army Soldier and Biological-Chemical Command (SBC-COM) in 1998 as a result of an Army reorganization.

National Academies of Sciences (NAS)
500 Fifth Street, NW
Washington, D.C. 20001
(202) 334-2000
Internet: http://www.nas.edu/

The NAS is a private, nonprofit society of distinguished and independent scholars engaged in scientific and engineering research, dedicated to the furtherance of science and technology and to their use for the general welfare. The National Research Council is the main agency under the NAS that advises Congress on the chemical demilitarization program and the CB defense program, although the NAS's Institute of Medicine can be involved in particular CB defense-related issues. Its reports are available to the public on-line and through its National Academy Press.

National Defense Industrial Association (NDIA)
2111 Wilson Boulevard
Suite 400
Arlington, Virginia 22201-3061
(703) 522-1820
Internet: http://www.ndia.org/committees/chembio/index.cfm

The NDIA is a group of 950 companies from the entire spectrum of defense and national industrial bases, including organizations that sell goods and services to the various government agencies of the U.S. executive branch. The group provides a legal and ethical forum for the interchange of ideas between the government and industry to resolve problems of concern to both, such as research and development, procurement, and logistics support. There is a CB defense division within NDIA that coordinates meetings between government and industry to exchange information and constructive counsel on current CB defense topics.

NBC Industry Group
P.O. Box 2781
Springfield, Virginia 22152
Internet: http://www.nbcindustrygroup.com/

The NBC Industry Group is composed of about 100 companies, nonprofit organizations, and consultants who support NBC defense activities. Their purpose is to provide information on NBC civil and military matters to the U.S. military forces, other appropriate agencies of the United States, and the general public. Their statement of purpose also includes improving understanding of the importance of NBC defense and its contributions to U.S. ability to carry out its global responsibilities. This group meets quarterly to discuss NBC defense issues with various government and industry representatives, exchanging information on current events in this area and discussing emerging trends and requirements. They are not lobbyists but, rather, a collection of interested businesses with a common interest in maintaining a warm industrial base in this sector.

Nuclear Threat Initiative (NTI)
1747 Pennsylvania Avenue, NW
Seventh Floor
Washington, D.C. 20006
(202) 296-4810
Internet: http://www.nti.org/

Ted Turner and former Senator Sam Nunn founded the NTI in January 2001. This organization's mission is to strengthen global security by reducing the risk of use and preventing the spread of nuclear, biological, and chemical weapons. It accomplishes this through increasing public awareness, promoting studies in particular program areas, and investigating areas that governments could execute on a larger scale. Its web site includes a research library that includes information on CB warfare issues as well as a tutorial on weapons of mass destruction.

Office of the Deputy Assistant to the Secretary of Defense for Chemical and Biological Defense (DATSD[CBD])
The Pentagon
Washington, D.C.
Internet: http://www.acq.osd.mil/cp/index.html

The DATSD(CBD) falls under the assistant to the secretary of defense for nuclear and chemical and biological defense programs (ATSD[NCB]), who reports to the undersecretary of defense for acquisition, technology, and logistics (USD[AT&L]). This office acts as the single focal point within the Office of the Secretary of Defense (OSD) responsible for oversight, coordination, and integration of the DOD's Chemical and Biological Defense Program. This office develops the DOD Annual Report to Congress on CB Defense in addition to providing other related reports and testimonies to congressional committees. These reports can be accessed at its web site.

Organization for the Prohibition of Chemical Weapons (OPCW)
2517 JR
The Hague
The Netherlands

+ 31 (70) 416-3300
Internet: http://www.opcw.org/

The OPCW is charged with implementing the provisions of the
Chemical Weapons Convention in order to achieve the vision of a
world free of chemical weapons and in which cooperation in
chemistry for peaceful purposes for all is fostered. The headquarters proposes policies for implementing the convention to the
member states that have signed the CWC, and it develops and
delivers programs with and for the members.

Pine Bluff Arsenal
Commander, U.S. Army Pine Bluff Arsenal
Attn: Public Affairs Office
Pine Bluff, Arkansas 71604
(870) 540-3000
Internet: http://www.pba.army.mil/

Pine Bluff Arsenal was established in 1941 to load incendiary
bombs and chemical munitions. For a short time in the 1950s and
1960s, it was the site of a biological weapons production plant,
and in the 1980s, of a binary chemical weapons production facility. Today it is the second-largest stateside chemical weapons
stockpile site, and it continues to fill smoke and white phospho-
rus munitions. It also rebuilds and repairs protective masks, fab-
ricates and tests CB filters, and provides other maintenance functions for CB defense equipment.

Program Executive Office for CB Defense (PEO CBD)
5203 Leesburg Pike
Suite 1609
Falls Church, Virginia 22041-3203
(703) 681-9600
Internet: http://www.jpobd.net
http://www.sbccom.apgea.army.mil/RDA/pmnbc/

The Army recently reorganized its acquisition practices to create
a PEO for all CB defense research and development programs it
executes. This included combining the Joint Program Office for
Biological Defense at Falls Church, Virginia, with the Project
Manager for NBC Defense Systems at Aberdeen Proving Ground,
Maryland, under one organization. The new group will also
include a Project Manager for CB Medical Systems, covering the

research at Fort Detrick. In April 2003, the USD(AT&L) elevated this organization to become a joint PEO, responsible for all DOD CB defense systems.

Program Manager for Chemical Demilitarization (PMCD)
4585 Parrish Road
Building E
Aberdeen Proving Ground
Aberdeen, Maryland 21010-4005
(410) 436-3629
Internet: http://www.pmcd.army.mil/default.asp

The PMCD was established in 1985 to dispose of the 31,000 tons of chemical agents and munitions located at nine chemical weapons stockpiles. Although the U.S. Army Soldier and Biological-Chemical Command (SBCCOM) manages the safe storage of these munitions, PMCD is charged with constructing the disposal facilities at each of the nine sites and executing the disposal process in line with environmental and health safety regulations. Its mission was to complete disposal within the CWC deadline of April 2007, but congressional insistence on the use of alternative technologies other than incineration has lengthened that mission, possibly to 2012. The PMCD web site describes the organization and its mission but is primarily a tool to educate the public about ongoing issues at the chemical stockpile sites.

Stockholm International Peace Research Institute (SIPRI)
Signalistgatan 9
SE-169 70 Solna, Sweden
+ 46-8-655 97 00
Internet: http://projects.sipri.se/cbw/cbw-mainpage.html

SIPRI is an international research foundation, established in 1966, that examines questions of conflict and cooperation toward international peace and security, with the aim of contributing to an understanding of the conditions for peaceful solutions of international conflicts and for a stable peace. It supports several research areas, including arms control, export controls, military expenditures and technology, and, of course, CB weapons.

U.S. Air Force Counterproliferation Center (CPC)
325 Chennault Circle
Maxwell Air Force Base, Alabama 36112

(334) 953-2119

Internet: http://www.au.af.mil/au/awc/awcgate/awc-cps.htm

The CPC is hosted by the Air University at Maxwell Air Force Base and funded to undertake and direct counterproliferation research and education. This includes assessing NBC and missile proliferation threats and the means of addressing these threats. It also includes research and education on related topics as appropriate. The CPC hosts research projects, organizes Air Force counterproliferation (CP) conferences, sets up a CP speakers series and a CP information depository and clearing house, publishes books and occasional papers, provides CP courses and briefings for senior officers, and provides CP curriculum and faculty development support to the Air University.

U.S. Army Chemical School and Center (USACMLS)
320 MANSCEN Loop
Fort Leonard Wood, Missouri 65473-8929
(573) 563-8053
Internet: http://www.wood.army.mil/usacmls/

The Chemical School is the Army's center for doctrine, training, and leader development for the Chemical Corps. The Air Force, Navy, and Marine Corps also have training detachments located at Fort Leonard Wood. In addition to the schoolhouse activities, the Chemical Defense Training Facility allows students to enter an actual toxic-agent environment as a confidence-building measure to assert that the protective ensembles, detectors, and decontaminants all do work.

U.S. Army Medical Research Institute for Chemical Defense (USAMRICD)
3100 Ricketts Point Road
Aberdeen Proving Ground, Maryland 21010-5400
(410) 426-3628
Internet: http://chemdef.apgea.army.mil/

USAMRICD is a subordinate organization of the Army's Medical Research and Materiel Command (MRMC) at Fort Detrick, Maryland. Its mission includes researching and developing medical countermeasures to CW agents and training medical personnel in the medical management of chemical casualties. Although its name dates back to 1981, the Edgewood-based organization has been responsible for medical chemical defense since 1922 under other names.

**U.S. Army Medical Research Institute
for Infectious Diseases (USAMRIID)**
1425 Porter Street
Fort Detrick, Maryland 21702-5011
Internet: http://www.usamriid.army.mil/

USAMRIID, also a subordinate organization under the Army's Medical Research and Materiel Command (MRMC), conducts research to develop strategies, products, information, procedures, and training programs for medical defense against both BW threats and naturally occurring infectious diseases that require special containment. Its research covers all medical countermeasures, vaccines, and drugs used by the military for BW defense, and it has one of only two laboratories in the country with the capability to study highly hazardous viruses at biosafety level 4 (BL-4), or maximum biological containment. The other BL-4 suite is at the CDC in Atlanta, Georgia.

U.S. Army Nuclear and Chemical Agency (USANCA)
7150 Heller Loop
Suite 101
Springfield, Virginia 22150-3198
(703) 806-7870

USANCA's mission is to provide expert technical support and assistance to Army elements worldwide and to other U.S. government agencies and NATO agencies engaged in NBC programs. This includes managing an NBC weapons effects database, establishing NBC contamination survivability standards, and participating in international standardization of NBC defense matters. Its experts also work on chemical surety matters and support the Army's Chemical Stockpile Emergency Preparedness Program.

U.S. Army Research Laboratory (ARL)
Swan Creek Inn
Building 2207
Aberdeen Proving Ground, Maryland 21005
(410) 278-5964
Internet: http://www.arl.army.mil/slad/Services/
Chem-Bio-new.html

ARL conducts much of the research required to determine NBC contamination survivability standards and to develop data that permit the Army to construct equipment that is resistant to the effects of CB weapons and to the corrosive nature of decontaminants.

U.S. Army Soldier and Biological
Chemical Command (SBCCOM)
5183 Blackhawk Road
Building E5101
Aberdeen Proving Ground, Maryland 21010-5424
(410) 436-4345
Internet: http://www.sbccom.apgea.army.mil/

SBCCOM is the Army's major command overseeing Edgewood and Natick's research, development, and acquisition programs, which account for more than 60 percent of all military CB defense development efforts as well as the eight state-side chemical weapons stockpiles and the Alternative Chemical Weapons Assessment program. This command also oversaw the Domestic Preparedness Program, which sent trainers to more than 100 cities to train their emergency responders on responding to potential CB terrorism incidents. The organization oversees Rocky Mountain Arsenal as it cleans up decades of weapons and chemical production. It also oversees the fielding and surveillance of Army CB defense equipment, such as the masks, chemical detection equipment, decontamination systems, and collective protection systems, through its offices at Rock Island Arsenal in Illinois. This organization is reorganizing in 2003, but whatever organization replaces it will still be at Aberdeen and will still be focusing on CB defense issues.

U.S. Army Technical Escort Unit (TEU)
5183 Blackhawk Road
Attn: AMSSB-OTE-PAO
Aberdeen Proving Ground, Maryland 21010-5424
(410) 436-6455
Internet: http://teu.sbccom.army.mil/

The Army's TEU provides the DOD and other federal agencies with a unique, immediate, and global response capability for CBW material. This includes sampling, detecting and monitoring, rendering safe, packaging, escorting, and disposing of the material, be it a leaking chemical munition, a terrorist device, or a battlefield weapon. Originally formed in 1944 to escort U.S. chemical weapons to and from the United States, it now supports a wide host of agencies with its CB munitions and material expertise during peace and war.

9

Print and Nonprint Resources

There are many resource materials about chemical and biological warfare and related issues, but there are only a limited number of recent books on this topic. Many publishers see CB warfare as a specialty field and not an issue of interest to the general public, and so, unfortunately, there is not a great variety of books available, but there are several very good ones out there. There were three general "surges" in literary publications corresponding with increased public interest: one following the Dugway Proving Ground incident in 1968, one during the military's campaign to develop binary chemical weapons in the 1980s, and one recently with the interest in biological terrorism caused by the anthrax-tainted letters. There are certainly more books available on various CBW topics than are listed here, especially on such specific issues as bioterrorism, the World War II accidental release of mustard agent into the port at Bari, Operation Ranch Hand, and others. The following list is focused more on the general topic of CB defense rather than on specific issues.

There are a few journals and magazines, newsletters, and government documents available that one may be able to obtain upon request through the right channels. The General Accounting

Office, for instance, has a wide variety of documents available at no cost through the Internet. Most of the journals and newsletters listed below tend to focus on current issues, but they often touch upon historical background material.

The real blessing for those interested in this subject is the World Wide Web, with its variety of information sources on CB warfare, weapon systems, and pictures of defense equipment. A great deal of information on the industries associated with CB defense programs can be found on the Internet, for instance. There is some repetition of information on particular issues, the sources may not be entirely objective, and it may take some cross-checking of the facts before these sources can be used, but those are the risks one takes with information on the Internet. Chapter 8 listed several Internet sites associated with particular agencies; the web sites listed below are not associated with major CB defense agencies but have well-developed information sources.

Books and Journal Articles

Alibek, Ken, with Stephen Handelman. *Biohazard: The Chilling True Story of the Largest Covert Biological Weapons Program in the World. Told from Inside by the Man Who Ran It.* New York: Random House, 1999.

Ken Alibek defected to the United States in 1992 after reaching the post of deputy chief of Biopreparat, the Soviet Union's offensive biological weapons research and development program. His narrative covers from the mid-1970s to the early 1990s, discussing the enormous scope of the Soviet Union's offensive BW program and its views and interactions with the United States. Of particular interest is his firsthand account of the Sverdlovsk anthrax outbreak that occurred in 1979.

Brophy, Leo P., and George J. B. Fisher. *The Chemical Warfare Service: Organizing for War.* Washington, DC: Office of the Chief of Military History, 1959.

The Army's history office wrote a number of books after World War II to record its efforts; they are often called the "Army green books" because of their covers. This volume, the first of a three-part history of the Chemical Warfare Service, relays a great amount of technical, organizational, and historical facts relating to its leadership, organization, and programs executed during World War II. The first volume starts with the origins of the Chemical Warfare Service, its mission and roles during World War I and the interwar period, its development and continued growth through World War II, field units, personnel management, and the training of chemical specialists, general soldiers, and civil defense officers.

Brophy, Leo P., Wyndham D. Miles, and Rexmond Cochrane. *The Chemical Warfare Service: From Laboratory to Field.* Washington, DC: Office of the Chief of Military History, 1966.

This is the second of three books in the Army's historical collection on the Chemical Warfare Service's work during World War II. The volume covers the research, development, procurement, and distribution of chemical warfare materiel. It also starts with research and development efforts undertaken in World War I and through the interwar period and discusses the toxic agents, incendiaries, smoke generators, and flamethrowers manufactured during this time as well as the protection equipment developed and fielded to the soldiers. It discusses in detail the industrial mobilization and procurement actions taken as well as transportation and storage issues. There is not much mention of the U.S. Army's offensive BW program (most of it was still classified), but there is a great deal of information on the development and use of chemical defense equipment, smoke generators, and incendiary munitions.

Brown, Frederic J. *Chemical Warfare: A Study in Restraints.* Westport, CT: Greenwood Press, 1981.

This book was originally published in 1968, but it has been reprinted due to high demand. Whereas the Army's "green books" focused on military developments during World War II, Brown's book covers from World War I into the interwar period and through the end of World War II. His book provides perhaps the most thorough coverage of U.S. CW military policy during this period even to this date. This review discusses the military's and political leadership's views and positions rather than technical points, intending to develop an understanding of the restraints that prevent the employment of chemical weapons during military conflicts.

Bryden, John. *Deadly Allies: Canada's Secret War, 1937–1947.* Toronto: McClelland and Stewart, 1989.

Unbeknownst to most people, Canada played a major role in the U.S. and U.K. CBW programs during World War II. This included developing anthrax and botulinum toxin as weaponized agents and conducting open-air CW trials at Suffield, Canada's parallel to Dugway Proving Ground. Although the Canadian program was much smaller in scale, this book offers a unique view into the U.S. and British programs that has not been seen elsewhere.

Clarke, Robin. *The Silent Weapons: The Realities of Chemical and Biological Warfare.* New York: David McKay, 1968.

Clarke's book is similar to a number of others written in this time, at the height of the U.S. CBW program and during the rise of environmental awareness movements. His book is very technically focused on the properties of CBW agents, but it offers a historical review in addition. There is a discussion on the potential employment of modern CBW agents and the use of herbicides in Vietnam.

Cole, Leonard A. *Clouds of Secrecy: The Army's Germ Warfare Tests over Populated Areas.* Totowa, NJ: Rowman and Littlefield, 1988.

Leonard Cole's first book on CB weapons tests undertaken by the U.S. military focuses on the open-air simulant tests executed in the United States during the 1950s and 1960s, including tests in Minneapolis, New York City, and San Francisco. He calls into question the legitimacy of the tests, the safety of the simulants used, and the U.S. government's lack of warning to the public. He examines the resurgence of the U.S. CBW program in the 1980s with a concern that such testing will be resumed in light of alleged Soviet threats.

Cole, Leonard A. *The Eleventh Plague: The Politics of Biological and Chemical Warfare.* New York: W. H. Freeman, 1997.

This book jumps across three main topics: open-air and human volunteer testing conducted in the 1960s that may have threatened the health and safety of the public, the military challenges posed by Iraq during the Gulf War with an interesting review of the civil defense effort by Israel, and the future challenges that nations face from BW terrorism and the continued proliferation of BW programs. Cole also discusses the challenges in developing a verifications protocol for the BWC.

Cordesman, Anthony H., and Abraham R. Wagner. *The Lessons of Modern War,* vol. 1, *The Arab-Israeli Conflicts, 1973–1989;* vol. 2, *The Iran-Iraq War;* and vol. 3, *The Afghan and Falklands Conflicts.* Boulder, CO: Westview Press, 1990. Vol. 4, *The Gulf War.* Boulder, CO: Westview Press, 1996.

Although this collection is not focused on CB warfare, the books do include excellent reviews of CBW threats and employment along with the discussions of the particular conflicts. These reviews include analysis of when and where CBW agents were allegedly used, what weapon systems delivered the agents, defensive measures taken, and the overall impact of CBW in each conflict. Cordesman's book on the Iran-Iraq War includes an excellent account of the chemical warfare incidents that occurred during that conflict, unparalleled in other books on the war. It has a similar level of detail on what occurred during the Gulf War in terms of CB warfare concerns and preparations.

Covert, Norman M. *Cutting Edge: A History of Fort Detrick, Maryland, 1943–1993.* Fort Detrick, MD: Public Affairs Office, 1993.

Although it could be easy to overlook this book as a strictly government public relations release and therefore biased, the book does relate a good history of Fort Detrick and its programs (BW-related and otherwise) since its inception in 1943. The book describes the various military activities located at Fort Detrick, its past commanders, and other relevant data. Photographs help illustrate the major facilities and former research efforts executed at the post, including the famous "8-ball" sphere where weaponized BW agents were tested.

Croddy, Eric, with Clarisa Perez-Armendariz and John Hart. *Chemical and Biological Warfare: A Comprehensive Survey for the Concerned Citizen.* New York: Copernicus Books, 2002.

This book is one of the most comprehensive and modern books written for the layman on CB warfare to date. Croddy covers threat agents and weapon systems; the countries that are developing these weapons; a history of CB warfare events, control, and disarmament issues; and CB terrorism. Even given the large area he covers, the author offers a practical and solid review of all the issues for those who lack a military background.

Dando, Malcolm. *Biological Warfare in the 21st Century: Biotechnology and the Proliferation of Biological Weapons.* London: Brassey's, 1994.

The author discusses research and development of BW agents and technologies, with some historical inputs, and leads into how one might execute nonproliferation efforts in the future. There is not much focus on military applications, but this book is very good reading for information on BW agents, research technologies, and arms control issues.

Douglass, Joseph D., and Neil C. Livingstone. *America the Vulnerable: The Threat of Chemical/Biological Warfare.* Lexington, KY: Lexington Books, 1987.

This book describes the proliferation of CBW agents and their potential use by the Soviet Union and nonstate actors through a series of vignettes and discussions on the issues. The authors emphasize the deadly nature of the threat and the need to implement actions—such as increased intelligence gathering, response teams, and arms control measures—to reduce vulnerability to the threat.

Falkenrath, Richard A., Robert D. Newman, and Bradley A. Thaher. *America's Achilles Heel.* Cambridge: MIT Press, 1998.

This book discusses the possibilities of both state and nonstate actors using NBC weapons in covert and terrorist applications. It attempts to answer the basic questions of what the known record is of attempts to acquire or use NBC weapons and what factors explain the character and frequency of past NBC weapons use. This book is more an examination of the policy of dealing with NBC weapons proliferation than a technical or historical review of NBC weapons per se.

Gilbert, Martin. *The First World War: A Complete History.* New York: Henry Holt, 1994.

Although many books on World War I overlook or minimize the role of gas attacks, Gilbert's book has a good deal of information on various CW attacks and on the impact of chemical warfare during this period. His book puts chemical warfare into perspective as a constant hazard that was dealt with as a matter of fact rather than an extraordinary condition of warfare. Other books, such as Liddell Hart's *A History of the World War* and S. L. A. Marshall's *World War I*, also cover chemical warfare well in their discussions on military operations during this war.

Haber, Ludwig Fritz. *The Poisonous Cloud: Chemical Warfare in the First World War.* New York: Oxford University Press, 1986.

Ludwig Haber is the son of Fritz Haber, the Nobel laureate and lead scientist for the German military's CW effort during World War I. Although written largely from the German perspective, the author's objective and frank findings are extremely valuable in understanding the true impacts of chemical warfare, minus the propaganda that has been spun about its use during the war since then. This book is perhaps the best sourcebook on chemical warfare during World War I. It is not in print now but is available through a print-on-demand program.

Harris, Robert, and Jeremy Paxman. *A Higher Form of Killing: The Secret Story of Chemical and Biological Warfare.* New York: Hill and Wang, 1982.

This book offers a critical look at the development of CB weapons, focusing mostly on the period between 1940 and 1980, with an opening chapter on World War I. Written by British authors, the book offers a good account of the offensive CBW research carried out by the United States and the United Kingdom during and after World War II. The authors' perspectives lean toward demonstrating that although CB weapons are indiscriminate terror weapons, attempts to rid the world of them have somehow failed.

Hart, Liddell. *A History of the World War.* Boston: Little, Brown & Co., 1935.

Hart's book on World War I (originally published in 1930) is an excellent, very complete account of the origins of this war and of the many battles fought on land and sea. Although it has few maps and no photos, the author more than makes up the deficit with his unblinking assessments of the triumphs and failures on both sides. He is one of the few authors who objectively assessed the use and impact of chemical weapons during the conflict.

What instantly won me over was the following passage: "The chlorine gas originally used was undeniably cruel, but no worse than the frequent effect of shell or bayonet, and when it was succeeded by improved forms of gas both experience and statistics proved it the least inhumane of modern weapons. But it was novel and therefore labelled an atrocity by a world which condones abuses but detests innovation."

Heller, Charles E. *Chemical Warfare in World War I: The American Experience, 1917–1918.* Washington, DC: Government Printing Office, 1984.

Major Heller wrote this study at Fort Leavenworth to show how the Army prepared for chemical warfare as the United States entered World War I and how the American Expeditionary Force adapted (or failed to adapt) to fighting in the first war that used chemical warfare on a mass scale. Well illustrated with numerous maps, sketches, and tables, this book shows the difference being prepared for chemical warfare can make, as the unprepared and untrained Americans quickly adapted to fight and win in this war. This is definitely the one book to read if one is looking for the American CW experience in World War I.

Hogg, Ian V. *Gas.* New York: Ballantine Books, 1975.

This book is part of Ballantine's Illustrated History of the Violent Century, Weapons Book number 43. In addition to covering the chemicals, weapon systems, and organizations developed for chemical warfare in World War I, the book contains what is probably the largest collection of photographs of both sides' personnel using defensive gear and offensive weapons. Although the text is short but accurate, the photographs more than make up for the brevity.

Jane's NBC Protection Equipment. Alexandria, VA: Jane's Information Group, 1988–.

Jane's military books are well known for their international coverage of equipment and current military issues. Their NBC protection equipment books, updated annually, are equally renowned as the source books to go to for summaries and photographs of existing CB defense equipment used by militaries all over the world. The book covers military and commercial detection, protection, decontamination, and medical CB defense equipment, with details on their use, sizes and weights, and manufacturers.

Journal of the American Medical Association **278, no. 5** (August 6, 1997).

This particular issue of *JAMA* has ten contributions from military and civil medical experts that deal with biological warfare and biological terrorism cases. Although *JAMA* features occasional articles on medical CBW issues throughout its issues, this particular issue is well worth digging out of the past-issues catalogue and reading. It includes historical summaries of the U.S. offensive BW program as well as commentaries on the nature of particular BW agents.

Kleber, Brookes E., and Dale Birdsell. *The Chemical Warfare Service: Chemicals in Combat.* Washington, DC: Office of the Chief of Military History, 1966.

This, the third volume of the Army's historical collection on the Chemical Warfare Service's work during World War II, is devoted to its overseas activities, including administration, logistics, and combat operations. Each theater had a distinct command-and-control function and a distinct emphasis on particular aspects of the Chemical Warfare Service's products. The Mediterranean theater of operations had some large-area smoke operations and made heavy use of the chemical mortars firing high explosives in support of combat operations. The European theater of operations saw heavy use of large-area smoke screens but also saw the chemical mortars supporting operations. In the Pacific, there was less interest in smoke operations but more use of flamethrowers and mortars. The book discusses specific employment of chemical units at specific battles in each theater. In all theaters, there were considerable preparations against the potential Axis employment of CB warfare.

Lavoy, Peter R., Scott D. Sagan, and James J. Wirtz, eds. *Planning the Unthinkable: How New Powers Will Use Nuclear, Biological, and Chemical Weapons.* Ithaca, NY: Cornell University Press, 2000.

This book features a diverse collection of essays on current countries developing offensive NBC weapons and what their motivations are. Countries discussed include Iraq, Iran, Israel, India, Pakistan, and North Korea, and it also discusses terrorist groups in general. The tone of the articles is more on the side of counterproliferation policy, trying to understand what drives these countries and what the U.S. government response should be.

Lederberg, Joshua, ed. *Biological Weapons: Limiting the Threat.* Cambridge: MIT Press, 1999.

Lederberg, a Nobel laureate, has collected a number of technical, historical, and arms control–oriented essays on the issue of biological warfare. In addition to a historical review, the essays discuss arms control, Iraq's BW program, detection and use of BW agents, and policies for responding to the threat of biological warfare. The introduction is written by former defense secretary William Cohen.

Lefebure, Victor. *The Riddle of the Rhine.* New York: Chemical Foundation, 1923.

This book, written during the arms control talks between the world wars, focuses mostly on the German industry that produced the chemicals and the German forces that employed them. The book's thesis is to identify what it took to develop this capability, and therefore what is required to disarm a nation that potentially has this capability. This is a dated book and obviously slanted against the German manufacturers, but it is a readily available text with good information about World War I agents and munitions.

Lewis, William H., and Stuart E. Johnson. *Weapons of Mass Destruction: New Perspectives on Counterproliferation.* Washington, DC: National Defense University Press, 1995.

The National Defense University often hosts symposia addressing challenges to U.S. national security, and in particular, NBC weapons and missiles as a means of delivery. This particular symposium featured several military and civilian experts discussing a range of issues from nonproliferation incentives and disincentives to ways to protect against proliferation when it occurs. The book has fifteen such discussions and concludes with a proposal on how nations might prevent future proliferation and craft policy to implement these decisions.

Marshall, S. L. A. *World War I.* New York: Houghton Mifflin Co., 2001.

Marshall's book on World War I, first printed in 1964, stands out as one of the most thorough and analytical reviews of this conflict. It is a very readable history, well illustrated with maps throughout the book, of a very complex conflict, and (more important for the reader of this book) it does not shrink from descriptions of the use of chemical warfare agents. One of the more famous photos of British soldiers, blinded by mustard gas but moving toward the aid station, is included in the book. Although the details of the chemical attacks are not as complete as one might wish, the author clearly demonstrates how the use of chemicals was merely another tool of war, used often and by both sides.

Mauroni, Albert J. *America's Struggle with Chemical-Biological Warfare.* Westport, CT: Praeger, 2000.

This book focuses on the development of U.S. military and national policy associated with CB warfare between 1968 and 1990, including discussions of the Army's technical developments, both offensive and defensive, during this time frame. The book touches on current events, such as the Gulf War, the chemical demilitarization program, and the DOD Domestic Preparedness Program that trained city emergency responders to respond to CB terrorism incidents.

Mauroni, Albert J. *Chemical-Biological Defense: U.S. Military Policies and Decisions in the Gulf War.* Westport, CT: Praeger, 1998.

This book discusses the Army's preparations and execution of CB defense for the coalition forces during the Gulf War. It discusses the Army leadership's deliberations in the Pentagon, at Aberdeen Proving Ground, and at Fort McClellan and the preparations of its forces in the Gulf. It also includes a chapter discussing the Khamasiyah depot incident in which it counters the popular view that military forces were exposed to nerve agents.

Mauroni, Albert J. *Chemical Demilitarization: Public Policy Aspects.* Westport, CT: Praeger, 2003.

Most efforts discussing the Army's chemical demilitarization program focus on the technologies and the struggles between the Army and its critics in light of leaks and accusations of insufficient safety measures. This book takes a public policy review of the program, examining how the Army developed its program starting in 1972, how the Army dealt with Congress and its critics, and how the Army could better execute chemical demilitarization and CB defense programs with the public and Congress, given a more appropriate public policy approach.

McDermont, Jeanne. *The Killing Winds: The Menace of Biological Warfare.* New York: Arbor House, 1987.

This book takes a critical look at the U.S. CB defense program in the 1980s, when critics saw the rapid influx of funds into the CBW program as a resurgence of military plans to develop an offensive program. In her review of current events, the author interviews people on both sides of the issues, military leaders as well as critics of the military's program. Issues covered include the Sverdlovsk incident in 1979, the "yellow rain" investigations, the Japanese BW research during World War II and the U.S. military's recruitment of Japanese scientists, open-air testing, and other controversial topics.

Miller, Judith, Stephen Engelberg, and William Broad. *Germs: Biological Weapons and America's Secret War.* New York: Simon and Schuster, 2001.

This book grew out of a number of investigative reports for the *New York Times* that began in 1998, focusing on national preparations for BW defense from the 1970s through the 1990s. It touches on arms control issues, the Gulf War, domestic BW terrorism, and what actions the government, at the highest levels, have taken (or not taken) to date. The authors portray a good sense of how the senior U.S. political and military leadership has dealt with this issue.

Norris, John, and Will Fowler. *NBC: Nuclear, Biological, and Chemical Warfare on the Modern Battlefield.* Cambridge: Brassey's, 1997.

This short book summarizes basic facts on nuclear weapon effects and CB agents and illustrates modern (and primarily British) NBC protective systems. Although the BW information is very brief, the book includes chemical structures for most CW agents and explains how military personnel use their defensive equipment.

Palazzo, Albert. *Seeking Victory on the Western Front: The British Army and Chemical Warfare in World War I.* Lincoln: University of Nebraska Press, 2000.

The author makes a strong argument in this book that the British Army, when faced with the threat of chemical weapons in World War I, did not reluctantly initiate an offensive program, but rather, recognized the need to incorporate these new weapons into their methods to reclaim the initiative. This book demonstrates how the British Army adapted its tactics to use a new technology and how it contributed to eventual victory.

Regis, Ed. *The Biology of Doom: The History of America's Secret Germ Warfare Project.* New York: Henry Holt, 1999.

This book describes the technical work conducted for the offensive BW program by the United States between 1940 and 1975. It covers the recruitment of Japanese scientists after World War II, the open-air and human volunteer trials, North Korean accusations in the 1950s, and CIA experiments. Because the book focuses on incidents in which the military was widely criticized, one might think the author had a bias against the military program, but he does portray both sides well.

Rothschild, J. H. *Tomorrow's Weapons: Chemical and Biological.* New York: McGraw-Hill, 1964.

After leaving the Army Chemical Corps, Brigadier General (retired) J. H. Rothschild wrote this book in an attempt to explain the strategic military policies and decisions behind the U.S. CBW offensive program to the general public. The book outlines the weapons, tactics, and rationale for developing these weapons, one of which is to allow the United States to retain an ability to win against superior forces without resorting to nuclear weapons.

Schneider, Barry R. *Future War and Counterproliferation: U.S. Military Responses to NBC Proliferation Threats.* Westport, CT: Praeger, 1999.

This book examines the threat of NBC weapons and outlines how the United States could develop an effective counterproliferation strategy to reduce the threat from adversaries armed with NBC weapons and missiles. It has ample examples using such nations as Iraq, North Korea, Syria, and Libya and a full discussion on CB defensive measures, and it is well footnoted.

Seagrave, Sterling. *Yellow Rain: A Journey through the Terror of Chemical Warfare.* New York: M. Evans, 1981.

Seagrave's book surfaced during the national debate on binary weapons. The author notes both the increased CW activity of the Soviet Union in Laos and Afghanistan and the increased U.S. interest in binaries. During this discussion, he reviews the history of CB warfare with a particular focus on the 1968–1980 period.

Spiers, Edward. *Chemical Warfare.* Urbana: University of Illinois Press, 1986.

———. *Chemical Weaponry: A Continuing Challenge.* New York: Macmillan, 1989.

———. *Chemical and Biological Weapons: A Study of Proliferation.* New York: St. Martin's, 1994.

This trilogy of books is a very complete discussion about the nature of modern chemical warfare, the doctrine and employment of chemical weapons, and the difficulties in trying to stop the proliferation of these weapons. The author discusses these complex issues at a level that is understandable to the general public without omitting critical facts. The first book presents a good summary of CBW issues during World Wars I and II prior to delving into an examination of Soviet and NATO programs and policies during the Cold War. The last book has one of the earliest public analyses of CB defense preparations by the coalition allies during the Gulf War.

Stockholm International Peace Research Institute (SIPRI). *The Problem of Chemical and Biological Warfare.* New York: Humanities Press, 1971–1975.

SIPRI's six-volume set of books on CB warfare is perhaps the most complete technical source of unclassified data on the subject up to the mid-1970s. The books may be hard to find, but they are a great source on the subject, with a focus on Cold War offensive CBW programs across the globe. In addition to a complete history, this set has data on CB weapons, legal aspects, current (as of the mid-1970s) national programs, arms control issues, and defensive measures.

Tucker, Jonathan, ed. *Toxic Terror: Assessing Terrorist Use of Chemical and Biological Weapons.* Cambridge: MIT Press, 2000.

This collection features an in-depth review of terrorist incidents, from 1946 to 1998, that included the potential or actual use of CB agents, including the Aum Shinrikyo Tokyo subway incident of 1995. The author notes that there are far fewer cases of CB terrorism than would seem to justify the robust response that governments have raised to this threat. Tucker notes that although the technical hurdles of producing and disseminating these agents may have been overcome, it is unclear what would motivate a terrorist group to actually employ CB agents.

Waitt, Alden H. *Gas Warfare.* New York: Duell, Sloan, and Pearce, 1942.

Brigadier General Alden Waitt, the second-highest ranking Chemical Warfare Service officer at the time this book was published, wrote it to educate the public and the military forces on CW issues. The book includes a detailed discussion of CW agents, chemical weapons, and their use in battle and of protection and first aid both for military and civil defense purposes. Although dated, the book offers a perspective on how the U.S. Army intended to use chemical weapons and to defend against them in World War II.

Journals, Bulletins, and Newsletters

Armed Forces Journal International
8201 Greensboro Drive
Suite 611
McLean, Virginia 22102
(703) 848-0493
Internet: http://www.afji.com/

This monthly journal is not focused solely on military CB defense issues, but it does from time to time feature articles and commentaries associated with current national and international military CB defense issues. It is more likely to be found in a military library than the neighborhood library. Not all of its articles are online, but the magazine can be ordered.

Army Chemical Review
320 MANSCEN Loop
Suite 210
Fort Leonard Wood, Missouri 65473-8929
Internet: http://www.wood.army.mil/CHBULLETIN/

The *Army Chemical Review* is the official publication of the Army Chemical Corps, offering articles and information about ongoing CB defense issues within the military. Because of recent concerns about government CB defense issues being available on the Internet, this magazine is not available on-line. It can be ordered through the Government Printing Office at http://www.access.gpo.gov.

Bulletin of the Atomic Scientists
6402 South Kimbark
Chicago, Illinois 60637
(773) 702-0077
Internet: http://www.bullatomsci.org/

This arms control journal focuses primarily on nuclear weapon arms control, but it occasionally discusses CB arms control issues. It is available through subscription and in some libraries.

The CBIAC Newsletter
Building E-3330
P.O. Box 196
Aberdeen Proving Ground, Maryland 21010-0196
(410) 676-9030
Internet: http://www.cbiac.apgea.army.mil/awareness/newsletter/intro.html

The *CBIAC Newsletter* is a quarterly newsletter that includes articles on current events and recent news in the CB defense community, as well as listings of contract awards and upcoming conferences. It is available through subscription as well as on-line, and past issues are available on-line.

The CBW Chronicle
Henry L. Stimson Center
11 Dupont Circle, NW
Ninth Floor
Washington, D.C. 20036
(202) 223-5956

Internet: http://www.stimson.org/cbw/?sn=cb20011221166

This quarterly on-line chronicle reviews current domestic and international events in the CB defense community, chemical demilitarization programs, and CB arms control issues.

The CBW Conventions Bulletin
Harvard-Sussex Project
7 Divinity Avenue
Cambridge, Massachusetts 02138
(617) 495-2264
Internet: http://fas-www.harvard.edu/~hsp/bulletin.html

Each issue of this quarterly bulletin, available by subscription with past issues available on-line, includes articles on arms control issues and a detailed summary of articles on CB defense and arms control issues that appeared in newspapers within the preceding quarter.

The CPC Outreach Journal
U.S. Air Force Counterproliferation Center
325 Chennault Circle
Maxwell Air Force Base, Alabama 36112
(334) 953-2119
Internet: http://www.au.af.mil/au/awc/awcgate/awc-cps.htm

This biweekly journal recaps U.S. news articles on counterproliferation issues, including CB defense issues. It is distributed through an electronic mail subscription list. To join it, contact Jo Ann Eddy at the above web site.

The Dispatch
Chemical and Biological Arms Control Institute (CBACI)
1747 Pennsylvania Avenue, NW
Washington, D.C. 20006
(202) 296-3550
Internet: http://www.cbaci.org/

The Dispatch is a biweekly newsletter delivered by e-mail to subscribers. It summarizes CB defense issues in the news and includes international news as well as U.S. news sources.

Journal of Homeland Security
Analytic Services, Inc.

2900 South Quincy Street
Arlington, Virginia 22206
(703) 416-3597
Internet: http://www.homelandsecurity.org/journal/

The Institute of Homeland Security hosts an on-line journal that prints original articles from subject-matter experts on counter-proliferation, terrorism, and homeland security. The institute also features a weekly newsletter summarizing recent news articles and upcoming events.

National Defense
2111 Wilson Boulevard
Suite 400
Arlington, Virginia 22201-3061
(730) 522-1820
Internet: http://www.ndia.org/

This monthly journal is not focused solely on CB defense, but it often has industry and military perspectives on CB defense issues and equipment. Like the *Armed Forces Journal*, it is probably not available in the neighborhood library but should be in many military libraries.

Government Documents and Agency Publications

Chemical Casualty Care Office. *Medical Management of Chemical Casualties.* 3rd ed. Aberdeen Proving Ground, Aberdeen MD: U.S. Army MRICD, 2000.

This pocket-size book is, not surprisingly, a reference book for medical professionals who might have to deal with CW casualties. For each of the modern CW agents, there is a historical summary, a listing of signs and symptoms, toxicity information, and detection/protection methods. Available on-line at http://www.vnh.org/CHEMCASU/titlepg.html.

Chemical Warfare Review Commission. *Report of the Chemical Warfare Review Commission.* Washington, DC: Government Printing Office, 1985.

In compliance with congressional direction, President Ronald Reagan tasked the Chemical Warfare Review Commission to review the need for binary chemical weapons. Its report covers a good deal of U.S. policy on the justification for a retaliatory chemical weapons capability and also gives a good history of the U.S. military stockpile.

Department of Defense. *DOD Annual Report to Congress on CB Defense.* Washington, DC: Office of the Secretary of Defense, April 2003.

The publication of this annual report is a congressional requirement (public law P.L. 50 US Code 1523). It reviews the current DOD management structure, research and development activities, logistics readiness, training, and CWC compliance measures. Available on-line at http://www.acq.osd.mil/cp/index.html.

Department of Defense. *Plan for Integrating National Guard and Reserve Component Support for Response to Attacks Using Weapons of Mass Destruction.* Washington, DC: Office of the Secretary of Defense, January 1998.

This report, prepared by a DOD "WMD Tiger Team" led by Brigadier General Roger Schultz, documents the efforts of the Army in its proposal to develop a reserve component force that would support the consequence management response to CB terrorism. Initially called Rapid Assessment and Initial Detection (RAID) elements, this concept would eventually take shape as the National Guard's WMD Civil Support Teams. Available on-line at http://www.defenselink.mil/pubs/wmdresponse/.

Department of Defense. *Proliferation: Threat and Response.* Washington, DC: Office of the Secretary of Defense, January 2001.

This publication identifies the nations suspected of sponsoring offensive CBW programs and the DOD's planned nonproliferation and counterproliferation responses to this threat. Available on-line at http://www.defenselink.mil/pubs/ptr20010110.pdf.

Department of Defense. *Quadrennial Defense Review Report.* Washington, DC: Office of the Secretary of Defense, September 2001.

The *Quadrennial Defense Review Report* outlines the DOD defense strategy and explains how the department plans to reshape its forces and doctrine to execute the strategy. The 2001 report in particular emphasized the CBW threat. Available on-line at http://www.defenselink.mil/pubs/qdr2001.pdf.

Department of Defense. *Report of the Defense Science Board Task Force on Persian Gulf War Health Effects.* Washington, DC: Defense Science Board, June 1994.

The Defense Science Board was asked to review information regarding the possible exposure of people to CB weapons and other hazardous material during the Gulf War and its aftermath. The board found no evidence that either chemical or biological weapons were used against U.S. service members, nor could it find epidemiological evidence of any coherent "syndrome." The board emphasized that this was a review of currently available information and that the medical and scientific communities needed to continue their work to better understand the problems of Gulf War veterans who are ill. Available on-line at http://www.acq.osd.mil/dsb/persianhealth.pdf.

General Accounting Office (GAO). *Chemical and Biological Defense: Emphasis Remains Insufficient to Resolve Continuing Problems.* Washington, DC: General Accounting Office, March 1996.

————. *Chemical and Biological Defense: Improved Risk Assessment and Inventory Management Are Needed.* Washington, DC: General Accounting Office, September 2001.

————. *Chemical and Biological Defense: Observations on DOD's Risk Assessment of Defense Capabilities.* Washington, DC: General Accounting Office, October 2002.

————. *Chemical and Biological Defense: Observations on Nonmedical Chemical and Biological R&D Programs.* Washington, DC: General Accounting Office, March 2000.

————. *Chemical and Biological Defense: Units Better Equipped, but Training and Readiness Reporting Problems Remain.* Washington, DC: General Accounting Office, November 2000.

————. *Chemical Warfare: DOD's Successful Effort to Remove U.S. Chemical Weapons from Germany.* Washington, DC: General Accounting Office, February 1991.

————. *Chemical Weapons: DOD Does Not Have a Strategy to Address Low Level Exposures.* Washington, DC: General Accounting Office, September 1998.

————. *Chemical Weapons: FEMA and Army Must Be Proactive in Preparing States for Emergencies.* Washington, DC: General Accounting Office, August 2001.

————. *Chemical Weapons and Materiel: Key Factors Affecting Disposal Costs and Schedule.* Washington, DC: General Accounting Office, February 1997.

————. *Combating Terrorism: Need to Eliminate Duplicate Federal Weapons of Mass Destruction Training.* Washington, DC: General Accounting Office, March 2000.

————. *Weapons of Mass Destruction: DOD's Actions to Combat Weapons Use Should Be More Integrated and Focused.* Washington, DC: General Accounting Office, May 2000.

Congress has asked the GAO to review the DOD CB Defense Program, chemical demilitarization program, and other related topics many, many times. These reports and others are good tools for summarizing particular aspects of the DOD's programs at particular points in time. Although I do not always agree with their recommendations, the data are very good. All unclassified reports are available on-line at www.gao.gov.

Joint Publication 3-11, *Joint Doctrine for Operations in Nuclear, Biological, and Chemical (NBC) Environments.* Washington, DC: Joint Chiefs of Staff, 2000.

Joint Publication 3-11 offers the official joint doctrine and concepts of operation for how the military as a whole intends to survive and sustain combat operations in a CB-contaminated environment. This document is updated every three to five years. Available on-line at http://www.dtic.mil/doctrine/jel/new_pubs/jp3_11.pdf.

Jollenbeck, Lois, Lee Zwanziger, Jane Durch, and Brian Strom, eds. *The Anthrax Vaccine: Is It Safe? Does It Work?* Washington DC: National Academy Press, 2002.

The National Academy of Sciences' Institute of Medicine prepared this congressionally mandated report for the Department of Defense to review the efficacy and safety of the currently licensed anthrax vaccine. This book describes in detail how the disease works, how the vaccine works, and how the DOD research measures up to the charges of its critics.

Kortepeter, Mark, George Christopher, Ted Cieslak, Randall Culpepper, Robert Darling, Julie Pavlin, John Rowe, Kelly McKee, and Edward Eitzen, eds. *Medical Management of Biological Casualties.* 4th ed. Fort Detrick: U.S. Army MRIID, 2001.

Like its chemical counterpart, the Chemical Casualty Care Office's *Medical Management of Chemical Casualties,* this is a pocket-size reference tool for medical experts who might have to deal with casualties exposed to BW agents. Information includes BW agent histories, signs and symptoms, treatments and prophylaxis, and detection and protection measures. Available on-line at http://www.usamriid.army.mil/education/bluebook.html.

National Research Council (NRC). *Chemical and Biological Terrorism: Research and Development to Improve Civilian Medical Response.* Washington, DC: National Academy Press, 1999.

———. *Disposal of Chemical Munitions and Agents: A Report.* Washington, DC: National Academy Press, 1984.

———. *Evaluations of Chemical Events at Army Chemical Agent Disposal Facilities.* Washington, DC: National Academy Press, 2002.

———. *Recommendations for the Disposal of Chemical Agents and Munitions.* Washington, DC: National Academy Press, 1994.

The NRC has executed a large number of studies to review and recommend actions in relation to the Army's chemical demilitarization program, in addition to other chemical defense topics. The three NRC reports on chemical weapons disposal listed above are probably the more valuable ones that review the entire disposal program; there are other NRC reports on individual sites and projects within the disposal program as well. The report on CB terrorism discusses the requirements and materiel available to respond to CB terrorism incidents and is not just focused on medical response, as the title suggests. Most NRC reports can be accessed and ordered on-line through the National Academy

Press at http://www.nap.edu/. Sections of the newer books can be read on-line, offering readers a chance to see exactly what they are purchasing.

Presidential Advisory Committee on Gulf War Veterans' Illnesses. *Final Report.* Washington, DC: Government Printing Office, 1996.

Congress received this final report from a twelve-member panel of experts reviewing the government's response to veterans' complaints of postwar illnesses, the nature of these illnesses, and what health risks there were in the Gulf to which veterans could have been exposed. The recommendations of this panel were a major factor in the formation of an OSD office for a special assistant for Gulf War illnesses and a host of continued studies into the various potential causes of Gulf War illnesses.

Program Manager for Chemical Demilitarization. *Chemical Stockpile Disposal Program: Final Programmatic Environmental Impact Statement.* Aberdeen Proving Ground, Aberdeen, MD: U.S. Army, 1988.

Although this report is not available on-line and is not liable to be in many libraries, it is a great reference for understanding the chemical demilitarization program. It exhaustively covers the chemical warfare agents and their effects, potential strategies and risks in disposing of the munitions and agents at the stockpile sites, and the public responses to the draft environmental impact statement.

Shuey, Robert. *Nuclear, Biological, and Chemical Weapons and Missiles: The Current Situation and Trends.* Washington, DC: Congressional Research Service, August 2001

A great unclassified source for identifying countries that are developing offensive CB weapons programs. Although short (only thirty-three pages), it packs a good deal of information and analysis on these nations and what their programs mean to the United States. Its assessment notes that "although the potential scale of NBC warfare has diminished with the end of the Cold War, the number of countries or groups that could initiate a nuclear, biological, or chemical attack may be increasing." Available on-line at http://www.cnie.org/NLE/CRS/abstract.cfm? NLEid=21578.

Sidell, Frederick, Ernest Takafuji, and David Franz, eds. *Medical Aspects of Chemical and Biological Warfare.* Washington, DC: Office of the Surgeon General, 1997.

This book discusses the medical management of CBW casualties in considerable depth, drawing upon the knowledge of some of the most learned professionals in the United States. It includes historical overviews of CB warfare and descriptions of the threat agents and CB defense equipment, with numerous pictures and references. Although focused on medical issues, this book is very readable by the layman as well as the general military history enthusiast. Available on line at http://www.nbc-med.org/SiteContent/HomePage/WhatsNew/MedAspects/contents.html.

U.S. Congress Office of Technology Assessment. *Proliferation of Weapons of Mass Destruction: Assessing the Risks.* Washington, DC: Government Printing Office, 1993.

This book reviews the nature of nuclear, biological, and chemical threats, what countries are developing these weapons, and what nonproliferation measures are available to reduce this threat. This book was written prior to the announcement of the DOD's Counterproliferation Initiative.

Internet Information Sources

Army Special Weapon Facilities
GlobalSecurity.org
http://198.65.138.161/wmd/facility/army.htm

This site summarizes information about the Army's chemical and (former) biological weapons storage sites.

Biowar: The Nixon Administration's Decision to End U.S. Biological Warfare Programs.
The National Security Archive
http://www.gwu.edu/~nsarchiv/NSAEBB/NSAEBB58/

Through the Freedom of Information Act, the National Security Archive has acquired several documents from the Nixon library that focus on the studies and recommendations leading up to

President Nixon's announcement on November 25, 1969, to end the country's offensive BW program.

Chemical and Biological Weapons Resource Page
Center for Nonproliferation Studies
http://cns.miis.edu/research/cbw/index.htm

The web site of the Center for Nonproliferation Studies contains links to books, news releases, reports, briefings, and other resources related to CB arms control, characteristics, warfare and defense, chemical demilitarization, terrorist use, and specific country profiles.

Chemical and Biological Weapons Site
Center for Defense Information (CDI)
http://www.cdi.org/issues/cbw/

The CDI's web site has several good links to articles and information on CB warfare, including information on the CWC and BWC and links to other agencies involved in this area.

Chemical Warfare Agents and Associated Health Guidelines
U.S. Army Center for Health Promotion and Preventive Medicine
http://chppm-www.apgea.army.mil/hrarcp/CAW/

The on-line documents at this web site present physical and chemical characteristics of CW agents.

Defending against the Threat of Biological and Chemical Weapons
Ministry of Defence (United Kingdom)
http://www.mod.uk/issues/cbw/index.htm

This site features an eight-chapter discussion on chemical and biological defense, including a history, facts on the warfare agents, UK policy on facing the battlefield and terrorist use of CB warfare agents, protective measures, research conducted at Porton Down, and a glossary.

DefenseLINK
Department of Defense
Anthrax vaccine: http://www.anthrax.osd.mil/
Arms control treaties: http://www.defenselink.mil/acq/acic/treaties/treaties.htm

Smallpox vaccine: http://www.smallpox.army.mil
WMD civil support teams: http://www.defenselink.mil/
specials/destruction/

These are the official DOD information sites on specific military CB defense topics.

DeploymentLINK
Office of the Special Assistant for Military Deployments
http://www.deploymentlink.osd.mil/current_issues/
shad/shad_intro.shtml

When the Office of the Special Assistant for Gulf War Illnesses stopped its investigation and closed down, its personnel transferred to this new office and continued to focus on the health and welfare of military personnel during military deployments. This site includes fact sheets on the SHAD cases, which took place in the 1960s.

Dugway Proving Ground Registry
of Atmospheric Survivors (RATS)
http://home.attbi.com/~kknowlto/index.html#cmlc

This site addresses the potential health consequences to military personnel who participated in the U.S. Army's atmospheric testing of CBR warfare agents. There is a great deal of information on Dugway tests as well as on human volunteer tests conducted in the 1950s and 1960s.

GulfLINK
Office of the Special Assistant for Gulf War Illnesses
http://www.gulflink.osd.mil

This web site is no longer updated, but it remains accessible. It holds all the raw data as well as investigations into cases where there was a possibility that U.S. forces might have been exposed to CB weapons during the Gulf War. The information papers go into great detail on CB defense equipment and on the exact events as documented from the personnel involved.

Homeland Defense
U.S. Army Soldier and Biological-Chemical Command (SBC-COM)

http://hld.sbccom.army.mil/

SBCCOM has played a significant role in developing capabilities for emergency responders to respond to potential CB terrorist incidents. This web site has several information products and related resources that focus on homeland defense issues.

How Biological and Chemical Warfare Works
How Stuff Works
http://www.howstuffworks.com/biochem-war.htm

This site is a short and simple tutorial on, well, how CB warfare works. The information on this page is good for younger audiences, people that just want the facts, and those with short attention spans.

Jim Placke's NBC Links
http://www.nbc-links.com/

This site, run by an active-duty chemical officer in his spare time, offers a very extensive list of connections to just about every CBW-related Internet site available, from news articles to military units to industry sources and private agencies that work in this line of business. It is perhaps one of the most well-populated and current sites for finding links to any source of CB defense information on the net.

Last Battle of the Gulf War
PBS *Frontline*
http://www.pbs.org/wgbh/pages/frontline/
shows/syndrome/

PBS's *Frontline* ran a special discussing Gulf War illness issues. This site features information on the series and discussions on the various aspects under investigation, including the possibility that chemical or biological warfare agents could have caused these illnesses.

Medical NBC Online Information Server
U.S. Army Office of the Surgeon General
http://www.nbc-med.org/others/

Although its front page is graphic intensive, this site hosts current news clips of interest in addition to updated military medical references, Internet resources, and numerous links to related military and civilian CB defense sites.

NBC Defense Programs
U.S. Army Soldier and Biological-Chemical
Command (SBCCOM)
Historical documents: http://www.sbccom.army.mil/hooah/
pubs.htm
NBC defense programs: http://www.sbccom.army.mil/
products/nbc.htm

The first web site has several documents relating to the Army's research and development areas going back to the formation of the Chemical Warfare Service in 1917. The second web site features the latest CB defense equipment under development and being fielded to military units.

Plague War
PBS *Frontline*
http://www.pbs.org/wgbh/pages/frontline/shows/plague/

Another PBS special, this one focused on the growing threat of biological weapons. It includes a fascinating perspective on the rise and fall of the Soviet offensive BW program. This site features information on the series and discussions on the various aspects under investigation.

Preventing Biological Warfare
University of Bradford, UK
http://www.brad.ac.uk/acad/sbtwc/

This site focuses on BW arms control topics, including up-to-date reports on the conferences held by the BWC review group, the BWC protocol text, current issues, and ad hoc group working papers. This site has an international focus.

Public Health Emergency and Response
Centers for Disease Control
Chemical warfare agents:
http://www.bt.cdc.gov/Agent/agentlistchem.asp
Biological warfare agents:
http://www.bt.cdc.gov/Agent/agentlist.asp

Radiological health hazards: http://www.cdc.gov/nceh/
radiation/response.htm
Chemical demilitarization: http://www.cdc.gov/nceh/demil/
factsheets/oversight.htm

There are many references to health studies and information on
the various CBR hazards on the CDC site, in addition to what
HHS is doing to ensure that a government emergency response
capability exists in the event of a biological terrorist event.

Rocky Mountain Arsenal
Department of Defense
http://www.pmrma.army.mil/

Rocky Mountain Arsenal's past association with the development
of chemical weapons often draws attention from the media and
aspiring authors. This web site reviews its history, the cleanup
effort, and the plans to eventually make it a national wildlife
refuge.

Terrorism Incident Annex
Federal Emergency Management Agency (FEMA)
http://www.fema.gov/rrr/frp/frpterr.shtm

The Federal Response Plan outlines how federal agencies will
respond to various emergencies in which the states call for federal assistance, from natural disasters, such as hurricanes, to
human-caused disasters, such as rioting. This annex to the Federal Response Plan defines the federal government's policies and
procedures to respond to a CB terrorist incident. The FBI and
FEMA are the official lead federal agencies to respond to a CB terrorist incident, with DOD being a major supporter of both.

U.S. Air Force Counterproliferation Center
U.S. Air Force Air War College
http://www.au.af.mil/au/awc/awcgate/awc-cps.htm

This site was produced by the Air War College in the interest of
advancing concepts related to national defense. Although the
briefings, reports, and links to agencies on this page are not officially sanctioned DOD products, they cut across the entire spectrum of nonproliferation and counterproliferation topics and can
be a valuable source of information for both casual and serious
students.

U.S. Navy Chemical-Biological Defense
U.S. Navy Counterproliferation Office
http://www.cbd.navy.mil/index.htm
http://www.dcfp.navy.mil/index.htm (at the CBR-D link)

Although the Navy does not have a full-time specialty for CB defense, it is very active in ensuring that it has the proper equipment and training to protect sailors and marines. This site features the programs in which it is participating, in addition to Navy reference publications and related web sites.

WMD Resources
Federation of American Scientists (FAS)
http://fas.org/bwc/index.html
http://fas.org/nuke/index.html

The FAS hosts this site to provide information on special weapon capabilities around the world. It includes current news and information on arms control agreements, delivery systems, military doctrine, associated organizations, and facilities.

Glossary

Acetylcholinesterase   An enzyme that hydrolyzes the neuro-transmitter acetylcholine, which must be inactivated in order to terminate impulse transmissions at cholinergic synapses within the nervous system. The action of this enzyme is inhibited by nerve agents, which causes an accumulation of acetylcholine, which further causes continuous stimulation of the affected organ.

Active defense   Measures taken to detect, divert, or destroy enemy NBC weapons and delivery means while en route to their targets.

Aerosol   A liquid or solid composed of finely divided particles suspended in a gaseous medium. Examples of common aerosols are dust, mist, fog, and smoke. Particle size may vary from 0.01 micrometers to 100 micrometers.

Anthrax vaccine   An inactivated vaccine made from protective antigen of organisms, approved by the FDA in 1970 for inhalation and percutaneous anthrax cases. The vaccine may be less effective if the subject is faced with an overwhelming quantity of inhaled spores.

Atropine   A compound used as an antidote for nerve agents. It works by inhibiting the actions of excess acetylcholine in the parasympathetic nervous system. (This affect is more effective at muscarinic sites than at nicotinic sites.)

Bacteria   A class of single-celled microorganisms that live in soil, water, organic matter, or the bodies of plants and animals. Their complex structure allows them to reproduce on their own by cell division. Diseases caused by bacteria often respond to treatment with antibiotics.

Binary chemical munition   A munition whose chemical agent is composed of two separate components. The components are separated in the round in two sections, each containing precursor chemicals that combine and react during flight, releasing a chemical warfare agent either upon impact or upon detonation of the fuse in flight. The toxicity of the two precursor chemicals is less than their toxicity when they are combined. The U.S. binary weapons were 155 mm GB-filled artillery rounds, VX-filled MLRS warheads, and VX-filled Bigeye bombs.

Biological warfare (BW) agent   A living organism, or material derived from living organisms, that causes disease in personnel, plants, or animals or causes the deterioration of materiel, the intentional use of which is to cause incapacitation or death; also known as "agents of biological origin."

Biological weapon   An item of materiel that projects, disperses, or disseminates a BW agent, including arthropod vectors (fleas, ticks, mosquitoes, and the like).

Blister agent   A chemical agent that injures the eyes and lungs and irritates or blisters the skin and mucous membranes; also called vesicant agents. They are primarily nonlethal incapacitant and persistent agents but can cause death if a person is exposed to large amounts. Blister agents include mustard agent and lewisite.

Blood agent   A chemical compound that affects bodily functions by preventing the normal utilization of oxygen by body tissues. They are primarily lethal and nonpersistent agents. Blood agents include cyanogen chloride and hydrogen cyanide.

Chemical, biological, radiological, and nuclear (CBRN) hazards Toxic chemical, biological, radiological, and nuclear hazards that may be employed by adversarial nations or nonstate actors against U.S. forces or civilians, not necessarily in quantities that could cause mass casualties. CBRN hazards include those created from a release other than attack, toxic industrial chemicals (specifically toxic inhalation hazards), biological diseases of operational significance, and radioactive matter as well as those created as a result of deliberate employment of NBC weapons during military operations.

Chemical demilitarization   The process of destroying chemical agents and munitions to the point that the CW agents cannot be reconstituted back into their original lethal form. The U.S. program for chemical demilitarization includes the Chemical Stockpile Disposal Program (CSDP), the Non-Stockpile Chemical Materiel (NSCM) project, and the Alternative Technology and Approaches Project (ATAP). The Chemical Stockpile Emergency Preparedness Program (CSEPP) and the Alternative Chemical Weapons Assessment (ACWA) program are also associated with the program.

Chemical warfare (CW) agent   Any toxic chemical agent intended for use in military operations for the incapacitation or death of exposed personnel through its physiological effects. Riot-control agents, herbicides, and incendiary munitions are chemical munitions but are not considered toxic chemical agents.

Chemical weapon   Together or separately, a munition or device filled with a CW agent, specifically designed to cause death, injury, or other harm through the toxic properties of CW agents.

Choking agents   Chemical agents that cause irritation and inflammation of the breathing apparatus. They are generally lethal nonpersistent agents. Choking agents include chlorine, phosgene, and diphosgene.

Ciprofloxacin   An antibiotic drug useful in treating bacterial infections. Ciprofloxacin has recently been cleared by the FDA for use by civilians exposed to anthrax spores as a result of BW terrorism. Another related antibiotic is doxycycline.

Collective protection   Protection provided to a group of individuals in a nuclear, biological, or chemical environment, which provides a contamination-free working environment and permits people to work without continuously wearing protective gear. Collective protection can be subdivided into stand-alone shelters and integrated systems (that is, systems built into buildings and vehicles).

Consequence management   Measures taken to protect public health and safety, restore essential government services, and provide emergency relief to governments, businesses, and individuals affected by the consequences of a CBRN incident.

Contamination   The deposit, absorption, or adsorption of chemical or biological agents or radioactive material on or by structures, areas, personnel, or objects.

Counterforce   Operations that divert, deny, degrade, or destroy an adversary's capability to develop, manufacture, stockpile, or employ NBC weapons before they can be used.

Counterproliferation   Activities to combat proliferation. These efforts span the full range of U.S. government activities and include the use of military power to protect U.S. forces and interests; intelligence collection and analysis; and support to diplomacy, arms control, and export controls; with particular responsibility for assuring U.S. forces and interests can be protected should they confront an adversary armed with NBC weapons.

Decontamination   The process of making any person, object, or area safe by absorbing, destroying, neutralizing, ventilating, making harmless, or removing chemical or biological agents, or by removing radioactive material clinging to or around it. The military defines four levels: immediate decontamination for lifesaving measures, operational decontamination to reduce the spread of contamination, thorough decontamination to allow the resumption of unprotected operations, and restoration decontamination to allow peacetime use of equipment and areas.

Detection   The determination of the presence of a CBR hazard but not necessarily the identification of its exact nature. Detection is generally split into manual detection (requiring an operator) and automatic detection (running without operator assistance).

False positive   An erroneous detection indicating the presence of a CBW agent, particularly due to interferents or other equipment malfunctions. A "false negative" would be the erroneous lack of detection and of subsequent warning in the presence of a CBW agent; a false negative is more dangerous than a false positive.

Gas   The molecular form of a substance in which molecules are dispersed widely enough that they have little attraction on each other. "Gas" is also typically the slang form used for all chemical warfare agents.

Hazardous materials   Any flammable, corrosive, explosive, toxic, poisonous, etiological, radioactive, nuclear, or unduly magnetic material; or any oxidizing agent, chemical agent, biological research material, compressed gas, or other material that, because of its quantity, properties, or packaging, may endanger human life or property.

Identification   The determination of the exact identity of the CBR hazard, for instance, sarin nerve agent as opposed to mustard agent, or anthrax as opposed to smallpox.

Immunization   The administration of either a nontoxic antigen to confer active immunity or an antibody to confer passive immunity to a person or animal to render them unsusceptible to the toxic effects of pathogens or toxins.

Incapacitants   In this venue, chemical or biological warfare agents that temporarily disable personnel for hours to days after exposure has ceased, given a moderate and not excessive dosage. Examples of incapacitants include mustard agent, SEB toxin, psycho-chemicals, and riot-control agents.

Individual protection   Actions taken by individuals to survive and continue their mission under CBR hazard conditions. Individual protection is usually divided into nonmedical means (the use of individual protective equipment, such as suits and masks) and medical means (the use of vaccines, countermeasures).

Individual protective equipment (IPE)   The protective ensemble worn by military personnel, including the protective jacket, trousers, boots, gloves, and mask; also known as personal protective equipment (PPE).

Investigational new drug   Any new drug or biological product that is not formally approved by the FDA, which may be administered to humans with FDA approval.

LCt_{50}   The vapor or aerosol exposure necessary, in terms of concentration and time, to cause death in 50 percent of an exposed population. There are also incapacitating concentrations (ICt) and effective concentrations (ECt), and dosages can be expressed that affect or kill 5 percent or 25 percent of those exposed. Dosages are often expressed in terms of milligrams of agent-minutes/cubic meter.

LD_{50}   The dose that will cause death in 50 percent of an exposed population by routes of administration other than respiratory (often ingested or percutaneous). There are also incapacitating doses (ID) and effective doses (ED), and dosages can be expressed that affect or kill 5 percent or 25 percent. Dosages are often expressed in terms of milligrams of agent per kilograms of body weight.

Miosis   The contraction of the pupil of the eye, specifically when the pupil is unable to dilate and remains contracted, causing an effect as if the lights have suddenly dimmed. This effect can be caused by exposure to low levels of nerve agent vapors and can last from hours to days, depending on the dose received.

Mission-oriented protective posture (MOPP)   A flexible system of individual protective equipment that allows one to balance protection against the ability to carry out one's work in light of threat levels, the mission, humidity, and temperature.

NBC contamination survivability   The capability of a defense system and its crew to withstand an NBC-contaminated environment and relevant decontamination without losing the ability to accomplish the assigned mission. There are three components: hardening the system against NBC warfare agents, hardening the system against the corrosive nature of decontaminants, and compatibility with individual protective equipment.

Nerve agent   A potentially lethal chemical agent that interferes with the transmission of nerve impulses by inhibiting the cholinesterase enzyme and elevating the acetylcholine level in the body. Nerve agents are often divided into the G-series, developed in the 1930s and 1940s (tabun, sarin, soman), and the V-series, developed in the 1950s and 1960s.

Nonpersistent agent   A CW agent that, when released, dissipates or loses its ability to cause casualties after ten to fifteen minutes. These agents are primarily an inhalation hazard. They generally last as liquids for minutes to hours, and exposed equipment does not usually require decontamination.

Nonproliferation   The use of the full range of political, economic, informational, or military tools to prevent the proliferation of NBC weapons and missiles, to reverse it diplomatically, or to protect U.S. interests against an opponent armed with NBC weapons

Nuclear, biological, and chemical (NBC) weapons   Weapons that are characterized by their capability to produce mass casualties using NBC means and whose threat or use introduces individually diverse and distinct challenges to the planning and conduct of military operations. These weapons do not include riot-control agents or herbicides, but they may include toxic industrial chemicals (specifically toxic inhalation hazards) and radiological materials that are weaponized for employment against personnel.

Passive defense Defensive measures (rather than the offensive measures in counterforce and active defense) that enable friendly forces to survive, fight, and win military operations despite the enemy's employment of NBC weapons or agents.

Pathogen A disease-producing microorganism. Pathogens can be bacteria, viruses, rickettsia, and fungi.

Persistent agent A CW agent that when released does not immediately dissipate or evaporate and that through its contact hazard can cause casualties for an extended duration (hours to days). Equipment contaminated with persistent agents requires operational and thorough decontamination prior to use by unprotected persons.

Precursor A chemical that can be combined with another substance to form a CW agent. Most precursors are controlled through international efforts and have commercial uses as well as military uses.

Prophylaxis Medical measures taken to preserve an individual's health and prevent the spread of disease. Prophylactic measures can include those taken after exposure to CB agents but prior to the onset of symptoms, in contrast to medical treatment, which occurs after the onset of symptoms.

Protective ensembles Generally a camouflage-colored, expendable, two-piece overgarment consisting of a coat and trousers (aircrew ensembles are typically one-piece overgarments). These garments provide protection against chemical agent vapors, liquid droplets, biological agents, and radioactive alpha and beta contamination. Protective qualities last from thirty to forty-five days once the garment is removed from its bag, depending on the particular suit, and the garments provide twenty-four hours of protection against exposure to liquid or vapor chemical agents.

Protective mask A respirator that is designed to protect the wearer's face and eyes and to prevent the wearer from breathing air contaminated with CBR hazards. They are often erroneously referred to as "gas masks," when they will also protect against the inhalation of biological and radiological particles.

Psychochemicals A group of incapacitant chemical agents that alter the nervous system, causing visual and aural hallucinations, a sense of unreality, and changes in thought processes and behavior.

Quarantine   The detention, isolation, or restriction of the activities of people or animals exposed to a communicable disease
during the incubation period (period of time in which the disease
can be transmitted to another) to prevent the spread of the disease
to others.

Reconnaissance   The process of obtaining information,
through visual and other detection methods, on the activities and
resources of an enemy or (in the case of CB defense) the process
of securing data on the potential contamination or lack of contamination of a particular area or route.

Riot-control agent   Any chemical compound that can rapidly
produce temporary sensory irritation or disabling physical effects
in humans; the effects normally disappear within a short time following the termination of exposure; also commonly known as
tear gases.

Simulant   A chemical that has some physical or physiological
feature(s) of a chemical or biological warfare agent. Simulants are
used to allow test and evaluation agencies to assess the effectiveness of defense equipment without using actual toxic CBW
agents.

Survey   The directed effort to determine the location and nature of the CBRN hazard in a defined area.

Thickened agent   An agent to which a polymer or plastic has
been added to retard evaporation and to cause it to adhere to surfaces.

Threshold Limit Value   The smallest amount of toxic substance that can produce the first recognizable injuries (for example, irritation of the skin, nausea, or miosis). The term may also
refer to the level of a chemical that shall not be exceeded for even
and instant (TLV-C, or threshold limit value–ceiling). Some other
common threshold doses are TLV-STEL (threshhold limit
value–short-term exposure), which is a level of exposure that cannot be exceeded for more than fifteen minutes, four times per day
with an hour in between each exposure; TLV/TWA (threshold
limit value/time weighted average), which is the amount of a
product a person can be exposed to repeatedly during an eight-
hour day/forty-hour week with no toxic effects; and TLV/Skin
(threshold limit value/skin), which is the amount of material that
causes skin irritation or that can be absorbed into the skin.

Toxic inhalation hazard   A gas, vapor, or aerosol that can cause damage to a person as the result of asphyxiation, topical damage to the respiratory system, systemic damage to the organs, or allergic response.

Toxins   Poisonous substances produced by living organisms. Examples include ricin, derived from castor beans, and botulinum toxin.

Vaccine   A substance administered to induce immunity in the recipient. Vaccines can be further subdivided into FDA-licensed vaccines and Investigational New Drug (IND) vaccines. The latter require the subject to volunteer to take the vaccine with a full understanding of the potential side effects.

Vapor   The gaseous state of a substance that at normal temperature would be a solid or a liquid. Generally, vapors condense back into a liquid state and thus may have both an inhalation and percutaneous effect.

Virus   Any of the various submicroscopic pathogens consisting of a core of a single nucleic acid surrounded by a protein coat, characterized by a total dependence on living cells for reproduction and a lack of independent metabolism.

Vomiting agent   A chemical compound that produces a strong pepper-like irritation in the upper respiratory tract, with irritation of the eyes and tearing. These chemicals cause violent, uncontrollable sneezing, coughing, nausea, vomiting, and general discomfort for minutes to hours after exposure.

Weapons of mass destruction   Weapons that are capable of a high order of destruction or of being used in such a manner as to destroy large numbers of people. Such weapons include chemical, biological, radiological, and nuclear weapons or high explosives. This arms control term generally refers to the NBC weapons threat posed by adversarial nations or nonstate actors or to their offensive programs developed to asymmetrically counter U.S. or coalition ally strengths.

Index

About the Author

Al Mauroni is a senior military analyst with Analytic Services, Inc. He has worked on Department of Defense chemical and biological defense issues for more than seventeen years, seven of them in the U.S. Army as a chemical officer. He has written three books and several magazine articles on chemical-biological defense topics. He lives with his wife, Roseann, and their three dogs in Alexandria, Virginia.